Literature 5
Student Guide

3rd Edition

Illustrations Credits

All illustrations © K12 Inc. unless otherwise noted

About K12 Inc.

K12 Inc., a technology-based education company, is the nation's leading provider of proprietary curriculum and online education programs to students in grades K–12. K¹² provides its curriculum and academic services to online schools, traditional classrooms, blended school programs, and directly to families. K12 Inc. also operates the K¹² International Academy, an accredited, diploma-granting online private school serving students worldwide. K¹²'s mission is to provide any child the curriculum and tools to maximize success in life, regardless of geographic, financial, or demographic circumstances. K12 Inc. is accredited by CITA. More information can be found at www.K12.com.

ISBN 978-1-60153-469-9

Manufactured in the United States by RR Donnelley, September 2015, Lot 092015

Table of Contents

Unit 3

Unit 4

Unit 5

Unit 8

Unit 9

Unit 10

Unit 12

Unit 13

Unit 14

Unit 16

Unit 17

Unit 19

Unit 21

Unit 22

Unit 23

Unit 24

Unit 26

Name _____   Date _____

Foundational Skills

Learn about what to expect in this course and review some strategies for understanding what you read. Then answer questions about reading strategies.

In This Course

Complete this online activity to learn about the course that you are about to begin. You will learn about resources in the course and review reading strategies for being a better, more effective reader.

Check Your Listening

Complete this online activity to answer questions about your understanding of reading strategies.

Name _____   Date _____

"Salt and Bread"

A father learns a lesson about love he will never forget.

Vocabulary
You will find these words in today's reading.

rumor: (n.) a story, which may or may not be true, that is passed from person to person
It isn't nice to repeat unkind stories that you hear because that is how *rumors* begin.

lavish: (v.) to give or spend in a generous way
The child *lavished* love and attention on her new puppy.

banish: (v.) to force a person to leave his or her country or home as a punishment
"Because you have betrayed me," said the king to the traitor, "I *banish* you from this kingdom forever."

expose: (v.) to make known; reveal
The newspaper reporter *exposed* the truth about the dangerous conditions in the factory.

Think Ahead
Have you ever heard the expression, "Listen to your heart"? What do you think this means?

Read
"Salt and Bread" in *Classics for Young Readers,* Vol. 5A, pages 6-8

Questions
Answer the following questions in complete sentences in your
Reading Notebook.

1. How do the two older girls feel about their youngest sister?
2. Why does the father decide to test his daughters' love for him?
3. What does the youngest daughter tell her father about her love
   for him?
4. What happens when the youngest daughter is sent into the woods?
5. What does the youngest daughter leave off the tables at her
   wedding banquet?
6. What happens to the older daughters at the end of the story?

Discuss
1. Why are salt and bread valuable?
2. What lesson does the father learn at the youngest daughter's
   wedding?
3. What qualities in the youngest daughter do you admire?

Dear King
Imagine you are an advice columnist for the *Royal Gazette*, a
newspaper that serves the local kingdoms in your area. You
receive the following letter:

> Dear Sir or Madam:
> I am very upset and not sure what to do. I have three daughters and I love
> them all. I am certain they all love me, but lately I have been hearing
> rumors that my youngest child cares very little for me. In my heart, I love
> her dearly, and I believe she loves me. But I want to test all three children
> so I can be sure. What do you think?
> > Yours truly,
> > An Uncertain King

In your Reading Notebook, write a paragraph or more in which you
reply to this king. In your reply, use examples from "Salt and Bread."

Characters and Conflicts

A *conflict* is a clash or struggle between people, ideas, or feelings. When you read, you will find that characters have different kinds of conflicts.

A character can have a conflict with:

- Another character or group of characters. For example, Cinderella has a conflict with her stepmother and stepsisters.

- His or her own thoughts and feelings. For example, in the story of "Beauty and the Beast," when the Beast allows Beauty to return to visit her family, Beauty experiences a conflict in her own feelings. Her loyalty to the Beast makes her want to return to him, but her love for her family makes her want to stay with them.

- His or her society or the natural world. For example, in the story of "The Leak in the Dike," the little Dutch boy faces a conflict against the powerful seas that threaten to force their way through the leak.

In a story, characters usually need to *resolve*, or work out, their conflicts. Having conflicts with other people is hard, but having conflicts within yourself can be even harder.

In "Salt and Bread" there is more than one conflict that needs to be resolved. Fill in the Characters and Conflicts page with details from "Salt and Bread."

Guidelines for Peer Discussion

Share your thoughts, ideas, questions, and feelings about a text with a peer or others. Listen carefully to what everyone has to say about the text. During your discussion, follow these guidelines.

1. Be prepared to discuss what you think about the text. You should have already read the assignment. Come prepared to discuss your ideas and use examples from the text to support your thoughts and answers.

2. You will be asked questions about the text. Be ready to answer them, and bring some questions of your own to ask others, such as:

   "Who was your favorite character? Why?"

   "What was your favorite part of the text? Why?"

   "What fact did you enjoy learning? Why do you find this fact interesting?"

   "What question would you ask if you had the chance to meet the author?"

3. Listen if it's not your turn to speak. Pay attention to what others say so that you can add your ideas. Speak clearly and in complete sentences.

4. If you don't understand what someone says, ask a question.

   "What do you mean when you say . . . ?"

   "Can you give an example of . . . ?"

5. If you don't agree with what someone says, explain why.

   "I don't agree with that because . . . "

6. Keep discussions positive! You can disagree, but don't argue. Be respectful.

Name _____   Date _____

Characters and Conflicts

Use the details from "Salt and Bread" to help you answer the following questions in complete sentences.

1. What is the conflict between the youngest daughter and her two older sisters?

_____

_____

_____

2. At first, how does the King feel about his youngest daughter?

_____

_____

_____

3. What conflict takes place inside the King? (Hint: Does he listen to his heart or listen to others?)

_____

_____

_____

6

Characters and Conflicts

4. How are the conflicts resolved at the end of the story?

_____

_____

_____

_____

_____

_____

_____

Name _____   Date _____

"Ali and the Magic Stew"

In this tale set in old Persia, Ali ibn Ali learns a lesson he will never forget from an unlikely person.

Vocabulary

You will find these words in today's reading.

imperious: (adj.) commanding
The queen spoke with an *imperious* tone when she ordered her page to bring her gown.

audible: (adj.) able to be heard
The speaker's voice was so low that it was barely *audible* to the people sitting in the back row.

delicacies: (n.) rare or special foods that are pleasing to eat
Frog's legs, caviar, and snails were a few of the *delicacies* on the restaurant's menu.

belied: (v.) contradicted
The woman climbed the stairs with a grace that *belied* her elderly appearance.

invalid: (n.) someone who is very sick or disabled
We brought flowers and gifts to cheer up the *invalids* in the hospital.

Think Ahead

1. Have you ever learned a lesson from someone unexpected? What did you learn and how did that experience change you?

2. This story is set in a country that used to be called Persia. In 1935, Persia became known as Iran. Locate Iran on a map or globe.

3. Have you ever heard the saying, "Walk a mile in someone else's shoes"? What does that saying mean to you?

Read

"Ali and the Magic Stew" in *Classics for Young Readers,* Vol. 5A, pages 9-16

Questions

Answer the following questions in complete sentences in your Reading Notebook.

1. What does "he was the apricot of his parents' eyes" mean?
2. How does Ali's mother say a true Muslim behaves?
3. What does Ali's father ask for when he is ill?
4. What does Ali do to help his father?
5. At the end of the story, the beggar tells Ali to keep the cloak. What is the cloak supposed to remind Ali of?

Discuss

1. Describe Ali ibn Ali at the beginning of the story.
2. Why do you think the healing stew needs to be made with ingredients bought with coins begged from the street?
3. What lessons does Ali ibn Ali learn from his experience begging? How might this change him in the future?
4. At the end of the story, the beggar says, "I am going and I am staying…I am staying and I am going." What do you think this means?

Thank You, Sir

At the beginning of the story, Ali is not grateful for what he has, and he judges the beggar harshly. He speaks rudely to others. But by the end of the story, Ali learns some important lessons about himself and the kind of person he is, and about how to treat others.

The painful experience of begging for the coins teaches Ali a lesson in *humility*. Humility means being humble—not speaking too proudly of yourself or your own accomplishments, talents, or possessions. Find one example in the story that shows Ali has learned humility.

At the end of the story, the beggar tells Ali to keep the cloak "as a reminder of the pain unkindness brings." Ali acts unkindly at first, but he learns to be kind. He learns a special kind of kindness called *compassion.* To be compassionate means to feel the suffering of others and to want to help them. Find one example in the story that shows Ali has learned compassion.

Pretend you are Ali ibn Ali and write a thank-you letter to the beggar in which you explain the lessons you learned and how you will act in the future. Among the lessons you learned, include humility and compassion, as well as any others you wish. Be sure to include details from the story. You may write your letter in your Reading Notebook.

Name _____   Date _____

"The Fire on the Mountain"

In this Ethiopian folktale, a servant faces many conflicts, and his master learns a lesson.

Vocabulary

You will find these words in today's reading.

accentuate: (v.) to emphasize
Whenever I start to complain, my mother reminds me of a song that says to "*accentuate* the positive."

durra: (n.) grain grown in warm, dry lands
At the time of the harvest we will pick wheat, corn, and *durra*.

ordeal: (n.) a terribly hard or painful experience
It is an *ordeal* for me to have my teeth drilled by the dentist.

tantalizing: (adj.) desirable and extremely tempting, but out of reach
The neighbors' swimming pool was *tantalizing* on such a hot day, but it was behind a locked gate and we didn't have permission to use it.

Think Ahead

1. Has there ever been a time when you were treated unfairly? What did you do about it?

2. A folktale is a kind of story that is told and retold from one generation to the next. Often, folktales are not written down, but are part of an oral tradition, which means they are spoken from memory instead of being read from a book. Folktales are part of most cultures, and are often told to share important ideas or lessons. Can you name any folktales that you have been told?

3. This folktale is from Ethiopia, a country on the continent of Africa. Locate Ethiopia on a world map or globe.

Read

"The Fire on the Mountain" in *Classics for Young Readers,* Vol. 5A, pages 17-22

Questions

Answer the following questions in complete sentences in your Reading Notebook.

1. Who is Arha?
2. What question does Haptom want answered?
3. What will Arha gain if he wins the bet with Haptom?
4. How does the wise old man help Arha while he is on Mount Sululta?
5. Why does Haptom think that Arha did not fulfill the conditions of their bet?

Discuss

1. Why do you think the wise old man's fire helps Arha survive the cold?
2. After the judge rules against Arha, the old man tells his friend not to lose hope. He says, "More wisdom grows wild in the hills than in any city judge." What do you think this means?
3. What lesson do Haptom and the judge learn at the feast?

Arha's Conflicts

You have learned that a conflict is a clash or struggle between people, ideas, or feelings. A character can have a conflict with other characters, his own feelings, his society, or the natural world.

In "Salt and Bread," the youngest daughter has a conflict with her sisters, and the king has a conflict within himself.

In "The Fire on the Mountain," Arha experiences many conflicts.

Use details from the story to answer questions on the Arha's Conflicts page.

Name _____   Date _____

Arha's Conflicts

A character can have a conflict with:
- Another character or group of characters
- His or her own thoughts and feelings
- His or her society or the natural world

In a story, characters usually need to resolve, or work out, their conflicts.

Use the details from "The Fire on the Mountain" to answer the following questions in complete sentences.

1. Describe Arha's conflict with the natural world when he spends the night on Mount Sululta.

   _____

   _____

   _____

   _____

2. How does Arha resolve this conflict with nature?

   _____

   _____

   _____

   _____

Arha's Conflicts

3. What is the conflict between Arha and Haptom?

_____

_____

_____

_____

4. Arha goes to the judge, but the judge rules against him. When this happens, Arha faces a conflict with society because the judge stands for the rule of law in Arha's society. How does Arha feel when the judge rules against him?

_____

_____

_____

_____

5. Arha's conflicts with Haptom and with society are resolved with the help of Hailu. What does Hailu do to help resolve Arha's conflicts?

_____

_____

_____

_____

Name _____   Date _____

Summarizing a Story

Think about the main events in a story in order to write a plot summary.

Think Ahead

1. Why do you think folktales like "Salt and Bread" and "The Fire on the Mountain" are retold from generation to generation? What makes stories like this last?

2. So far you have read three stories in which characters learn important lessons:
   - "Salt and Bread"
   - "Ali and the Magic Stew"
   - "The Fire on the Mountain"

   For each story, in one or two sentences, identify who learns the lesson and what he or she learns.

A Plot Summary

The *plot* of a story is what happens in the story. It is the sequence of actions or events. When you *summarize* the plot of a story, you tell only the most important parts and ideas. You do not include details and examples, but only the main events. You tell these main events in the order in which they happen in the story.

For example, here is a plot summary of "Cinderella":

> After Cinderella's father dies, she goes to live with her cruel stepmother and stepsisters. The stepmother forces Cinderella to do all the hard housework. When the Prince invites all the young ladies in the kingdom to attend a ball, the stepmother refuses to let Cinderella go. But Cinderella's fairy godmother appears and sends her to the ball dressed in a beautiful gown and glass slippers. At the ball, the Prince falls in love with Cinderella. But when midnight comes, the magic spell ends and Cinderella runs away. The Prince finds only one glass slipper that has fallen from her foot. He searches the kingdom to find the girl whose foot fits the slipper, and when he finally finds Cinderella, they marry and live happily ever after.

Summarize the plot of one of the stories you have read so far: "Salt and Bread," "Ali and the Magic Stew," or "The Fire on the Mountain." In your plot summary, include only the main events of the story. Write your plot summary in your Reading Notebook.

Name _____   Date _____

"The Sword of Damocles"

Wouldn't it be wonderful to be as rich and powerful as a king?
Or would it?

Pronunciation
Dionysius (diy-uh-NISH-ee-uhs)

Vocabulary
You will find these words in today's reading.

> **dread:** (n.) great fear, especially fear that something bad is
> going to happen
> As the roller coaster climbed to the top of the hill, a feeling of
> *dread* swept over me.

> **tyrant:** (n.) a ruler who is cruel or unfair
> The cruel and unjust queen was considered a *tyrant* by most of
> her subjects.

Think Ahead
1. Do you know the saying, "The grass is always greener on the
   other side of the fence"? What does that saying mean to you?
   Have you ever felt that someone else's grass was greener than
   your own?

2. People sometimes say, "Be careful what you wish for." Think
   about that saying as you read today's story.

Read
"The Sword of Damocles" in *Classics for Young Readers,* Vol. 5A,
pages 23-24

Questions

Answer the following questions in complete sentences in your Reading Notebook.

1. Who is Dionysius? What does he live in fear of?
2. At the beginning of the story, how does Damocles feel about Dionysius's life?
3. What does Dionysius suggest that he and Damocles do?
4. What dangles over Damocles's head? Why is it there?
5. What lesson does Damocles learn?

Discuss

1. Why do you think Dionysius wants Damocles to see what his life is like by trading places?
2. Why do you think Damocles does not see Dionysius's life for what it really is until they trade places?

A Matter of Perspective

There is more than one way to look at any situation. It all depends on your *perspective*—on how you see and think about the situation. For example, imagine that it's a hot, dry summer and it hasn't rained for weeks, when suddenly there's a big rainstorm. If you were a gardener eagerly waiting for rain, your perspective on the rainstorm would be very different from the perspective of a person who has made big plans to go to the beach.

Think about the different perspectives of Damocles and Dionysius. At the beginning of the story, Damocles has his own perspective on Dionysius's life, a perspective that is very different from Dionysius's.

On the Comparing Perspectives page, compare and contrast the perspectives of these two characters

Stories and Sayings

You've heard two sayings that apply to the story of Damocles:

- The grass is always greener on the other side of the fence.
- Be careful what you wish for.

Did you know that the story of Damocles is the source for a saying? Even today, when people feel that something bad or dangerous lies ahead, they speak of having "a sword of Damocles" or "a sword hanging over their heads." For example:

> Jenny and Maggie both have a piano recital coming up. In one week, they will perform before a large audience. Jenny has been practicing every day. "I can't wait for the recital!" she says to Maggie. But Maggie, who has not been practicing, groans and says, "I can wait—I feel like I have a sword hanging over my head."

Tell a very brief story, like the one about Jenny and Maggie, in which someone might use any one of the three sayings you've learned in today's lesson. Write your story in your Reading Notebook.

Name

Date

Comparing Perspectives

Just how good is the life of the wealthy Dionysius? It depends on your perspective. Use the glasses below to compare the perspectives of Damocles and Dionysius. In the left lens, write two or more sentences about how Dionysius sees his own life. In the right lens, write two or more sentences about how Damocles sees the king's life at the beginning of the story. Use "I" and write in the voice of each character.

Name _____   Date _____

"As Rich As Croesus"

Croesus, who is said to be the richest man in the world, thinks he is the happiest man in the world. But is he?

Pronunciation
Croesus (KREE-suhs)

Vocabulary
You will find these words in today's reading.

prosperous: (adj.) successful
The *prosperous* business was able to give raises to all of its employees.

feeble: (adj.) weak
After the surgery, the man was very *feeble* and needed time to recover.

splendor: (n.) magnificent or beautiful appearance
When the curtain rose, we were impressed by the *splendor* of the scenery and costumes.

Think Ahead
When you were younger, you probably read stories that ended with, "And they lived happily ever after." What does it mean to be happy? List three things happiness means to you.

Read
"As Rich As Croesus" in *Classics for Young Readers,* Vol. 5A, pages 25-29

Questions

Answer the following questions in complete sentences in your Reading Notebook.

1. Describe Croesus.
2. Why does Solon think that Tellus was the happiest man?
3. What happens to Croesus's kingdom?
4. Fill in the blanks: People still say that a very wealthy man is as rich as _____, and that a very wise man is as wise as _____.

Discuss

1. Why do Solon's answers make Croesus unhappy?
2. What lesson does Croesus learn?
3. At the end of the story, why does Cyrus let Croesus go free?

Two Ideas of Happiness

The *theme* of a story is the important idea or message the story is trying to communicate. A story may have more than one theme.

One theme of "As Rich As Croesus" has to do with happiness. What does the story say about what it means to be happy? Complete the Thinking About Theme page. Be sure to use details from the story to support your answers.

Name _____ Date _____

Thinking About Theme

One theme of "As Rich As Croesus" is happiness. Croesus and Solon have very different ideas of what makes a person happy. Explain what happiness means to each character. Write as though you were speaking in the voice of the character. (Assume that you are speaking for Croesus at the beginning of the story, before he has lost all his wealth.) Use details from the story in your answers.

I, Croesus, am the happiest man in the world because _____

_____

_____

_____

_____

I, Solon, say this: _____

_____

_____

_____

In your own words, what is the theme of the story?

_____

_____

_____

Name _____   Date _____

"The Three Questions"

Meet a king in search of answers to three important questions.

Vocabulary
You will find these words in today's reading.

administrators: (n.) people in charge of directing or managing something
The office *administrators* trained the new employees to do their jobs well.

diverse: (adj.) unlike one another; different
The United States is a nation of *diverse* people.

hermit: (n.) a person who lives alone or away from others
The *hermit* lived in a cabin deep in the forest, far away from any town or village.

vengeance: (n.) the act of punishing or getting back at someone for a wrong or injury that he or she has committed
After the raiders robbed the village, the captain cried out to his men, "Let us seek *vengeance* upon those who have done such great harm to us!"

reconcile: (v.) to settle differences, to make up after a fight or argument
The two friends shook hands and were happy to be *reconciled* after their argument.

assaulted: (v.) attacked with force or violence
The soldiers took up their spears and swords and *assaulted* the castle of their enemy.

Think Ahead

1. Leo Tolstoy, a Russian author of novels and short stories, wrote "The Three Questions." He lived from 1828 to 1910. He is most famous for his great novels, including *War and Peace.* Find Russia on a world map or globe.

2. The king in this story wants to know the answers to three important questions. Think about how you would answer the following questions:
   - Who is the most important person to you?
   - When is the right time to do something?
   - What is the most important thing to do?

Read

"The Three Questions" in *Classics for Young Readers,* Vol. 5A, pages 30-34

Questions

Answer the following questions in complete sentences in your Reading Notebook.

1. For what three questions does the king want answers?
2. Why does the king decide to look for answers from the hermit?
3. What does the king help the hermit do?
4. Why does the wounded man ask for forgiveness?
5. What are the hermit's answers to the king's three questions?

Discuss

1. Paraphrase—explain in your own words—the hermit's answers to the king's three questions.
2. Why do you think the hermit doesn't answer the king's questions right away when he is first asked?
3. Were you surprised by the hermit's answers to the king's questions? Do you agree with the answers?

Write a Diary Entry

Choose one of the following characters: the king, the hermit, or the wounded man. Pretend you are that character and, in your Reading Notebook, write a diary entry about what happens to you in the story. Use details from the story to explain the lessons you learned or taught.

Name _____ Date _____

Roll and Write

Reflect on the details, characters, and lessons learned in these stories: "The Sword of Damocles," "As Rich As Croesus," and "The Three Questions."

Think Ahead
You've read about three kings: Dionysius, Croesus, and the king who asks the three questions. Which of these kings seems wisest to you? Why?

Roll and Write
Gather the Roll and Write activity page. Cut out the pattern on the page, fold on the lines, and tape it together to create a "review cube." Each side of the cube asks a different question.

Roll the cube. Read the question that lands face up and answer it using details and examples from one of the stories: "The Sword of Damocles," "As Rich As Croesus," or "The Three Questions." Write your answer in your Reading Notebook.

Repeat the process until you have answered a total of three questions, one question about each of the three stories.

Name _____   Date _____

Roll and Write

Who are the main characters in the story? Provide at least two details to describe each character.

What part of the story did you find most interesting? Describe the part and tell why you thought it was the most interesting

When and where does the story take place? Provide at least two details to describe the setting.

Summarize the plot of the story. What happens?

What important lesson do the character or characters learn?

Predict how you think the character or characters will behave now that they have learned an important lesson.

■ ■ ■ ■ ■ ■ cut
───── fold

Name _____ Date _____

Looking Back

Tie it all together. Think back on the lessons learned, and then write about two characters.

The Moral of the Story

When you were younger, you probably read or heard fables. For example, do you know the fable of the Tortoise and the Hare? That fable tells how the slow but patient Tortoise wins a race against the speedy but careless Hare. Like many fables, it ends with "the moral of the story."

A *moral* is a lesson that a story teaches. In the fable of the Tortoise and the Hare, the moral is, "Slow and steady wins the race."

Think back on the stories you have read in this unit. In these stories, the characters have learned important lessons. How would you boil down each of these lessons to a "moral of the story"?

Look back to the stories and use your Reading Notebook to help you complete the Moral of the Story page.

Character Study

In a story, sometimes an author will tell you exactly what a character is like. For example, in "As Rich As Croesus," the author tells us that Solon is wise and "noted for his wisdom."

At other times, however, you have to look for clues to understand a character. You need to pay attention to what the character says and does, and what other characters say about him.

For example, read the following passage from "Ali and the Magic Stew."

"Disgusting grapes!" A handful of fruit flew through the air. Ali was sitting cross-legged with Layla, his small black monkey, on his shoulder. "They are fit only for the beggar who fouls our gate!"

From this passage, what would you say are two adjectives to describe Ali at this point in the story?

Ali is_____and _____.

Why did you choose those adjectives?

Now complete the Character Study page.

Name _____   Date _____

The Moral of the Story

Think about each story in the unit. Draw a line from the title in the left column to the best moral—the lesson learned—for that story in the right column.

Story	Moral
"Salt and Bread"	Have compassion and humility.
"Ali and the Magic Stew"	Treasure the present moment and the people in it.
"The Fire on the Mountain"	Listen to your heart to hear the truth.
"The Sword of Damocles"	Be fair and just when dealing with others.
"As Rich As Croesus"	Be satisfied with your life and do not envy other people.
"The Three Questions"	Do not place your happiness in wealth and power because no one knows what the future may bring.

Name _____ **Date** _____

Character Study

Pick any **two** of the characters below. Look back to the story to remind yourself of what each character is like. Come up with two adjectives to describe the character. Then use evidence from the story to explain why you chose those adjectives.

"Salt and Bread"
- The king
- The youngest daughter

"Ali and the Magic Stew"
- Ali
- The beggar

"The Fire on the Mountain"
- Arha
- Haptom

"The Sword of Damocles"
- Damocles
- Dionysius

"As Rich As Croesus"
- Croesus
- Solon

"The Three Questions"
- The king
- The hermit

Note: If a character changes in the story, then you might pick one adjective to describe him before he changes and one to describe him after he changes.

1. _____is _____and _____

   (name)   (adjective)   (adjective)

_____is _____because _____

_____

_____

_____

Character Study

_____ Is _____ because _____

_____

_____

_____

_____

2. _____ Is _____ and _____

       (name)   (adjective)   (adjective)

_____ Is _____ because _____

_____

_____

_____

_____ Is _____ because _____

_____

_____

_____

Name _____   Date _____

"The Story of Mulan": Session 1

Doing the right thing is not always easy. Meet a young woman from China who had the courage to make a difficult decision.

Vocabulary

You will find these words in today's reading.

whimper: (v.) to make a low whining or crying sound
The baby foxes began to *whimper* when the mother fox left the den.

flinch: (v.) to suddenly pull away from something in fear or pain
Even though the shark was in a tank, when it swam near us, I *flinched.*

reproach: (n.) disapproval
My mother looked at me with *reproach* when I pulled my sister's braid.

satchel: (n.) a small bag used for carrying
I put my library books in my *satchel,* put the strap over my shoulder, and walked home.

Think Ahead

1. Have you ever heard of Superman, Hercules, William Tell, or Brave Margaret? They are not real people. They are fictional characters. In their stories, each of those characters is a *hero.* What kinds of things do these heroes do? What words describe them?

2. Today's story is about a hero from China. Find China on a map or globe.

Read

Chapter 1 of "The Story of Mulan" in *Classics for Young Readers,* Vol. 5A, pages 36-46

Questions

Answer the following questions in complete sentences in your Reading Notebook.

1. Why does Mulan say her father cannot go to war?
2. What will happen if no one from Mulan's family goes to war?
3. Write two things Mulan does to get ready to leave.

Discuss

1. Do you think Mulan is brave? Why or why not?
2. Mulan does not have to go to war. Why do you think she decides to take her father's place in the army?

Making Inferences

Sometimes, to understand a character, we have to go beyond the words in the story. We have to *make inferences.* When we make an inference, or *infer,* we use the words in the story as clues. What a character says, thinks, and does are all clues that help us make inferences. We think about the evidence in the story, and then we draw conclusions based on that evidence.

For example, think back to "Ali and the Magic Stew." What can we infer about Ali? When we first see him in the story, he is proud and selfish. He calls the beggar a "pig." But he puts on the beggar's cloak and begs enough coins to buy the ingredients for his father's stew, even though people jeer at him and scorn him. So, we can infer that Ali's love for his father is greater than his pride and selfishness. At the end of the story, we see Ali put his arms around the beggar and ask him to stay. What do you think we can we infer from this?

Think about the characters in "The Story of Mulan" and make inferences to answer the following questions.

1. How do Mulan's parents feel about her decision to take her father's place? What evidence in the story helped you come to this conclusion?

_____

_____

_____

_____

2. After Mulan decides that she will take her father's place, she buys a saddle and a horse, she dresses in disguise, and she rides away without looking back. What do Mulan's actions tell you about her?

_____

_____

_____

_____

Guidelines for Peer Discussion

Share your thoughts, ideas, questions, and feelings about a text with a peer or others. Listen carefully to what everyone has to say about the text. During your discussion, follow these guidelines.

1. Be prepared to discuss what you think about the text. You should have already read the assignment. Come prepared to discuss your ideas and use examples from the text to support your thoughts and answers.

2. You will be asked questions about the text. Be ready to answer them, and bring some questions of your own to ask others, such as:

   "Who was your favorite character? Why?"

   "What was your favorite part of the text? Why?"

   "What fact did you enjoy learning? Why do you find this fact interesting?"

   "What question would you ask if you had the chance to meet the author?"

3. Listen if it's not your turn to speak. Pay attention to what others say so that you can add your ideas. Speak clearly and in complete sentences.

4. If you don't understand what someone says, ask a question.

   "What do you mean when you say . . . ?"

   "Can you give an example of . . . ?"

5. If you don't agree with what someone says, explain why.

   "I don't agree with that because . . . "

6. Keep discussions positive! You can disagree, but don't argue. Be respectful.

Name _____   Date _____

"The Story of Mulan": Session 2

Will Mulan be discovered? Will she ever see her family again?
Find out in today's reading.

Vocabulary

You will find these words in today's reading.

cascade: (v.) to fall like water
The blue silk *cascaded* over the edge of the sewing table like a
rippling stream.

tresses: (n.) long locks of hair
Rapunzel's long blond *tresses* reached from the high tower
window to the ground.

marshal: (v.) to bring together and put in order
After the battle, the general *marshaled* his scattered troops and
marched on.

insignia: (n.) the symbol or badge of a group or person
The king's messengers wore the royal *insignia* on their clothes.

indebted: (adj.) owing gratitude to someone else
I am *indebted* to you for taking care of my dog while I was on
vacation.

Think Ahead

1. Summarize what has happened so far in the story.
2. How do you think Mulan feels as she rides away from home?
   What do you infer from the statement that "she did not look
   back"?

Read

Chapters 2 and 3 of "The Story of Mulan" in *Classics for Young Readers,* Vol. 5A, pages 36-46

Questions

Answer the following questions in complete sentences in your Reading Notebook.

1. What is Mulan's rank in the army?
2. For how many years does Mulan fight the enemy?
3. What does Mulan ask for when the Emperor offers her anything she wants as a reward?
4. What does the Emperor give her?

Discuss

1. In Chapter 3, Mulan thinks, "I have disgraced my country and myself by lying." Do you agree or disagree? Why?
2. Do you think the Emperor knows that Mulan is a woman? What clues in the story make you think so?

How Others See Mulan

One way we learn about a character is by examining what other characters say about her and how they respond to her. Answer the following questions about Mulan. Go back through the story and find evidence to support your answers. Write your responses in your Reading Notebook.

1. Is Mulan a skilled warrior? What do the soldiers say about her?
2. How do you know the soldiers respect Mulan? What do they do after the battle?
3. Do Mulan's soldiers like having her as their general? What do they do after her speech?

The Hall of Heroes

Mulan is the first of many fictional heroes you will meet in this unit. Create a "Hall of Heroes" to remember her as you read about other heroes.

Write Mulan's name on the line on the Hall of Heroes page. Write a paragraph that tells why Mulan is a hero. Include two or more examples of things Mulan says and does that show why she belongs in the Hall of Heroes. If you want to, draw a picture of her in the box. Save this page.

Name _____   Date _____

The Hall of Heroes

_____

belongs in the Hall of Heroes because

_____

_____

_____

_____

_____   _____

Name _____   Date _____

"St. George and the Dragon"

There are many kinds of heroes. Can you find two in today's story?

Vocabulary
You will find these words in today's reading.

desolation: (n.) ruin, destruction
The fire cut a wide path of *desolation* through the countryside.

girdle: (n.) a belt or sash
The lady fastened a *girdle* of green velvet about her waist and tied her handkerchief to it.

yon: (adj.) an old-fashioned word for "yonder," meaning "far away, in the distance"
"*Yon* fortress," said the knight, pointing to the castle on the hill, "is where we shall feast this evening."

Think Ahead
1. Review "Mulan." What does Mulan do that makes her a hero?
2. "St. George and the Dragon" is a tale from England. Find England on a map or globe.

Read
"St. George and the Dragon" in *Classics for Young Readers,* Vol. 5A, pages 47-51

Questions

Answer the following questions in complete sentences in your Reading Notebook.

1. Why does St. George leave his peaceful, happy lands?
2. What is the Princess going to do to try to save the city?
3. What does St. George do to save the city?

Discuss

There are *two* heroes in this story: the Princess and St. George. What makes the Princess a hero? What makes St. George a hero?

The Hall of Heroes: St. George and the Princess

Have St. George and the Princess join the Hall of Heroes. Complete a Hall of Heroes page for each character.

Write the hero's name on the line. Then include two or more examples of things each character says and does that show why he or she belongs in the Hall of Heroes. If you want to, draw a picture of her in the box. Save this page.

Name _____   Date _____

The Hall of Heroes

_____

belongs in the Hall of Heroes because

_____

_____

_____

_____

_____

Name _____   Date _____

What Is a Hero?

You've met three heroes: Mulan, St. George, and the Princess.
Decide the most important qualities of a hero and write a
proclamation calling for a hero.

Think Ahead
1. Summarize the plot of each story.
2. Reread your Hall of Heroes pages.

The Qualities of a Hero
You've met three heroes: Mulan, St. George, and the Princess.
For each character, discuss the following questions.

- What heroic things does he or she do?
- What makes the hero different from the other characters in the story?
- Who is the hero trying to help?
- Why do you think each character is a hero?

Divide a sheet of paper into three columns. At the top of each column,
write the name of one hero: Mulan, St. George, and the Princess.
Underneath each name, list words and phrases that define why this
character is a hero. You may use the same word for more than one
character. For example, under all three, you might write "brave."

When you finish writing your list, review it. Which words and
phrases show up most often? Pick three words or phrases that you
think are the most important qualities of a hero. Write them here:

1. _____

2. _____

3. _____

A Royal Proclamation

Imagine that you are the king or queen of a land that is threatened by some danger—it might be a dragon, it might be invading armies, or something else—you decide. You need a hero to help save your land.

Use the Calling All Heroes page to write a royal proclamation in which you call for a hero to come to your aid. In each paragraph, name one of three important qualities for a hero (which you listed above), and give examples to illustrate that quality. For example:

> Like Mulan, you must be brave. Mulan showed her bravery by . . . .

You may look back at the stories and your Hall of Heroes pages for ideas and information.

Name _____ Date _____

Calling All Heroes!

Write a royal proclamation to bring aid to your land in a time of need.

Hear ye! Hear ye!

The most high and mighty _____

hereby calls for all heroes to come to the aid of their land.

Like _____, you must be _____

_____

_____

_____

_____

Like _____, you must be _____

_____

_____

_____

_____

_____

Calling All Heroes!

Like _____, you must be _____

_____

_____

_____

_____

_____

Heroes, come forth! Villains, beware!

Name _____   Date _____

"The Last of the Dragons"

The last of the dragons has been found in England! What do you think will happen to this unique creature?

Vocabulary
You will find these words in today's reading.

snout: (n.) an animal's nose
The pig wriggled its *snout* in the mud, searching for food.

unbend: (v.) to relax
After a long week at the office, my father looks forward to the weekend, when he can *unbend* and have fun.

presently: (adv.) an old-fashioned expression for "at once" or "very soon"
"Please go ahead without me," said the princess, "for I will join you *presently*."

fencing: (n.; verb *to fence*) a sport in which two athletes fight with long, slender swords
I put on my special face guard and padded jacket to prepare for my *fencing* lesson.

valor: (n.) bravery, courage, firmness in the face of danger
The king praised the knight for his great *valor* in battle.

philosophy: (n.) the study of basic truths, deep ideas, and great questions, such as, "What is truth?"
He read many books of *philosophy* because he wanted to answer the question, "What is the right way to live?"

neglect: (v.) to ignore, to fail to pay attention

Do not *neglect* the chores you have to do today, or you will only add to your duties tomorrow.

triumph: (n.) the joy of victory or success

The soccer team paraded through the town in *triumph* after winning the league finals.

retreat: (v.) to move back away from an enemy, to withdraw from a battle

After hours of fighting, the soldiers were forced to *retreat* into the woods.

gratitude: (n.) a feeling of thankfulness and appreciation

To express their *gratitude* to our coach, the parents all chipped in to buy him a big trophy.

Think Ahead

1. How do St. George and the Princess show that they are heroes?
2. From the story of "St. George and the Dragon," as well as other stories you've read or heard with dragons in them, what do you expect the dragon in today's story to be like?

Read

"The Last of the Dragons" in *Classics for Young Readers,* Vol. 5A, pages 52-61

Questions

Answer the following questions in complete sentences in your Reading Notebook.

1. Does the Princess want to be rescued by the Prince?
2. What does the dragon say about fighting for and eating the Princess?
3. What do the Prince and the Princess offer the dragon?
4. Why does the dragon cry?
5. What does the dragon want to drink?
6. What does the dragon turn into at the end of the story?

Discuss

1. What do people think the dragon is like? What is he really like?
2. The Princess says, "Everything can be tamed by kindness." What do you think that means?
3. What do you think the Princess means when she says, "You can't tame anything, even by kindness, if you're frightened of it"?

Expectations and Surprises

The author of "The Last of the Dragons" knows that we are likely to have certain expectations about a story with a prince, a princess, and a dragon. For example, you might have expected the dragon in this story to be a fierce and terrible monster, like the one in "St. George and the Dragon." But he turns out to be a surprisingly different creature.

Complete the Expectations and Surprises page. Under "Expectations," write what you think the author expects us to think. Under "Surprises," tell what actually happens in the story. Write at least one expectation and surprise for each of the main characters: the Princess, the Prince, and the dragon.

Name _____

Date _____

Expectations and Surprises

Under "Expectations," write things from "The Last of the Dragons" the author expects us to think. Under "Surprises," tell what actually happens in the story. Write at least one expectation and surprise for each of the main characters.

	Expectations		
The Princess			
The Prince			
The Dragon			

Name _____   Date _____

Turning a Hero Tale on Its Head

Discuss what makes a hero tale. Rewrite the ending of "St. George and the Dragon."

Think Ahead

Review the three stories you have read: "The Story of Mulan," "St. George and the Dragon," and "The Last of the Dragons." Which is your favorite? Why?

Compare and Contrast

"The Story of Mulan" and "St. George and the Dragon" are hero tales. Compare and contrast the hero tales with "The Last of the Dragons." Discuss the following questions.

1. Describe the main character in a hero tale. What is he or she like? What does the hero have to do?

2. Describe the battle the hero fights. Does it seem like the hero will win?

3. Who is supposed to be the hero in "The Last of the Dragons"? What is unusual about him?

4. Compare the Princess in "St. George and the Dragon" to the Princess in "The Last of the Dragons."

5. How is the dragon in "St. George and the Dragon" different from the dragon in "The Last of the Dragons"?

6. In "The Last of the Dragons," what do the characters do instead of fighting?

Turn a Hero Tale on Its Head

"The Last of the Dragons" has fun by turning the hero tale on its head. It plays with what we expect and gives us something unexpected.

Write your own story, or part of a story, in which you take what readers expect and surprise them with something unexpected.

Rewrite the end of "St. George and the Dragon." Begin at the point at which St. George first encounters the dragon. Think of an unexpected reason why the dragon has been destroying the land. For example, you might say the dragon doesn't *mean* to be destroying things. He has a cold, and his coughing knocks down trees, while his fiery sneezes burn the fields. How would the rest of the story change? Would the Princess and St. George try to help the dragon? How might they cure him?

Use that example if you want to, or imagine your own new ending.

Use your imagination—if you have fun writing, your readers will have fun reading what you write.

Name _____   Date _____

"Robin Hood and Allin-a-dale"

You've probably read tales of the outlaws of Sherwood Forest and their bold leader, Robin Hood, who robbed from the rich to give to the poor. Find out how Robin helped a young man win his true love.

Vocabulary
You will find this word in today's reading.

> **trip:** (v.) to dance or skip
>
> As the children returned from the circus, they *tripped* merrily down the sidewalk to their homes.

Think Ahead
1. Think about the heroes you've read about so far. What do all these heroes have in common?
2. This story comes from England. Which other two stories in this unit also come from England?

Read
"Robin Hood and Allin-a-Dale" in *Classics for Young Readers,* Vol. 5A, pages 62-65

Questions
Answer the following questions in complete sentences in your Reading Notebook.

1. Why do the men live in Sherwood Forest?
2. Why do the common people call Robin Hood their friend?
3. What does Allin-a-Dale promise he will do if Robin saves his bride?
4. What does Robin disguise himself as to get into the church?
5. What happens when Robin Hood blows his horn?

Discuss

1. The story says that the rich old man "went home in a great rage." Do you think he has a right to be angry?
2. Compare Robin Hood as a hero to St. George. Does Robin Hood do anything that you think St. George would not do?

Robin Hood and St. George

Compare and contrast Robin Hood and St. George. Are they very different or do Robin Hood and St. George share some of the same qualities?

Divide a sheet of paper into two columns. Label the first column "Robin Hood" and the second column "St. George." Look back through the stories and answer the following questions for each:

1. How does he spend his time?
2. What words does the author use to describe him?
3. How does he treat others?
4. What do his actions tell you about him?

Write two paragraphs about Robin Hood and St. George. In the first paragraph, tell at least two ways that the characters are alike. In the second paragraph, tell at least two ways they are different.

Write your paragraphs in your Reading Notebook.

Name _____   Date _____

"Robin Hood and the Golden Arrow"

Will the Sheriff of Nottingham outsmart Robin Hood? Read this story and find out!

Vocabulary
You will find these words in today's reading.

thatch: (n.) plant material, like grasses or straw, used for roofing
The woman laid bundles of *thatch* together to make a roof for her hut.

thoroughly: (adv.) completely
I was *thoroughly* embarrassed when I got to baseball practice and realized that I'd accidentally put my jersey on inside-out.

Think Ahead
1. Why do the poor people in England consider Robin Hood their friend?
2. If you've read tales of Robin Hood before, then you might have met a character in today's story—Robin's foe, the Sheriff of Nottingham. What do you know about the Sheriff?

Read
"Robin Hood and the Golden Arrow" in *Classics for Young Readers,* Vol. 5A, pages 66-74

Questions
Answer the following questions in complete sentences in your Reading Notebook.

1. Reread the second paragraph of part 1. What does the sheriff's wife worry about most?

2. What does the sheriff's wife think of the advice the king gives the sheriff?
3. Why does the sheriff fail to catch Robin Hood at the archery contest?
4. Why does Robin Hood want to give the arrow back to the sheriff?
5. Who are the monks at the end of the story? How do you know?

Discuss

1. The sheriff thinks of himself as a "great man." Do you think he is? Why?
2. What does Robin Hood mean when he says, "If the proud sheriff had but borrowed a woman's wit to help him, he'd have put me in the deepest dungeon cell by now"?

Debate at the Hall of Heroes

An enormous crowd has gathered around the doors of the Hall of Heroes. Some are making speeches. Others are carrying signs. Tomorrow, a vote will be held to decide whether to add Robin Hood to the Hall of Heroes. Half the crowd wants to add Robin Hood. The other half wants to keep him out.

Write a speech that tells why Robin Hood should or should not be added to the Hall of Heroes.

Remember, in your speech you are trying to *persuade* people. You want them to agree with your opinion. Make sure you give *examples* of Robin Hood's behavior that support your opinion, and compare him to at least one other character in the Hall of Heroes.

Name _____   Date _____

The Hall of Heroes

_____

belongs in the Hall of Heroes because

_____

_____

_____

_____

_____   _____

Name _____   Date _____

"The Horse of Power": Session 1

Listen for the thunder of iron hooves as you read this old Russian tale about a young archer and his wise horse.

Pronunciation
Tsar (zahr)

Vocabulary
You will find these words in today's reading.

archer: (n.) a man or woman who uses a bow and arrow
The skilled *archer* could shoot an arrow through a leaf from a hundred paces away.

scarcely: (adv.) hardly
My brother used so much hot water for his shower, there was *scarcely* any left for me.

maize: (n.) corn
The chickens pecked at the golden kernels of *maize* the girl scattered on the ground.

flagon: (n.) a large bottle
The servants brought three enormous *flagons* of wine up from the cellar for the king's feast.

Think Ahead
1. Look back at the three most important qualities of a hero you selected for "Calling All Heroes." Keep those qualities in mind as you read "The Horse of Power."
2. Today's story is from Russia. Find Russia on a map or globe.

Read
Chapter 1 of "The Horse of Power" in *Classics for Young Readers,* Vol. 5A, pages 75-82

Questions
Answer the following questions in complete sentences in your Reading Notebook.

1. Describe the horse of power.
2. What does the horse of power say will happen if the archer picks up the firebird's feather?
3. Why does the archer pick up the feather, even though the horse warned him not to?
4. What does the Tsar say will happen to the archer if he doesn't bring the Princess Vasilissa?

Discuss
1. Why isn't the Tsar satisfied with what the young man brings him?
2. The horse of power gives this advice: "Do not be frightened yet, and do not weep. The trouble is not now; the trouble lies before you." What do you think he means by that? Do you think it's good advice? Why?

Journal Entry
Imagine that you are the Tsar, and that you are telling what has happened so far. You might begin like this:

> A few days ago, one of my archers burst into my palace and laid a firebird's feather at my feet. What other ruler in the world has one of those? I couldn't bear the thought of someone else having one, so I told the man to go and fetch me the rest of the firebird, or else he would lose his head!

Now pretend you are either the horse of power or the young archer. Write a journal entry in which you summarize what has happened so far in the story. Write in the voice of the character you choose. Write in your Reading Notebook.

Name _____   Date _____

"The Horse of Power": Session 2

Will the archer be able to meet the Tsar's demands?

Vocabulary
You will find these words in today's reading.

casket: (n.) a small box
I put my best jewelry in the silver *casket* my grandmother gave me.

cauldron: (n.) a large pot
The *cauldron* was so large that the cook could make soup for thirty people in it.

seethe: (v.) to boil
The water in the hot spring *seethed* and steamed.

Think Ahead
1. What has happened so far in the story?
2. Predict what will happen next. Why do you think that will happen?

Read
Chapter 2 of "The Horse of Power" in *Classics for Young Readers,* Vol. 5A, pages 82-87.

Questions
Answer the following questions in complete sentences in your Reading Notebook.

1. How does the horse of power catch the tsar of all the lobsters?
2. What happens when the archer jumps into the boiling water?
3. What happens when the Tsar jumps into the boiling water?

Discuss

1. Who is the villain in this story? Do you think he deserves what happens to him? Why or why not?

2. Do you think the archer gets what he deserves? Why or why not?

What Characters Say

We can learn about a character by looking at how the author describes him and by what the character says and does. In this activity, you will make inferences about what the character says. First, identify who says each of the quotations below. Then, in your Reading Notebook, write what you can learn about the character from what he says.

1. Who says these words?_____

"As you have known how to take the firebird, you will know how to bring me the bride I desire. If you do not bring her, then, by my sword, your head will no longer sit between your shoulders!"

What inferences can you make from what he says?

2. Who says these words?_____

"Well, do not be frightened yet, and do not weep. The trouble is not now; the trouble lies before you."

What inferences can you make from what he says?

Hero or Not?

Think back to the essay you wrote about what makes a character a hero. Do you think the archer is a hero? How is he like and unlike the other heroes you've read about?

- Is he brave like Mulan, St. George, and the Princess?
- Does he face dangers to help others, like Robin Hood and St. George?
- Can you find examples in the story where you think the archer acts like a hero?
- If you think the archer is a hero, is he a different kind of hero from Mulan and St. George? If so, explain.

In your Reading Notebook, write a paragraph of at least five sentences telling whether you think the archer is a hero. Be sure to provide examples from the story to support your opinion.

Name _____   Date _____

Let's Talk Heroes

Discuss the heroes you've met while reading "The Last of the Dragons" and the stories about Robin Hood. But first, learn some important tips for having a productive and enjoyable discussion of a story.

Speaking and Listening

Complete the online activity to learn how to participate in a discussion about something you've read.

Think Ahead

1. Who are your favorite heroes in literature? Who are some people that you consider to be real-life heroes?

2. How can a hero in real life be different from a hero in a story?

Discussion: Different Types of Heroes

After completing the online activity and thinking about real-life examples of heroism, share your thoughts about the prince and princess in "The Last of the Dragons" and about Robin Hood. Listen as others share their thoughts with you. Discuss the following questions:

- How are these characters like other heroic characters found in story books?

- How are these characters different from other heroes in literature? What qualities do they demonstrate that make them unique?

- In what ways are these characters like real people?

- Which of these characters do you admire most? Why?

- If you could trade places with one of these characters, which one would it be? Which character would you not want to trade places with? Why?
- If you were in trouble and needed help, which of these characters would you most want to help you? Why?

During discussion, don't interrupt others, ask and answer specific questions, and try to build on the points that others make.

Name _____   Date _____

From The Prince and the Pauper

Have you ever wished to be someone else? Find out what happens when two boys get their wish.

Vocabulary

You will find these words in today's reading.

pauper: (n.) a very poor person
The charity collected food, toys, and clothing for the *paupers*.

long: (v.) to want something very much
She *longed* to be a great violinist, so she made sure to practice every day.

courtly: (adj.) polite, elegant, in the manner of a royal court
The family had such *courtly* manners that people who had dinner at their house felt as if they were dining with a king and a queen in a grand castle.

pampered: (adj.) being given an extreme amount of care and attention
The *pampered* canary had dozens of toys, a golden water dish, and a huge cage with a small tree inside.

fiend: (n.) an evil or wicked person
He was no ordinary bully; he was so mean to the other children that they called him a *fiend*.

rickety: (adj.) not stable, likely to fall down
The table with the cracked leg was so *rickety* that it would collapse if you touched it.

passion: (n.) a strong love or desire
My neighbor's *passion* is gardening; his yard blazes with colorful flowers, bushes, and trees that he carefully tends every day.

Think Ahead

The Prince and the Pauper is a novel written by an American author named Mark Twain. The fictional story is set in England in the 1500s, and it begins on the day Edward Tudor, the Prince of Wales, is born. Everyone in the city of London is celebrating because when Prince Edward grows up, he will become the next King of England.

Read

from *The Prince and the Pauper* in *Classics for Young Readers,* Vol. 5A, pages 88-92

Questions

Answer the following questions in complete sentences in your Reading Notebook.

1. Where and when does the story take place?
2. Name and describe the two boys who are born on the same day.
3. Describe Tom's real life.
4. What does Tom imagine he is?

Discuss

1. Do you admire Tom? Use examples from the story to explain why or why not.
2. How does Tom feel about his life?

Character Study

We learn about characters by paying attention to what they say and do, and what others say about them. And sometimes, to understand a character, we go beyond the words in the story. We *make inferences.* To make an inference, or *infer,* means to think about the evidence in the story, and then draw conclusions based on that evidence.

To make inferences about Tom Canty, begin by discussing these questions. Look back to the story for specific evidence.

- What does the priest teach Tom? What kinds of stories does Tom read and hear?
- What does Tom dream about afterwards?
- How do Tom's behavior and ideas change? What does he think about and wish for?
- How do other people react to the changes in Tom?

Using your answers to the questions above, draw conclusions about Tom Canty. In your Reading Notebook, write a paragraph describing the kind of person he is. Use evidence from the story to support your ideas.

Guidelines for Peer Discussion

Share your thoughts, ideas, questions, and feelings about a text with a peer or others. Listen carefully to what everyone has to say about the text. During your discussion, follow these guidelines.

1. Be prepared to discuss what you think about the text. You should have already read the assignment. Come prepared to discuss your ideas and use examples from the text to support your thoughts and answers.

2. You will be asked questions about the text. Be ready to answer them, and bring some questions of your own to ask others, such as:

   "Who was your favorite character? Why?"

   "What was your favorite part of the text? Why?"

   "What fact did you enjoy learning? Why do you find this fact interesting?"

   "What question would you ask if you had the chance to meet the author?"

3. Listen if it's not your turn to speak. Pay attention to what others say so that you can add your ideas. Speak clearly and in complete sentences.

4. If you don't understand what someone says, ask a question.

   "What do you mean when you say . . . ?"

   "Can you give an example of . . . ?"

5. If you don't agree with what someone says, explain why.

   "I don't agree with that because . . . "

6. Keep discussions positive! You can disagree, but don't argue. Be respectful.

Name _____ Date _____

"The Prince and the Pauper" (A Play) Session 1

Will Tom Canty get his wish? Will he get more than he wished for? Find out as you read this play based on Mark Twain's story.

Vocabulary

You will find these words in today's reading.

glimpse: (n.) a quick look
We caught a *glimpse* of the hummingbird as it darted past our window.

indignantly: (adv.) filled with anger because of an injustice
When Tommy saw the tiger pacing back and forth in its cage at the zoo, he cried *indignantly*, "They should send that poor animal back to the jungle!"

stature: (n.) height
When he stood up, he rose to such a *stature*, he looked like a giant to me.

differ: (v.) to have different opinions, to disagree
Sometimes my parents and I *differ* about what time I should go to bed.

crave: (v.) to want very much
After two hours in the noisy, busy store, I began to *crave* the peace and quiet of home.

hesitantly: (adv.) not being sure of oneself, holding back
The baby bird crept *hesitantly* to the edge of the nest, spread its wings for the first time, and flew.

etiquette: (n.) correct behavior
It is proper *etiquette* to keep your elbows off the table while eating dinner.

Think Ahead

1. Summarize the chapters your read from *The Prince and the Pauper*. Include the following in your summary:
   - The author's name
   - The main character's name
   - What Tom's life is like
   - What Tom wishes

2. Today you will see how a writer has dramatized *The Prince and the Pauper*—that is, how she has turned Mark Twain's novel into a play. Find the play "The Prince and the Pauper" in the Table of Contents and turn to it in the book. How does this play look different on the page from the stories you've been reading?

3. Who are some of the characters in the play?

4. Just as books are sometimes divided into chapters, plays are sometimes divided into *scenes.* Identify the setting (the time and place of the action) of Scene 1.

5. Today you are reading a *script* of a play. The script provides the written words that the actors say on stage. The script also provides *stage directions,* which give the actors information about where to go on stage or how to say a particular line. Stage directions, usually written in parentheses, are not read aloud. Find the stage directions in the following lines. How should the characters speak their lines?

   > LORD ST. JOHN (*Concerned*): True, true, I did forget myself. Yes, he must be the Prince. There could not be two in the land who look so much alike.

   > HERTFORD (*A little doubtfully*): An impostor would claim to be the Prince. Has there ever been an impostor who would deny this? No, this must be the Prince gone mad. We must help him all we can. Ah, it is the Lord Head Cook.

Read

Scenes 1 and 2 of "The Prince and the Pauper" in *Classics for Young Readers,* Vol. 5A, pages 93-101

Questions

Answer the following questions in complete sentences in your Reading Notebook.

1. How do Tom and Prince Edward meet?
2. What do the boys decide to do?
3. What is unusual about the boys' appearances?
4. What happens to the real Prince?
5. What do the members of the court think has happened to their Prince?

Discuss

1. Is Tom happy being a prince? Why or why not?
2. Based upon what you have learned about Tom, predict what he will do.

Exploring Language

When Mark Twain wrote *The Prince and the Pauper*, he wanted to make the characters sound the way he thought people spoke in sixteenth-century England. This play uses some of that old-sounding language. How is the language in this play different from the language you usually see in books and stories?

Write the following phrases in your Reading Notebook. Then rewrite them in your own words.
   1. "He's always had a fancy for royalty, and now he's gone stark mad."
      2. "Methinks I have forgotten about that, too!"

Character Study

One way you can learn about a character is by paying attention to what he or she says. You can also make inferences about the character by paying attention to *how* the character speaks.

For example, read aloud the lines below. What do you notice about the way Prince Edward speaks and the things that concern him? What can you infer about him? (Hint: Does Prince Edward ask for things?)

- "Guards! How dare you treat a poor lad like that! Release him!"
- "Well, that is better! Tell me more about your life at Offal Court. What do you do for fun there?"
- "Would you really like that? Then it shall be. I'll call the servants to clear the table. While they do that, you and I will have time to go into the next room and exchange clothing. *(Calls)* Page!"

Based upon what you have inferred about the Prince from the way he talks, write a paragraph in your Reading Notebook about the following topic:

Predict what will happen to Prince Edward while he is at the Canty house. (For example, how will the Prince react when John and Gammer Canty give him orders?) Explain your reasons for your prediction.

Name _____   Date _____

"The Prince and the Pauper" (A Play) Session 2

Tom becomes a prince and the Prince becomes a pauper. How much are the boys really alike and different?

Vocabulary

You will find these words in today's reading.

cackle: (v.) to laugh harshly or cruelly
"Too bad you can't come to the ball," Cinderella's wicked stepsisters *cackled*, slamming the door as they left.

fatigue: (n.) exhaustion
After running twenty miles to deliver the letter, the messenger collapsed with *fatigue*.

reluctantly: (adv.) not willingly, hesitantly
Bobby made a very sour face as he *reluctantly* ate his spinach.

impostor: (n.) a person pretending to be someone else
The wolf tried to sneak into the flock by wearing a sheep skin, but when the sheep saw his hairy paws, they knew he was an *impostor*.

imperiously: (adv.) commandingly
He spoke so *imperiously* that everyone rushed to follow his orders.

ward: (n.) a person who is guarded or protected
"You shall be my *wards*," said the knight to the orphans, "and I promise you shall always have food to eat, clothes to wear, and a safe place to live."

bearing: (n.) the way a person acts or carries himself
He had such a noble *bearing* that everyone who saw him was filled with admiration.

Think Ahead

1. Summarize the first two scenes of "The Prince and the Pauper."
   In your summary, explain the following:
   - how Tom and the Prince meet
   - what they decide to do
   - what is unusual about the boys' appearances
   - how they get separated

2. Describe Tom and the Prince. How are they alike and different?

Read

Scenes 3 and 4 in "The Prince and the Pauper" in *Classics for Young Readers,* Vol. 5A, pages 101-108

Questions

Answer the following questions in complete sentences in your Reading Notebook.

1. How do the Cantys treat the Prince?
2. What do Hugo and Ruffler tell the Prince that surprises him?
3. What question does Lord St. John ask the Prince that proves he is telling the truth?
4. What happens to Tom at the end of the play?

Discuss

1. After changing places with Tom, what do you think the Prince learns? What do you think he will do differently in the future?
2. What do you think Tom learns after changing places with the Prince?

Compare and Contrast Characters
Were there ever two boys more alike *and* more different than Tom Canty and Prince Edward? Compare and contrast the two characters. Look back to both the story and the play.

On page 1 of the Compare and Contrast Characters page:
- Write the character's full name.
- Describe the character's life before the boys trade places.
- Describe the character's personality, giving examples from the play to support your opinion.
- Tell something each character learns by trading places.

Then, on page 2 of the Compare and Contrast Characters page, write a paragraph to answer each question.

If you'd like to, draw a picture of each character.

Optional: The Curtain Rises
What part of the play did you like the best? Was there a scene that you found particularly interesting or exciting?

Choose the scene that you most enjoyed and try reading it aloud or acting it out. Remember to follow the stage directions and read with expression.

Name _____

Date _____

Compare and Contrast Characters

	Character's name:	Character's name:
What each boy's life was like before they traded places		
A description of each boy's character		
Something each boy learned by trading places		

Compare and Contrast Characters

Write answers to the following questions:

Tom and Prince Edward look alike. But, in your opinion, what is the most important thing they have in common?

_____

_____

_____

_____

_____

Tom is a pauper and Edward is a prince. But, in your opinion, what is the most important way they are different?

_____

_____

_____

_____

_____

_____

Name _____ Date _____

Summer

In this lesson you will be *comparing and contrasting* poems that describe the season of summer. That means you will be noticing how the poems are alike and different.

First Reading: "June" and "That Was Summer"

Think Ahead

When you think of summer, what colors, images, or scenes come to mind?

Read

Read "June" and "That Was Summer" once silently and a second time aloud.

Discuss

1. In your own words, describe what is happening in each poem.

2. Write the names of each of your five senses.

   _____ _____ _____ _____ _____

3. Both poems appeal to your senses. But each poem appeals to a different sense. "That Was Summer" is mostly about *smells.* What summery smells does the poet describe?

4. Have you ever done what the speaker in "June" is doing? What does it feel like to walk barefoot in grass?

5. Which of your senses does "June" mostly appeal to? (You can name more than one sense.) Point to words and lines in the poem that appeal to this sense or senses.

6. These two poems are alike because they appeal to your senses. They are different because each poem mostly appeals to a different sense. In what other ways are these poems different?

Second Reading: Two Poems Called "Summer Rain"

Vocabulary

You will find these words in the next pair of poems you will read today.

scythe: (n.) a tool for cutting grain
The farmer used a *scythe* to cut the wheat.

uproar: (n.) loud, noisy excitement
There was an *uproar* in the gym after the home team won the game.

pageant: (n.) a parade, or a fancy play or celebration
In the Christmas *pageant,* I played the part of a shepherd.

dread: (adj.) causing great fear
The young knight trembled as he approached the cave of the *dread* dragon.

tread: (n.) heavy step
Jack could hear the Giant's *tread* behind him as he started to climb down the beanstalk.

tangy: (adj.) having a sharp, pleasant flavor
I enjoyed the *tangy* taste of the lemonade.

Think Ahead

If you say, "It is raining today," you are making a *literal* statement about the weather. But if you say, "It is raining cats and dogs today," you are speaking *figuratively*. Be on the lookout for figurative language in the next two poems.

Read

Read both poems titled "Summer Rain" once silently and a second time aloud. Start with the poem by Elizabeth Coatsworth.

Discuss

1. In the first poem, where do you think the people are standing?

2. Which of your five senses does the first stanza of the first poem most appeal to? Point to specific words or phrases that appeal to this sense.

3. Which words in the second poem appeal to your five senses?

4. The second poem describes the rain as "a shower, a sprinkle." Is that *literal* or *figurative* language?

5. The second poem also says that the rain is "like stars on your toes" and like "a million-dot freckle." Is that *literal* or *figurative* language?

Name _____   Date _____

Describing Summer

Write a poem or a paragraph in which you use figurative language to describe summer. You can describe the whole season or focus on one special place or event. In your description, use at least one simile or metaphor. To help warm up your imagination, first answer the following questions:

1. Close your eyes and think of summer. What do you see? What images and colors come to mind?

   _____

   _____

   _____

2. List at least two sounds you associate with summer:

   _____

3. List at least two tastes you associate with summer:

   _____

4. Describe the smells you associate with any two of the following:

   the beach _____

   a swimming pool _____

   the playground or park _____

   a sports field _____

   a field or meadow _____

Describing Summer

5. Fill in each blank with a simile. Use your imagination!

In summer, it is as hot as_____.

The sun shines as bright as_____.

During a summer storm, the thunder sounds like_____.

6. Fill in each blank with a metaphor.

The summer rain is_____.

The summer breeze is_____.

Use what you have written above to help you write your description of summer or some part of summer. Appeal to your reader's senses. Try to make your reader see, hear, smell, taste, and touch what summer means to you. Remember, use at least one metaphor or simile in your poem or paragraph.

_____

_____

_____

_____

_____

_____

_____

Describing Summer

_____

_____

_____

_____

_____

_____

_____

_____

_____

_____

_____

_____

_____

_____

Guidelines for Peer Discussion

Share your thoughts, ideas, questions, and feelings about a text with a peer or others. Listen carefully to what everyone has to say about the text. During your discussion, follow these guidelines.

1. Be prepared to discuss what you think about the text. You should have already read the assignment. Come prepared to discuss your ideas and use examples from the text to support your thoughts and answers.

2. You will be asked questions about the text. Be ready to answer them, and bring some questions of your own to ask others, such as:

   "Who was your favorite character? Why?"

   "What was your favorite part of the text? Why?"

   "What fact did you enjoy learning? Why do you find this fact interesting?"

   "What question would you ask if you had the chance to meet the author?"

3. Listen if it's not your turn to speak. Pay attention to what others say so that you can add your ideas. Speak clearly and in complete sentences.

4. If you don't understand what someone says, ask a question.

   "What do you mean when you say . . . ?"

   "Can you give an example of . . . ?"

5. If you don't agree with what someone says, explain why.

   "I don't agree with that because . . . "

6. Keep discussions positive! You can disagree, but don't argue. Be respectful.

Name _____ Date _____

Autumn

In this lesson you will compare and contrast poems about the season of autumn.

First Reading: "The City of Falling Leaves" and "The Leaves Do Not Mind at All"

Think Ahead

1. When you think of autumn, what colors, images, or scenes come to mind?
2. If you say that "the wind sang through the branches," or that "the leaves danced in the breeze," are you speaking literally or figuratively? One of the poems you're about to read uses figurative language. Look for it as you read.

Read

Read "The City of Falling Leaves" and "The Leaves Do Not Mind at All" once silently and a second time aloud.

Discuss

1. In your own words, describe what is happening in each poem.

2. What are the colors of the leaves in "The City of Falling Leaves"? Which verbs show how the leaves fall? Is this description of the falling leaves mostly *literal* or *figurative*?

3. In "The Leaves Do Not Mind at All," the leaves almost seem to be human. For example, they "don't mind" that they are falling. Can you find other lines in the poem that describe something the leaves do that a person would usually do?

4. In "The Leaves Do Not Mind at All," are the descriptions of the falling leaves mostly *literal* or *figurative*?

5. In "The Leaves Do Not Mind at All," the poet uses a *simile* to describe a falling leaf. A simile compares two things, usually using the words *like* or *as*. What is the simile in this poem?

Second Reading: "Autumn Woods" and "Fall"

Vocabulary
You will find this word in the fourth poem you will read today.

withered: (adj.) dried up
My mother emptied the vase and threw away the *withered* flowers.

Think Ahead
Picture the trees you see in autumn. Do they look the same at the beginning of the season as they do at the end of the season? How are they different?

Read
Read "Autumn Woods" and "Fall" once silently and a second time aloud.

Discuss
1. In "Autumn Woods," what does the speaker like best about autumn? What can he do in autumn that he cannot do at any other time of the year?

2. Which of your senses does "Autumn Woods" appeal to? Point to words and lines in the poem that appeal to these senses.

3. In "Fall," the people "lock the garden gate" and "put the swings away." They already have taken the screens off the windows and put them in the attic and taken all the toys and outdoor furniture off the porch. What are they preparing for?

4. In "Fall," the poet uses the words *withered, deserted,* and *alone.* What do you feel when you hear words like this?

5. Is the language in these two poems more literal or figurative?

Name _____   Date _____

Painting a Picture of Fall

Poets and painters both paint pictures. The painter can use watercolors or oil paints. The poet uses words. Today you will paint pictures of fall with figurative language.

1. Close your eyes and think about a fall day. Are you in your yard raking leaves? At a football game? At a bonfire in a pumpkin patch drinking hot cider? Describe some of the images you feel, see, taste, smell, or hear.

   _____

   _____

   _____

2. Now complete these *similes*. Use your imagination!

   The dry leaves sound like_____.

   The smoke from the burning leaves smells like_____

   _____.

   The fall wind feels like_____.

3. Use a *metaphor* to describe at least one of the objects below.
   Example: A rake: <u>a comb that loosens the tangle of leaves from the grass</u>

   Leafless trees:_____

   The ground covered with leaves: _____

   Flocks of migrating birds: _____

Painting a Picture of Fall

4. Use *personification* to complete at least one of these sentences.

    Example: The leaf <u>danced and somersaulted through the air</u>.

    The ladybug_____.

    The autumn wind_____.

5. In one or two sentences, compare and contrast the seasons of summer and fall using *imagery*—language that appeals to the senses.

    Example: In summer the air feels sticky and heavy. In fall the air feels cool and sharp.

    _____

    _____

    _____

    _____

Now, if you want to, you can turn from poet to artist. Using crayons, colored pencils, chalk, or watercolors, create your own picture of autumn, complete with the scenes and images you have described above.

Name _____   Date _____

Winter

In this lesson you will be comparing and contrasting poems that describe the season of winter.

First Reading: "Winter the Huntsman" and "Falling Snow"

Vocabulary

You will find these words in the first poem you will read today. Study each word and how it is used in a sentence.

asunder: (adj.) apart, into pieces
The lightning bolt struck the tree trunk and tore it *asunder*.

reynard: (n.) the name for a fox in some legends and fables
Mr. Tod is the *reynard* in Beatrix Potter tales.

glade: (n.) an open space in a forest
As we walked through the woods, we came upon a pleasant *glade,* and there we had our picnic.

Think Ahead

The tone of your voice says almost as much as the words you speak. Imagine saying "Come here!" to a friend. Try saying it now. First say it in an excited tone, then an angry tone, and then a gentle tone.

Just as you let someone know how you feel by the tone of your voice, a poem has a tone as well. The tone of a poem comes through the words and images the poet uses to express his or her attitude and emotions. The tone might be happy or sad, confident or anxious, serious or playful.

As you read today's poems, think about the tone of each. See if you can tell how each poet feels about winter.

Read
Read "Winter the Huntsman" and "Falling Snow" once silently and a second time aloud.

Discuss
1. In "Winter the Huntsman," winter is described as a Huntsman on horseback, crashing through the woods, tearing apart things in his path. This is a *figurative* description. In your own words, describe what *literally* is happening in the poem.

2. How would you describe the tone of this poem? Is it harsh or pleasant? Point to specific verbs and sounds in the poem that create a pleasant or harsh tone.

3. Much of the imagery in "Winter the Huntsman" appeals to your sense of hearing. Point to words and lines in the poem that appeal to this sense.

4. In your own words, describe what is happening in "Falling Snow." Is the poet describing the falling snow literally or figuratively?

5. Does the poet in "Falling Snow" like the snow? Which words are your clues?

6. Compare the *tone* of the two poems. Which poem has a more negative tone about winter? Which poem has a more positive tone?

Second Reading: "On a Snowy Day" and "Snowflakes"

Think Ahead
Close your eyes and imagine a sandbox full of different toys. Now imagine a blizzard blowing in and covering all the toys with snow. The toys become hidden and transformed into various white shapes. What do these white shapes look like to you?

Read
Read "On a Snowy Day" and "Snowflakes" once silently and a second time aloud.

Discussion

1. You just imagined what toys in a sandbox covered with snow might look like. What are the *literal* snow-covered objects the poet describes in "On a Snowy Day"?

2. The snow changes the way these objects look, doesn't it? The poet *personifies* them in the poem—she describes them acting or doing things like people. Point to the words and lines that describe the snow-covered objects in these human ways.

3. In both poems, the poets use *metaphor* to describe the snow and snowflakes. They compare the snow to unlike things. Find at least one metaphor in each poem. Explain what each metaphor is comparing.

4. How would you describe the tone of these two poems? Do the poets seem to like the subjects they are writing about?

Name _____   Date _____

Winter at Your Fingertips

You will use "Winter the Huntsman" as inspiration for a poem or paragraph with an extended metaphor—a comparison carried throughout your poem or paragraph. Before you begin writing, you will need to pick your characters and choose your scene.

1. Close your eyes and think of a winter scene. List the colors you see and the sounds you might hear.

   _____

   _____

   _____

2. How do you feel in this scene? Do you feel cozy or cold? Calm or anxious? Describe these feelings.

   _____

   _____

   _____

3. What smells or tastes do you associate with the scene you've imagined? Describe them.

   _____

   _____

   _____

Winter at Your Fingertips

4. Now describe some aspect of winter using a simile:

The snow falls through the air like_____.

The wind blows like_____.

The sleet pelts my back like_____.

5. In "Winter the Huntsman," the poet compared winter to a huntsman riding through the forest on his horse, blowing his horn and cracking his whip. The poet *extended* this metaphor through the whole poem. Now, think of another metaphor for winter. Instead of a huntsman, what other character could winter be? (Your character does not have to be human.)

Write your ideas here: _____

_____

_____

_____

6. The huntsman crashed through trees in a forest. Now, imagine your "winter character." Where is this character—in a forest or some other place? What is your character doing?

Write your ideas here: _____

_____

_____

_____

Winter at Your Fingertips

Now use some of the ideas you've written above to create your own paragraph or poem with an extended metaphor about winter. If you want to, use the prompts below to get started. If you choose to write a poem, it does not need to rhyme.

Winter is_____.

It _____ through the_____.

It_____over the _____

and it _____

_____

_____

_____
_____

_____

_____

_____

_____

_____

Name _____ Date _____

Spring

You've read poems about summer, fall, and winter—what's next? Spring, of course! In this lesson you will compare and contrast poems about spring.

First Reading: Two Poems Called "April"

Vocabulary

You will find this word in the first poem you will read today.

> **save:** (conjunction) an old-fashioned word for "but" or "except"
> I would love to visit Africa *save* that I am scared to fly.

Think Ahead

When you think of spring, what colors, images, or scenes come to mind? How is the beginning of spring different from the end of spring?

Read

Read both poems titled "April" once silently and a second time aloud.

Discuss

1. Both poems are called "April" and describe the beginning of spring, but each poem describes a different scene. In your own words, describe these two scenes.

2. Which of your senses does the first "April" poem appeal to? Point to the words and lines in the poem that appeal to these senses.

3. Which of your senses does the second "April" poem appeal to? Point to the words and lines in the poem that appeal to these senses.

4. In the second poem, the poet uses a *simile* to describe the tulips pushing up through the ground. What two things does she compare in this simile?

5. Explain the use of *personification* in the last line of the second poem.

Second Reading: "In Time of Silver Rain"

Think Ahead

Have you ever taken a walk in the rain? What was it like?
Do you think the rain has a color? What color?

Read

Read "In Time of Silver Rain" once silently and a second time aloud.

Discuss

1. When you think of the word "silver," what images come to mind? The poet describes a spring rain as "silver." What do you think he means?

2. In this poem, the flowers are blooming, the green grass is growing, butterflies are flying, and trees are putting forth new leaves. How is this different from the way spring is described in the last two poems you read?

3. At the end of the first stanza, why do you think the poet repeats "Of life" three times?

4. What sounds of spring does the poet describe in the second stanza? Which of these sounds are literal? (That is, which are real sounds?) Which are figurative? (That is, which are sounds you could only imagine?)

Third Reading: "Spring"

Vocabulary

You will find this word in the last poem you will read today.

gamboling: (v.) skipping about playfully
We watched the playful ponies *gamboling* in the field.

Think Ahead
Remember, a poet's attitude and emotions come through in the *tone* of a poem. The tone might be happy or sad, confident or anxious, serious or playful. As you read the next poem, think about how you would describe its tone.

Read
Read "Spring" once silently and a second time aloud.

Discuss
1. Instead of describing spring itself, this poem describes a person's reaction to spring. In the poem, the speaker does many things to welcome spring. What are some of these actions? (Hint: look for vivid verbs!)

2. Which of these actions are things a person *literally* (really) could do?

3. Which of these actions are *figurative?* That is, which describe things a person could only imagine doing?

4. The speaker uses *metaphor* to describe how she feels. She compares herself to other things. For example, she says, "I'm a rabbit." Point to at least two other metaphors in the poem.

5. How would you describe the *tone* of the poem? Does the speaker like spring?

Name _____   Date _____

Spring Has Sprung

Write two short verses or paragraphs describing spring but with different *tone*s.
Before you write, answer the following.

1. When you think of spring, what colors do you think of?

_____

_____

2. What smells and sounds do you associate with spring?

_____

_____

3. Complete these pairs of sentences with contrasting *similes*.
   Example:

   The spring wind felt like <u>a warm whisper</u>.
   The spring wind felt like <u>a blast of chilly air from the freezer.</u>

The rain on my umbrella sounded like_____.

The rain on my umbrella sounded like_____.

The tiny buds on trees looked like_____.

The tiny buds on trees looked like_____.

Spring Has Sprung

The soil in the garden smelled like_____.

The soil in the garden smelled like_____.

4. Compare the tone of the two verses below. What words would you use to
   describe the tone of each?

a) The cold wind makes me cry
   as it bites my nose and stings my eye.
   I miss the warmth of summer sun.
   I wish winter had not begun.
   There is nothing in the sleet and snow
   that makes me want to sing or glow.

The tone is_____.

b) I love to sail on summer days
   bounced and sprayed by salty waves.
   The air is warm; the scents are sweet.
   I sigh with happiness complete.

The tone is_____.

Now use some of what you've written above to create two short poems
or paragraphs that describe spring in different tones. Be creative!
(Your poems do not have to rhyme.)

_____

_____

_____

Spring Has Sprung

Name _____ Date _____

"Eating Like a Bird": Session 1

For some birds along the Florida seashore, grabbing a snack means standing silent and motionless for hours, a high-speed underwater chase, or a 30-foot high dive into the sea!

Vocabulary

You will find these words in today's reading. Look at each word and how it is used in a sentence. You will find any definitions not provided here in the *Curious Creatures* glossary.

marsh: (n.)
When our ball rolled into the *marsh*, we knew not to go after it because we couldn't tell how deeply we would sink into the soggy ground.

crustacean: (n.) a small water animal with a hard shell
Crabs, shrimp, and lobsters are three kinds of *crustaceans.*

mammal: (n.) a warm-blooded animal that has hair and whose young are fed with milk
Many people think that whales are fish, but they are warm-blooded, have hair, and feed their young with milk, so they are *mammals.*

prey: (n.) the hunted animal
The lioness silently followed the herd of gazelles, waiting for the right moment to pounce on her *prey.*

roseate: (adj.) light reddish-pink
The flamingo is a *roseate* bird, almost the color of cotton candy.

Think Ahead

1. What do you think you will learn about as you read the magazine? Do you think the articles are *fiction* or *nonfiction*? Why?
2. Look through the magazine. How is it organized? Are there any special parts?
3. Look up "Eating Like a Bird" in the table of contents.

Read

"Eating Like a Bird," *Curious Creatures*

Questions

Answer the following questions in complete sentences in your Reading Notebook.

1. Explain what the expression "eating like a bird" means. Is this true of the birds in the selection?
2. Describe the three ways that the birds in the article catch their food.

Discuss

1. What do all the birds in the article have in common?
2. Which bird do you think is the most interesting? Why?

What's the Main Idea?

There's a lot of information in each of these articles. Finding the main idea will help you remember the most important information in an article.

Sometimes finding the main idea requires a little detective work. In many articles, one sentence in the first paragraph tells the main idea. But in other articles, the main idea is *unstated*. *Unstated* means "not said." When the main idea is unstated, no one sentence in the paragraph tells the main idea.

To find an unstated main idea, read all the sentences in the paragraph and decide what the facts have in common. That will help you uncover the hidden or unstated main idea.

Find the unstated main idea in the paragraph below. First, read the sentences. Tell three facts the paragraph gives about dogs. Then decide what the facts have in common.

> Blind men and women use guide dogs to help them navigate busy city streets. Therapy dogs visit hospitals to bring cheer to patients. Hundreds of people lost in mountains or forests have been saved by rescue dogs.

Now think about three facts that are stated. What kinds of jobs can dogs do? What is the main idea?

Now find the unstated main idea in the first paragraph of "Eating Like a Bird." First, read the sentences. Tell three facts that the paragraph gives about birds, such as, "Some birds along the Florida seashore dive into the sea to catch their food."

Decide what the facts have in common. Then choose the unstated main idea of the paragraph from the sentences below.

1. There are many kinds of birds along the Florida seashore.
2. Birds along the Florida seashore work hard for their food.
3. Birds can't fly when their feathers are soaked with water.

Write the unstated main idea from paragraph 1 on the Details Chart page.

Next, describe the three ways that birds along the Florida seashore catch their food. (Hint: Look back to Question 2 in your Reading Notebook.)

Each of the three ways that birds catch their food is a *detail*. *Details* give more information about the main idea. The main idea of this article states that birds along the Florida coastline work hard for their food. Then the author gives more information, or *details*: he tells three difficult ways the birds catch their food.

Read the titles of the three columns on the Details Chart. In the article, the author also gives details about each of the three ways birds catch their food. For example, he tells the names of some of the waders and describes some of divers' amazing feats.

Write three details from the article about birds that wade, birds that follow, and birds that drop down on their prey in each column. You may write the birds' names, describe their unusual ways, or tell about problems certain kinds of birds have.

When you finish, review and discuss your work.

Name _____

Date _____

Details Chart

Write the main idea of the article on the lines below. Then add three details from the article to each column.

The main idea of the article is: _____

Birds That Wade	Birds That Follow Their Prey	Birds That Drop Down on Their Prey
• _____	• _____	• _____
• _____	• _____	• _____
• _____	• _____	• _____

Guidelines for Peer Discussion

Share your thoughts, ideas, questions, and feelings about a text with a peer or others. Listen carefully to what everyone has to say about the text. During your discussion, follow these guidelines.

1. Be prepared to discuss what you think about the text. You should have already read the assignment. Come prepared to discuss your ideas and use examples from the text to support your thoughts and answers.

2. You will be asked questions about the text. Be ready to answer them, and bring some questions of your own to ask others, such as:

   "Who was your favorite character? Why?"

   "What was your favorite part of the text? Why?"

   "What fact did you enjoy learning? Why do you find this fact interesting?"

   "What question would you ask if you had the chance to meet the author?"

3. Listen if it's not your turn to speak. Pay attention to what others say so that you can add your ideas. Speak clearly and in complete sentences.

4. If you don't understand what someone says, ask a question.

   "What do you mean when you say . . . ?"

   "Can you give an example of . . . ?"

5. If you don't agree with what someone says, explain why.

   "I don't agree with that because . . . "

6. Keep discussions positive! You can disagree, but don't argue. Be respectful.

Name _____   Date _____

"Eating Like a Bird": Session 2

"Eating Like a Bird" is full of interesting information. How would you tell people about it? Design a brochure for tourists to the Merritt Island National Wildlife Refuge.

Think Ahead

1. What is the difference between fiction and nonfiction?
2. What differences did you notice between the "Eating Like a Bird" article and some of the *Classics* stories you've read?
3. Summarize the article.
4. Review your Details Chart. Which birds did you find most interesting? Why?

Author's Purpose

An author can present information in many different ways. Writing a nonfiction article is one method of informing a reader. Review the article, then discuss the following questions:

- What did you like best about the article?
- What did you notice about the way the article is organized?
- Pretend you are a visitor to the Merritt Island National Wildlife Refuge in Florida, taking a tour through the park. What changes would you make to the article to make it easier for a tourist to use? Why?

Bird Watch Brochure

One way to present nonfiction information is to make a brochure. A brochure is a small pamphlet or booklet that gives readers quick information about the most important features of a place or thing.

Pretend you are a tour guide for the Merritt Island National Wildlife Refuge in Florida. How would you organize your brochure to help visitors find information quickly? Review your Details Chart. Then design a brochure to give visitors information about the birds they will see on the island.

Directions:
1. Fold a piece of paper in thirds. This will be your brochure.
2. Make a cover for the brochure.
3. Label each of the three inside pages "Birds That Wade," "Birds That Follow Their Prey," and "Birds That Drop Down on Their Prey."
4. Use your Details Chart. On each of the three inside pages, write two or more sentences that describe how each category of bird catches its food, and list at least two examples of birds that find their food that way. Then draw and label a picture of one of those birds.
5. On the page that folds over from the right, draw a map of Florida. Mark Merritt Island with a star. Underneath the map, write two or more sentences that persuade people to visit the wildlife refuge.

If you wish, you may do more research on the birds of Merritt Island National Wildlife Refuge to add to your brochure.

Name _____ Date _____

"The Ocean's Cleaning Stations": Session 1

Even fish need to take baths sometimes. Read today's article to learn about the unusual way it happens.

Vocabulary

You will find these words in today's reading. Look at each word and how it is used in a sentence. You will find the definitions in the *Curious Creatures* glossary.

parasite: (n.)
The veterinarian gave my dog medicine so he would not get *parasites*.

fungus: (n.)
Two kinds of *fungus*, mushrooms and mold, grew in the dead tree stump.

gullet: (n.)
The bird took such a big bite that the food got stuck in his *gullet*.

Think Ahead

1. Look up "The Ocean's Cleaning Stations" in the table of contents.
2. What other kinds of "cleaning stations" do you know about? What happens there? What do you think happens at an *ocean* cleaning station?

Read

"The Ocean's Cleaning Stations," *Curious Creatures*

Questions

Answer the following questions in complete sentences in your Reading Notebook.

1. What is a host fish? What is a cleaner fish?
2. Why do host fish, such as eels and parrotfish, go to the cleaning stations?
3. What do the cleaner fish do with the parasites they clean off the host fish?
4. What happens when all the cleaners are removed from an area?
5. What does the word *symbiosis* mean?

Discuss

1. Why do you think bonnet-mouths and parrotfish hang in the water with their heads or tails straight up when they want a cleaning?
2. How do fish that can change color help the cleaners? Do you think this is useful? Why?
3. Why do you think that some host fish shudder when they sense danger? How does this help the cleaner fish?

Simply Symbiosis

The main idea is the most important or main point the author makes. But sometimes a passage will contain an *unstated main idea.* Even if the main idea is not stated, you will still know it is the main idea because most of the details will be about this idea. Discuss the unstated main idea of "The Ocean's Cleaning Stations." Then use supporting details from the text to help you complete the Simply Symbiosis page.

Author's Style

Compare and contrast the first paragraphs of "The Ocean's Cleaning Stations" and "Eating Like a Bird." First, reread the first paragraph of "The Ocean's Cleaning Stations." What does the paragraph sound like?

Now reread the beginning of "Eating Like a Bird." The author opens with a question to the reader. He asks, "Has anyone ever told you that you eat like a bird?" Do you think this is a good beginning?

Which beginning is your favorite? Why?

Rewrite the beginning of "Eating Like a Bird" in the style of "The Ocean's Cleaning Stations." Choose your favorite bird from "Eating Like a Bird." Find details in the article that tell you about how the bird catches its food. Then describe the scene as if you were at the wildlife refuge watching it happen. Write your new opening paragraph in your Reading Notebook.

For example:

The brown pelican circles high in the sky, little more than a speck against the clouds. Suddenly, he drops out of the sky like a stone, plunges into the sea, and grabs a fish with his beak. This hungry predator certainly does not "eat like a bird." Nor do many of the other avian inhabitants of Merritt Island Wildlife Refuge, as you will see.

Name _____   Date _____

Simply Symbiosis

Use details from the text to answer the questions.

1. The main idea of the article is _____

_____.

2. In the relationship called *symbiosis,* each animal _____ _____

_____.

3. How does the cleaner fish help the host fish? _____

_____.

4. How does the host fish help the cleaner fish? _____

_____.

5. Do the birds and fish from "Eating Like a Bird" have a *symbiotic* relationship?

_____.

Simply Symbiosis

6. Why or why not? _____

_____.

7. In the box below, draw a symbol to represent *symbiosis.*

Name _____   Date _____

"The Ocean's Cleaning Stations": Session 2

Design a *fin*-tastic underwater travel guide to the ocean's cleaning stations for host and cleaner fish.

Think Ahead
1. What does *symbiosis* mean?
2. What does the host fish give and receive? The cleaner fish?
3. Why are cleaning stations so important?

Author's Purpose
An author has many options when he or she presents nonfiction information. Review the article, then discuss the following questions:

1. What did you like best about the article?
2. What did you notice about the way the article was organized?
3. If you wanted to give guidelines and directions for the ocean's cleaning stations, what changes would you make to this article? Why?

A Fish's Guide to Ocean Cleaning Stations
Have you ever used a cookbook, read the directions to a game, or picked places to visit from a travel guide? Another way to present nonfiction information is to make a manual that gives advice or directions.

Pretend you are writing a travel and how-to guide for host and cleaner fish that want to visit the ocean's cleaning stations.

Directions:

1. Staple the three pieces of paper together to make a book.

2. Design the cover. Choose a title that tells what the guidebook is about, and write one or more sentences to persuade host and cleaner fish to go to the cleaning station.

3. On the first page, write a guide for host fish. Title the page, "For Host Fish," and write three or more sentences about each of the following:
   - When to Go: When and why should a host fish go for a cleaning?
   - How to Approach: How should the host fish swim as it approaches the cleaning station?
   - What Will Happen: What will happen when the host fish goes to the cleaning station?

4. On the back of your cover, draw a host fish. Use pictures from the article to help you.

5. On the second page, write a guide for cleaner fish. Title the page, "For Cleaner Fish," and write three or more sentences about each of the following:
   - Where to Go: How will a cleaner fish know which host fish are ready for a cleaning?
   - What Kind of Fish: What kinds of fish and shrimp are cleaners? What kinds of markings do cleaners have?
   - What to Do: What should a cleaner fish do when a host fish comes for cleaning? Is it safe? Why?

6. On the back of page 1, draw a picture of a cleaner fish. Use pictures from the article as your guide.

7. On the back of the book, write a warning for false cleaners who might try to visit the cleaning station. You may illustrate this page if you wish.

Name _____ Date _____

"Stormflight": Session 1

After the storm, mist rises from the ground. But this mist is *alive.*
Find out why in today's reading.

Vocabulary

You will find these words in today's reading. Look at each word
and how it is used in a sentence. You will find any definitions not
provided here in the *Curious Creatures* glossary.

predator: (n.)
A hawk is a fierce *predator*; it dives down and catches small
rabbits, mice, and other rodents for its meals.

colony: (n.)
A *colony* of one hundred sparrows lives together in the same
big tree.

bush: (n.) wild, undeveloped land
Animals in Africa do not live in cities or towns, they prefer to live
in the *bush*.

Think Ahead

1. Give two or more examples of kinds of nonfiction writing.
2. Look up "Stormflight" in the table of contents. Find the article
   and look at it. Do you notice anything different from the other
   articles you have read?

Read

"Stormflight," *Curious Creatures*

Questions

Answer the following questions in complete sentences in your Reading Notebook.

1. In what month does the stormflight occur?
2. What are the "plumes of steam"?
3. Why are the conditions after the storm perfect for winged termites?
4. Explain what will happen to the termites that survive.

Discuss

1. Reread the first paragraph of the article. Think about the last sentence: "You stand on the veranda of your mud-walled house, excited that the rains have finally come." The author of the article writes in a way that he puts you, the reader, in the middle of the action. Why do you think he writes the article in this way?

2. Would you like to see a stormflight in person? Why or why not? What details did the author include that influenced your opinion?

It's All in the Details

The main idea is the most important or main point the author makes. When the main idea is not written as a sentence, it is called an *unstated main idea.*

You can discover an unstated main idea by looking closely at the details the author gives. Complete the It's All in the Details page. When you finish, review and discuss your work.

Author's Purpose

Authors have many options when giving their readers information. They can write articles in many different writing styles as you have already seen. Why do you think the author included a box of information at the end of the article? Use the box to complete the Mighty Termites page.

It's All in the Details

Answer the questions below. Write one detail from the story in each oval. Then write the unstated main idea in the box

1. What is the title of the article? _____

2. What is the main event that takes place in the article? _____

_____.

3. Why is that event important to the termites? _____

_____.

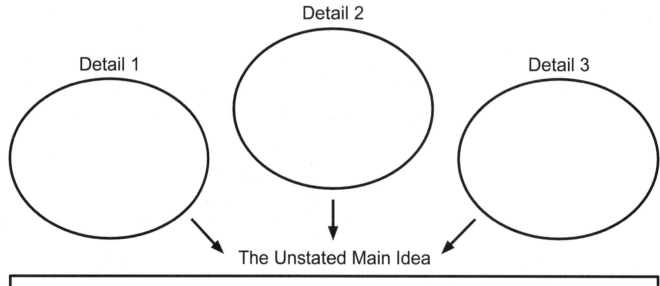

Detail 2

Detail 1

Detail 3

The Unstated Main Idea

Name _____   Date _____

Mighty Termites

Use the box of information on page 15 of *Curious Creatures* to complete this outline.

I. Where Termites Live
    A. Every continent except for Antarctica
    B. Colonies

II. Caste System
    A. Workers
        1. _____
        2. _____
        3. _____

    B. Soldiers
        1. _____
        2. _____
        3. _____

    C. King and Queen
        1. _____
        2. _____
        3. _____

III. What Termites Do
    A. _____
    B. _____

IV. What Termites Eat
    A. _____
    B. _____
    C. _____

Name _____   Date _____

"Stormflight": Session 2

A termite swarm? That's news to me! Rewrite "Stormflight" as a newspaper article.

Think Ahead
1. Summarize the article.
2. How was "Stormflight" like the other articles you read?
3. How was it different?

Author's Purpose
An author has many ways to choose from when he or she presents information. Review the article, then discuss the following questions:

1. What did you like best about the article?
2. What did you notice about the way the article was organized?
3. Now pretend you are writing an article about the stormflight for a newspaper. What do readers expect to find in a newspaper article? What changes would you make to "Stormflight" to make it like a newspaper article? Why?

Extra! Extra! Read All About It!
Every day, millions of people read or listen to nonfiction information: they read the newspaper or listen to the news on television or the radio. Writing a newspaper article and giving a news report are popular ways to share information.

Pretend you are a reporter for the National News. Turn the information from "Stormflight" into a short newspaper article.

Directions:
1. Complete the Extra! Extra! page to help organize your information.
2. Draft the body of your article.
3. Add a hook and a title.
4. Add a pull quote.
5. Publish your article! Write and illustrate a neat final copy in your Reading Notebook.

If you wish, pretend you are a television or radio news reporter. Read aloud or perform your piece.

Name _____ Date _____

Extra! Extra!

Answer the questions below using information from the article.

1. *What creatures* will your article be about? _____

2. *What event* will your article be about? _____

_____

_____

3. *Where* did the event take place? _____

4. *When* did the event take place? _____

5. *Why* did the event take place? _____

6. *Why* was the event important? _____

_____

_____

What will the main idea of your article be? _____

_____

_____

_____

Extra! Extra!

List three details that give more information about your main idea.

1. _____

_____

2. _____

_____

3. _____

_____

Name _____   Date _____

"A Mom with a Mission": Session 1

Deep in the tropical forests of Central America, one insect mom fights a deadly battle to keep her babies alive and safe.

Vocabulary

You will find these words in today's reading. Look at each word and how it is used in a sentence. You will find the definitions in the *Curious Creatures* glossary.

appendage: (n.)
Humans have four *appendages*: two arms and two legs.

molt: (v.)
When snakes *molt*, they shed their skins.

Think Ahead

1. Look up "A Mom with a Mission" in the table of contents. Look at the illustration. Predict what the article will be about.
2. What do you know about insects?

Read

"A Mom with a Mission," *Curious Creatures*

Questions

Answer the following questions in complete sentences in your Reading Notebook.

1. How are treehopper mothers different from most other insects?
2. List three things a treehopper does to care for and protect her young.
3. Why are the nymphs camouflaged?
4. When are the nymphs considered grown up?
5. How many clutches of young does a treehopper raise in her life?

Discuss

1. Why do you think the treehopper works so hard to protect her young?
2. Explain how camouflage and the pronotum help protect the treehoppers.

Discovering the Unstated Main Idea

The main idea is the most important or main point the author makes. An *unstated main idea* is not written out in a sentence. Describe how a reader can figure out an unstated main idea.

Write three important details from the article on one side of an index card. On the other side, write the main idea in your own words. Then find at least one more detail in the text that supports the main idea you chose.

Fact and Opinion

You know that nonfiction is writing about *facts*. Facts are statements that can be proven true. Look at the facts below and tell how you could prove them.

- There are seven continents.
- Snails have hard shells.
- Chocolate is made from cacao nuts.

Give two more facts and explain how you could prove them.

An *opinion* is what a person feels or thinks about something. Opinions are not true or false. People can have different opinions about the same thing without being right or wrong. Look at the opinions below, and then give your opinion about the subject.

- Cherry vanilla is the tastiest flavor of ice cream.
- Salamanders make great pets.
- Green is a pretty color.

Give two more opinions and find out what someone else's opinion is on the same subject. Complete the Fact and Opinion page. When you finish, review and discuss your work.

Name _____ Date _____

Fact and Opinion

Write "F" beside the facts and "O" beside the opinions. Then answer the questions using information from the text.

1. ____The Great Pyramid is located near the Nile River in Egypt.

2. ____ Carrots are tasty vegetables.

3. ____ Riding a horse is more fun than riding a bicycle.

4. ____ Pyramids are the most beautiful buildings in the world.

5. ____ Daffodils are usually white or yellow.

6. ____ Carrots grow underground.

7. ____ Daffodils smell nicer than any other kind of flower.

8. ____ Horses come in many breeds, colors, and sizes.

9. Which of these is a fact from "A Mom with a Mission"?
   a. Treehoppers live in Australia.
   b. Treehoppers are beautiful.
   c. Treehoppers protect their babies.

10. Write another fact from the article. _____

_____

11. Write your opinion about treehoppers. _____

_____

Name _____   Date _____

"A Mom with a Mission": Session 2

Zoom in on important events by making a timeline.

Think Ahead
Summarize the article. What does a treehopper do that is different from what other insects do?

Author's Purpose
An author can present nonfiction information in many ways. Review the article, then discuss the following questions:

1. What did you like best about the article?
2. What did you notice about the way the article was organized?
3. Pretend you want to learn about the life cycle of a treehopper. What information in the article would you find most useful? What information would you take out? Why?

Treehopper Timelines
Another way to present nonfiction information is to make a *timeline* of events. A timeline is a tool that lets you put events in the order in which they happened. The order starts with the earliest event and ends with the most recent.

For example, a timeline of a butterfly's life might look like this:

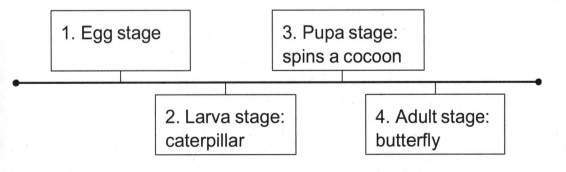

Pretend you are a famous entomologist, a scientist who studies insects. Reread the article. Then take a piece of paper and turn it sideways. Draw a horizontal line across it. Draw a timeline, putting the following events in the correct order:

- The treehopper mom guards her eggs.
- The adult treehoppers fly away from the branch and find mates.
- The nymphs move to the feeding holes and start sucking juices.
- The treehopper mom drills feeding holes into the branch.
- The adult female treehopper lays about 90 eggs on the end of a branch.
- The nymphs are six weeks old. They molt for the fourth time.
- The adult females lay eggs.

Cycle Diagrams
A cycle is a series of events that repeats. For example, the life cycle of a butterfly might look like this:

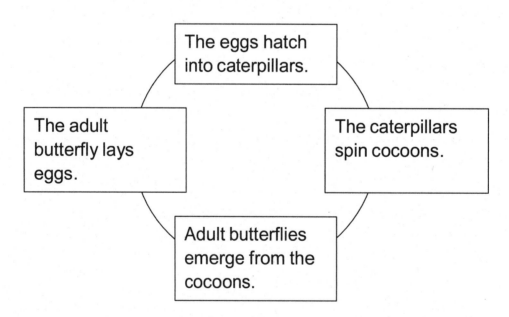

Complete the Life Cycle page. Use the seven events from your timeline and fill in the life cycle of the female treehopper. Remember, the first and last event in the cycle are always the same. If you wish, you may illustrate the life cycle or the timeline.

Name   Date

Life Cycle

Complete the life cycle of a female treehopper in the diagram
below. Remember to combine the first and last event in a
treehopper's life.

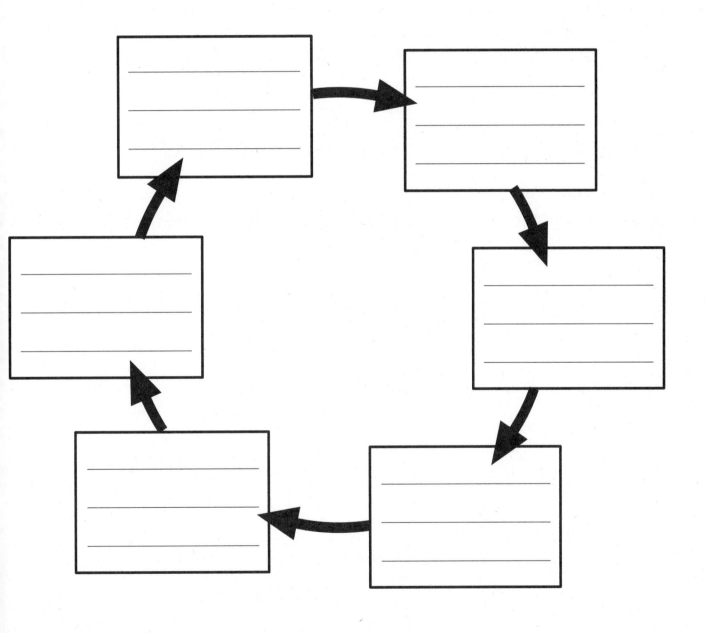

Name _____ Date _____

"Lingering Leeches"

Find out why the leech has been man's friend and foe for the past two thousand years.

Vocabulary

You will find these words in today's reading. Look at each word and how it is used in a sentence. You will find any definitions not provided here in the *Curious Creatures* glossary.

squeamish: (adj.) easily nauseated or disgusted
There is no way I could bait a fishhook with a worm; I am far too *squeamish.*

anesthetic: (n.)
The doctor gave me an *anesthetic* so I wouldn't feel pain when he gave me stitches.

anticoagulant: (n.)
Anticoagulants are sometimes used to help people with blood clots.

secrete: (v.)
When you exercise, you *secrete* sweat.

transplant: (n.)
The patient is on the waiting list for a heart *transplant* because he needs a new heart.

Think Ahead

1. Look up "Lingering Leeches" in the table of contents. What does the word *lingering* mean? What clue does that give you about leeches?
2. Look at the illustration. Predict what the article will be about.

Read
"Lingering Leeches," *Curious Creatures*

Questions
Answer the following questions in complete sentences in your
Reading Notebook.

1. Describe two ways leeches use their suckers.
2. Why did leech rental help spread diseases?
3. What do doctors today sometimes use leeches for?
4. Why doesn't a leech bite hurt?

Discuss
1. There's an old saying that goes, "Too much of anything is no
   good." How is that true for leeches? Give an example from the
   article in which leeches helped a person get better, and one in
   which they didn't.

2. Look at the gray box at the beginning of the article. Read this
   paragraph again. Why do you think the author chose to begin
   her article this way? What does this opening paragraph tell
   you?

Is That a Fact?
Nonfiction is writing about facts. What is a fact? Describe the
difference between a fact and an opinion. Then complete the Is
That a Fact? page.

It All Depends on Your Perspective
People can know the same facts about something, but have
different opinions about it. For example, Joe and Cindy both know
that it is usually cold in Alaska. Joe loves the cold and snow, so he
thinks it would be a nice place to live. Cindy prefers warm
climates. She would not like to live in Alaska. Joe and Cindy do not
share the same *perspective,* or *point of view.*

Think about the two children in the "Lingering Leeches" article: the author who was a child in Australia and the boy from Boston who is a surgical patient. Then discuss these questions:

1. What facts do both children know about leeches?
2. What is the girl's opinion of leeches? Find a sentence in the article that supports your answer.
3. What do you think the boy's opinion about leeches would be? Why?

On the lined side of one index card, write a postcard from the girl to the boy, explaining her opinion. On the other index card, write a postcard from the boy to the girl, explaining what you believe his opinion would be. Use details from the article to support the opinions of both children. Then decide: what is *your* opinion about leeches?

Name _____ Date _____

Is That a Fact?

Write "F" beside the facts and "O" beside the opinions. Then answer the questions using information from the text.

1. _____ Leeches are closely related to earthworms.

2. _____ Leeches are disgusting.

3. _____ Leeches live all around the world.

4. _____ Most leeches live in water.

5. _____ Not all leeches are bloodsuckers.

6. _____ Leeches should never be used to help people.

7. _____ Leech bites don't hurt.

8. _____ Leeches secrete hirudin to keep the blood from clotting.

9. Which of these is a fact from "Lingering Leeches"?
   a. Leeches almost became extinct during the eighteenth and nineteenth centuries.
   b. Leeches should have been made extinct during the eighteenth and nineteenth centuries.
   c. Napoleon rented leeches to soldiers in his army.
   d. Modern doctors don't know how to use leeches.

10. Write another fact from the article. _____

_____

11. Write your opinion about leeches. _____

_____

Name _____   Date _____

"The Story of Ruth"

In this Bible story, a young woman leaves her homeland and faces great difficulties for the sake of someone she cares about.

Vocabulary

You will find these words in today's reading.

famine: (n.) a time when there is not enough food for everyone
The year it did not rain, no crops grew, and there was a terrible *famine* in the land.

kindred: (n.) family or relatives
At the family reunion, I met many of my *kindred* whom I had only heard of before.

steadfast: (adj.) firm, unchanging, determined
The brave soldier stood *steadfast* at the gate, ready to guard it against any invaders.

sheaf: (n.) a bundle of grasses or plants that are tied together
We tied the stalks of wheat into *sheaves* and lined them up inside the barn.

Think Ahead

Today's story is from the Bible. The main character in the story has to make some very important choices. You make choices every day. Some are small choices, such as choosing what color shirt to wear or what to eat for lunch. But some are big, important choices, such as choosing to tell the truth. Tell about an important choice you have made. Was it hard to make the choice? Why or why not?

Read
"The Story of Ruth" in *Classics for Young Readers,* Vol. 5A, pages 110-114

Questions
Answer the following questions in complete sentences in your Reading Notebook.

1. Why did Naomi want to return to Bethlehem after her husband and sons died?
2. When she reached Bethlehem, what did Ruth do to take care of Naomi?
3. Why did Boaz marry Ruth?

Discuss
1. How do you think Ruth felt about leaving her home in Moab and traveling to a strange land?
2. Why do you think Ruth decided to leave her home and do hard work for Naomi's sake?

Choices and Consequences
In stories, characters make choices. These choices have consequences. Choices and consequences are an important part of a story's plot. Use details from the story to answer the questions on the Ruth and Her Choices page.

Bible Character Chart
Keep a chart to help you remember information about the characters in these stories. In the boxes write:
- the main character's name
- the title of the story
- two or three words or phrases to describe the character
- an important choice the character makes
- what matters most to the character in the story

Add Ruth to the Bible Character Chart.

Name _____

Date _____

Bible Character Chart

In the boxes below, write the character's name, the title of the story, two or three words or phrases that describe the character, an important choice the character made, and what mattered most in the story to the character.

Name	Title	Description	Choice	What Mattered Most

Name

Date

Bible Character Chart

Name	Title	Description	Choice	What Mattered Most

Name _____ Date _____

Ruth and Her Choices

Answer the questions using details from the story.

1. At the beginning of the story, Naomi faced many hardships. What were they?

_____

_____

_____

2. Why do you think Ruth decided to leave Moab and go to Bethlehem with Naomi?

_____

_____

_____

3. What did Ruth do when they arrived at Bethlehem?

_____

_____

_____

Choices and Consequences

4. Gleaning is hard work. Why do you think Ruth was willing to do it?

_____

_____

_____

5. Write two consequences of her choice.

_____

_____

_____

6. Describe Naomi's situation at the end of the story.

_____

_____

_____

7. What words would you use to describe Ruth?

_____

_____

Guidelines for Peer Discussion

Share your thoughts, ideas, questions, and feelings about a text with a peer or others. Listen carefully to what everyone has to say about the text. During your discussion, follow these guidelines.

1. Be prepared to discuss what you think about the text. You should have already read the assignment. Come prepared to discuss your ideas and use examples from the text to support your thoughts and answers.

2. You will be asked questions about the text. Be ready to answer them, and bring some questions of your own to ask others, such as:

   "Who was your favorite character? Why?"

   "What was your favorite part of the text? Why?"

   "What fact did you enjoy learning? Why do you find this fact interesting?"

   "What question would you ask if you had the chance to meet the author?"

3. Listen if it's not your turn to speak. Pay attention to what others say so that you can add your ideas. Speak clearly and in complete sentences.

4. If you don't understand what someone says, ask a question.

   "What do you mean when you say . . . ?"

   "Can you give an example of . . . ?"

5. If you don't agree with what someone says, explain why.

   "I don't agree with that because . . . "

6. Keep discussions positive! You can disagree, but don't argue. Be respectful.

Name _____   Date _____

"The Story of David": Session 1

A powerful enemy attacks Israel. Who will step forward to be the kingdom's champion?

Pronunciation Goliath
(guh-LIY-uhth) Philistine
(FIH-luh-steen)

Vocabulary
You will find these words in today's reading.

page: (v.) a helper who takes messages, does errands, and performs other services
"Come, *page*," said the prince to the boy, "and take this message to my father, the king."

defy: (v.) to challenge or dare
The knight *defied* the robber in the castle to come out and do battle.

scarce: (adj.) not plentiful, not much
Food was *scarce* during the famine; most families did not have enough to eat.

pillage: (v.) to rob, to take by force; (n.) something stolen or taken by force
After they raided the village, the band of robbers returned to their hideout to divide their *pillage.*

forage: (v.) to wander in search of food
When their supplies ran out, the explorers had to *forage* in the woods to survive.

upstart: (n.) a person who thinks he is more important than he really is
She is such an *upstart* that she thinks she ought to be first in line for everything.

Think Ahead

1. Summarize what you read in "The Story of Ruth." In your summary, tell the following things:
   - Ruth's mother-in-law's name
   - What Ruth did when they reached Bethlehem
   - What happened at the end of the story

2. Tell one choice Ruth made and the consequences of that choice.

3. The next Bible story you're going to read tells about the descendants of Ruth and Boaz. (If you don't know the meaning of *descendants,* check a dictionary.)

Read

Chapters 1-3 of "The Story of David" in *Classics for Young Readers,* Vol. 5A, pages 115-120

Questions

Answer the following questions in complete sentences in your Reading Notebook.

1. At the beginning of the story, why did David go to the palace?
2. What people invaded Israel?
3. What did the king offer as a reward to the person who killed Goliath?
4. Why didn't the king want David to fight Goliath?

Discuss

1. Describe Goliath. Why didn't any of the Israelite soldiers fight him?
2. David told the king, "Israel's heart should not fail because of a man" (page 119). What do you think David meant?
3. Why did David decide to fight Goliath? What reasons did he give to explain why he should?

Story Timeline

Use details from the story to answer the questions on the Story Timeline page.

Name _____ Date _____

Story Timeline

Use details from the story to answer the questions below.

1. Describe David's appearance. _____

_____

_____

2. How did David help the king? _____

_____

_____

3. Draw a symbol in the box to stand for David.

4. What happened while David was at the palace? _____

_____

_____

Story Timeline

5. Describe what happened after each army camped on its hill.

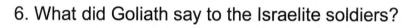

_____

6. What did Goliath say to the Israelite soldiers?

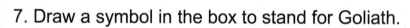

_____

7. Draw a symbol in the box to stand for Goliath.

Name _____   Date _____

"The Story of David": Session 2

David has chosen to meet Goliath in battle. What will be the consequences of his decision?

Vocabulary

You will find this word in today's reading.

assembly: (n.) a group of people who come together for a purpose, for example, to make laws, or to worship
The *assembly* gathered in the council hall to vote for the new mayor.

Think Ahead

1. Summarize what you have read so far in the story. In your summary, tell
   - how David helped the king
   - who invaded Israel
   - who challenged the Israelite army
   - what David decided to do

2. Do you think David is brave? Do you think he is wise? Why?

3. Predict what you think will happen next, and explain why.

Read

Chapter 4 in "The Story of David" in *Classics for Young Readers,* Vol. 5A, pages 120-122

Questions

Answer the following questions in complete sentences in your Reading Notebook.

1. Why didn't David wear the king's armor?
2. What did David take with him to the battle?
3. Copy the sentence in chapter 4 that tells if David was afraid of Goliath.
4. How did David kill Goliath?

Discuss

What words would you use to describe David? Use evidence from the story to explain why you would choose these words.

Bible Character Chart

Add David to the Bible Character Chart.

Name _____   Date _____

Choices That Count: Session 1

Making the right choice often means putting others before ourselves.

Think Ahead

1. *Loyalty* means being true to the people, places, and ideas we care about. Describe a time in "The Story of Ruth" or "The Story of David" when a character showed loyalty.

2. Loyalty sometimes requires people to put others before themselves. It means doing what's right instead of what is easy. Describe a time in "The Story of Ruth" or "The Story of David" when a character put others before him or herself.

Compare and Contrast Ruth and David

To compare and contrast characters means to tell how they are alike and different. Review the two stories and your Bible Characters Chart before discussing the following questions:

- What did each character do that was brave or difficult? Why did he or she do it?

- Who or what mattered most to each character? Why do you think so?

- How did each character's choice affect others? Did the character make a positive or negative difference in other characters' lives?

- Describe two ways the characters are alike.

- Describe two ways they are different.

Spotlight on Character

Complete a Spotlight on Character sheet for Ruth and David. Fill in a separate sheet for each character.

At the top of the sheet, write the character's name in the blank. Then in the circle at the center of the sheet, draw a picture of the character or a symbol of the character.

In each of the sections surrounding the circle, write two or more sentences on each of these four topics:

1. Tell about the character's important choice.
2. Explain how the character's choice affected other characters.
3. Describe how the character was loyal.
4. Tell what kind of person the character is and why you think so.

Name _____   Date _____

Spotlight on Character: _____

1. _____   2. _____

_____   _____

_____   _____

_____   _____

_____   _____

3. _____   4. _____

_____   _____

_____   _____

_____   _____

_____   _____

_____

Name _____ Date _____

Spotlight on Character: _____

1._____   2._____

_____   _____

_____   _____

_____   _____

_____   _____

3._____   4._____

_____   _____

_____   _____

_____   _____

_____   _____

Name _____ Date _____

"Daniel in the Lion's Den"

What should you do when someone asks you to do something you think is wrong? Should you stick to what you think is right? Think about how much harder it would be if you knew you might suffer for your decision.

Vocabulary
You will find these words in today's reading.

flatter: (v.) to praise untruthfully or insincerely
Do you really mean all those compliments or are you just trying to *flatter* me?

unwillingly: (adv.) not wanting to
When my parents asked me to go to bed in the middle of my favorite movie, I went, but very *unwillingly*.

alter: (v.) to change
Your drawing is perfect; I would not *alter* a single line.

Think Ahead
David helped the Israelites defeat the Philistines. Many years later, in the story you are about to read, Israel was defeated by the Babylonians, and the Babylonians, in turn, by the Persians.

The main character in today's story is Daniel. When he was young, he was captured and taken to the great city called Babylon. The Bible says that, because of his wisdom, Daniel became a trusted advisor to Babylonian and Persian kings.

Look at the map that goes with today's lesson. On the map, trace your finger around the Persian Empire. Then locate the following:
- Israel and Jerusalem
- Babylon

Read

"Daniel in the Lion's Den" in *Classics for Young Readers,* Vol. 5A, pages 123-126

Questions

Answer the following questions in complete sentences in your Reading Notebook.

1. Copy one sentence from the story that describes Daniel.
2. Why were the princes jealous of Daniel?
3. Why did the king choose to sign the law?
4. What did this law say?
5. Did Daniel obey the king's law?

Discuss

1. Did the king want to throw Daniel in the lion's den? Why did he?
2. What explanation did Daniel give for why the lions did not harm him?
3. When Daniel came out of the lion's den, how did he treat the king?

Bible Character Chart

Add Daniel to the Bible Character Chart.

Optional: Seeing Daniel

When you think of Daniel in the lion's den, what picture comes to mind? What do you think Daniel is doing? What are the lions doing? Why do you think this?

If you want to, draw a picture of Daniel in the lion's den. Then go online to see a painting on this website:
http://collectionsonline.lacma.org/mwebcgi/mweb.exe?request=ere cord&hilite=107539&id=12792&type=1

Look carefully at the painting and answer the questions in the box titled "Questions about the Artwork." Compare and contrast the way you pictured Daniel with the way he is shown in the painting.

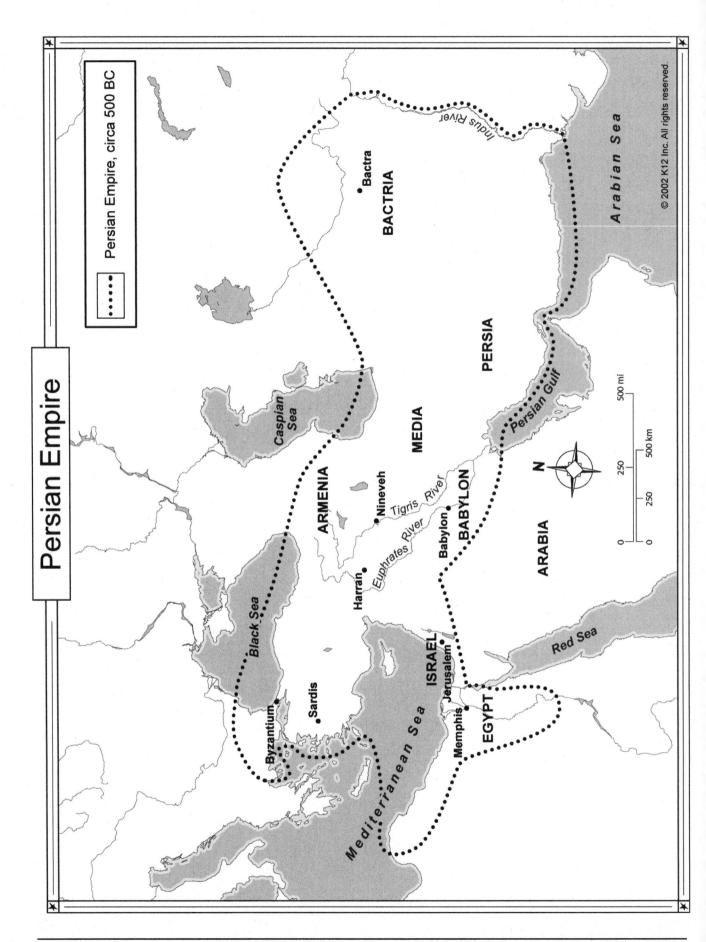

Persian Empire

Persian Empire, circa 500 BC

BACTRIA

Bactra

Indus River

Arabian Sea

© 2002 K12 Inc. All rights reserved.

PERSIA

Persian Gulf

Caspian Sea

MEDIA

500 mi

500 km

250

250

N

0

0

ARMENIA

Nineveh

Tigris River

Euphrates River

Harran

Babylon

BABYLON

ARABIA

Black Sea

Red Sea

ISRAEL

Jerusalem

Sardis

Byzantium

Memphis

EGYPT

Mediterranean Sea

Name _____ Date _____

Choices That Count: Session 2

Review the three Bible stories by focusing on the choices characters made and the consequences of their choices.

Think Ahead

Think about Ruth, David, and Daniel. What important choice did each character make?

Choices and Consequences

Ruth, David, and Daniel were called upon to make important choices about people, places, and beliefs they cared about.

Review their stories by completing the Choices and Consequences page. Look back to the stories in the book and to your Bible Character Chart pages. Use details from each story to support your answers.

Optional: Seeing Ruth and David

If you enjoyed viewing and discussing the painting of Daniel, then go online to see how two artists show Ruth and David.

To see a **painting of Ruth and Naomi**, go to:

http://www.amit.org.il/learning/english/JW/Ruth.htm

- What point in the story does this painting show?
- What emotion is expressed by the way the artist shows Ruth?

To see a **sculpture of David**, go to:

www.galleriaborghese.it/borghese/en/edavid.htm

- What point in the story does this sculpture show?
- What words would you use to describe David as this sculpture shows him?

Name _____   Date _____

Choices and Consequences

Write brief answers to the four questions about each character. Use details from each story to support your answers.

	Ruth	David	Daniel
What important choice did the character make?			
What hardships or dangers did the character face after making his or her choice?			

Name

Date

Choices and Consequences

	Ruth	David	Daniel
Why do you think the character decided to make the choice he or she did?			
What were the consequences of the character's choice?			

Name _____   Date _____

"Young Benjamin Franklin": Session 1

Read about the boyhood of Benjamin Franklin, who was called "the greatest man of the age and the country in which he lived."[1]

Vocabulary

You will find these words in today's reading:

studious: (adj.) paying careful attention to one's learning
The *studious* girl patiently worked on her lessons until she had done them correctly.

calculate: (v.) to solve a problem using math
You need to know the multiplication table to *calculate* the answer to this word problem.

object: (v.) to speak against or strongly disagree
He *objects* to walking across the muddy field because he wants to keep his new shoes clean.

promptly: (adv.) quickly or immediately
The librarian asked me to return the book *promptly*, because another person was waiting to borrow it.

endure: (v.) to suffer hardship or misfortune without giving in
Those who *endure* Mount Everest's icy weather and difficult climb are treated to an extraordinary view when they reach the top.

alarmed: (adj.) afraid, worried
I was *alarmed* to hear that it was supposed to rain on the day we planned to have our family picnic.

[1]James H. Hutson, "Franklin, Benjamin," World Book Online Americas Edition, http://www.worldbookonline.com/wbol/wbPage/na/ar/co/209260, June 27, 2002.

fatigued: (adj.) tired
After a long day sightseeing, we piled into the car *fatigued*, but content.

inquire: (v.) to ask
After my friend missed two days of soccer practice, I called her to *inquire* about her health.

Think Ahead

Today's reading, "Young Benjamin Franklin," begins in the year 1706. In 1706, the United States of America had not yet been formed. Only twelve of the thirteen colonies existed. But great changes were coming, and one little boy in Boston was growing up to become one of the greatest men of that extraordinary time.

Read

Chapters 1–3 of "Young Benjamin Franklin" in *American Lives and Legends,* pages 4–9

Questions

Answer the following questions in complete sentences in your Reading Notebook.

1. Why did Benjamin's father apprentice him to a printer?
2. Why did Benjamin choose to leave Boston?
3. Describe Benjamin's journey from Boston to Philadelphia.

Discuss

1. Benjamin Franklin said that going aboard the ship was one of the great *errata* of his life. Why do you think he said that? Do you agree or disagree with him?

2. Describe Benjamin Franklin's first day in Philadelphia.

Biography and Autobiography

A *biography* is a form of nonfiction writing that tells the story of a person's life.

An *autobiography* is the story of a person's life told by that person. In an autobiography, authors use the words *I, me,* and *mine* when writing about an event. In a biography, the author will use the words *he, him,* and *his.* Look at the two sentences below. One is from a biography of Benjamin Franklin, and the other is from his autobiography.

- Benjamin Franklin's parents were poor people who lived in a humble home on Milk Street, and he was the youngest son in the family of seventeen children.

- I then turned and went down Chestnut Street and part of Walnut Street, eating my roll all the way.

Discuss these questions:
- Which sentences give facts about Benjamin Franklin's life?
- Which sentence comes from Benjamin's biography? How do you know?
- Which sentence comes from Benjamin's autobiography? How do you know?

Look back at today's reading. Which chapters are a biography? Which are an autobiography?

Preserving the Past: Biography and Autobiography

If you listen carefully to the word *history*, you'll hear the word *story* in it. History is the story of what happened to people and places. We have many ways to *preserve,* or keep alive, history. One way we can preserve the past is to write a biography or an autobiography about the important events in a person's life.

Use facts from Benjamin Franklin's biography and autobiography to help you complete the Preserving the Past: Biography and Autobiography page.

Name _____   Date _____

Preserving the Past: Biography and Autobiography

Write five or more facts from "Young Benjamin Franklin" in his profile. Then answer the questions in complete sentences.

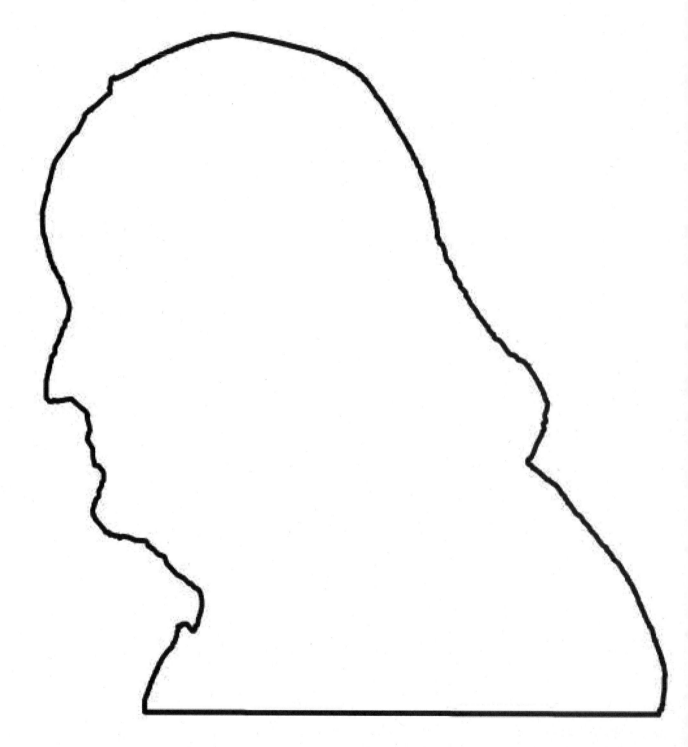

Preserving the Past: Biography and Autobiography

1. Write two adjectives that describe Benjamin Franklin. Give examples from the story to support your opinion.

_____

_____

_____

_____

2. Write one thing that was important to Benjamin Franklin. How do you know?

_____

_____

_____

_____

Guidelines for Peer Discussion

Share your thoughts, ideas, questions, and feelings about a text with a peer or others. Listen carefully to what everyone has to say about the text. During your discussion, follow these guidelines.

1. Be prepared to discuss what you think about the text. You should have already read the assignment. Come prepared to discuss your ideas and use examples from the text to support your thoughts and answers.

2. You will be asked questions about the text. Be ready to answer them, and bring some questions of your own to ask others, such as:

   "Who was your favorite character? Why?"

   "What was your favorite part of the text? Why?"

   "What fact did you enjoy learning? Why do you find this fact interesting?"

   "What question would you ask if you had the chance to meet the author?"

3. Listen if it's not your turn to speak. Pay attention to what others say so that you can add your ideas. Speak clearly and in complete sentences.

4. If you don't understand what someone says, ask a question.

   "What do you mean when you say . . . ?"

   "Can you give an example of . . . ?"

5. If you don't agree with what someone says, explain why.

   "I don't agree with that because . . . "

6. Keep discussions positive! You can disagree, but don't argue. Be respectful.

Name _____   Date _____

"Young Benjamin Franklin": Session 2

Young Benjamin Franklin loved reading books. When he grew up, he began writing his own. How many of his writings do you recognize?

Vocabulary

You will find these words in today's reading:

squander: (v.) to spend foolishly or waste
I *squandered* most of my allowance on treats, so I did not have enough money to buy the paints I wanted.

dissatisfied: (adj.) not happy, not pleased
He liked the head and the body of the shark he drew, but he was *dissatisfied* with the tail.

proprietor: (n.) owner
Jack loved books and reading so much that when he grew up, he became the *proprietor* of a bookstore.

coaxingly: (adv.) in a flattering or persuasive way
She called *coaxingly* to the kitten, hoping it would come and sit on her lap.

grave: (adj.) serious
Their faces were *grave* as they discussed the rules.

crestfallen: (adj.) ashamed, disappointed
I was *crestfallen* when I wasn't chosen for the team.

Think Ahead

1. Summarize what you have learned about the life of Benjamin Franklin so far. In your summary, include:
   - Where he grew up
   - The trade he learned
   - The city he moved to

2. What words would you use to describe Benjamin Franklin? Why?

Read

Chapters 4-5 of "Young Benjamin Franklin" in *American Lives and Legends*, pages 9-12

Questions

Answer the following questions in complete sentences in your Reading Notebook.

1. What is an *almanac?*
2. Who is the author of *Poor Richard's Almanac?*
3. What name did he use when he published the almanac?

Discuss

1. In your own words, explain why Benjamin Franklin continued to raise the price of the book that the man in his print shop was trying to buy.

2. A proverb is a brief, popular saying that contains a familiar truth, or useful thought. Find the proverb in Chapter 4. What does it mean? Do you agree or disagree? Why?

3. Choose one proverb from *Poor Richard's Almanac.* What does it mean? Is it good advice? Why?

People, Places, and Ideas

1. Benjamin Franklin was an author, but he was also a scientist, an inventor, and a statesman. Research the answers to the following questions and then write the completed sentences in your Reading Notebook. Add one more interesting fact that you learn as you read.

> Benjamin Franklin was one of the first people to experiment with _____. He flew a _____ during a thunderstorm, and proved that lightning was a kind of electricity. He invented the_____, which saved his and many other people's homes from being damaged when they were struck by lightning.

> Benjamin Franklin helped write the _____, which made the United States of America an independent country. He was the oldest person who signed it.

2. Look at the Important Places in American History map. Write the number of the sentence that describes Benjamin Franklin beside Philadelphia, the city in which he lived.

3. In what colony (now a state) was Philadelphia located?

4. Use the facts you have learned about Franklin to help you create a symbol for the man or one of his accomplishments. Draw a symbol in the box to represent Benjamin Franklin.

Ordinary People, Extraordinary Lives

Benjamin Franklin is the first of five people you will meet in this unit who led an extraordinary life. Write a brief biography to help you remember him as you read.

Write Benjamin Franklin's name and where he moved to on the lines on the Ordinary People, Extraordinary Lives page. Then write a paragraph that tells one thing Benjamin Franklin did that was extraordinary. Give at least one reason that explains why it was extraordinary. You may choose to illustrate your work. Save this page.

Name _____   Date _____

Important Places in American History

Match the number of the sentence to the person and place it describes. Then draw a symbol in the box to represent the person.

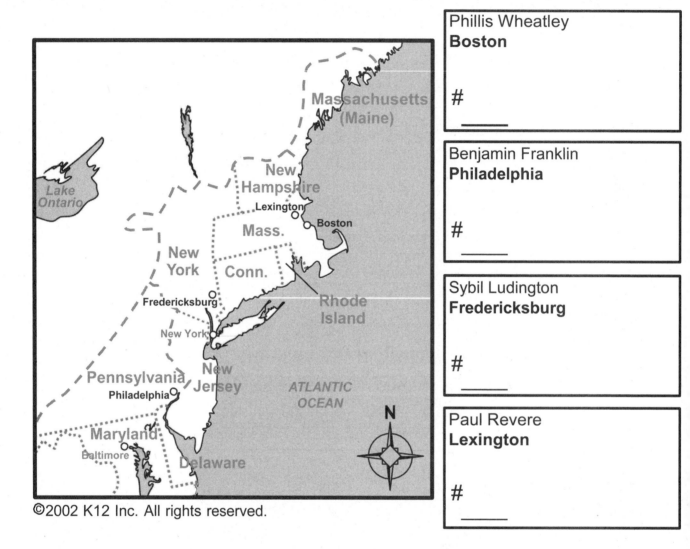

Phillis Wheatley
Boston

\#
_____

Benjamin Franklin
Philadelphia

\#
_____

Sybil Ludington
Fredericksburg

\#
_____

Paul Revere
Lexington

\#
_____

©2002 K12 Inc. All rights reserved.

1. This person saw two lights in a belfry, and then rode to warn farmers and townspeople that British soldiers were coming by sea to attack.
2. This person was a slave who became the first published African-American poet.
3. This person rode nearly 40 miles in one night to call American soldiers to gather and prepare for a British raid.
4. This person published *Poor Richard's Almanac.* He wrote the proverbs such as "A penny saved is a penny earned" and "Early to bed, early to rise, makes a man healthy, wealthy, and wise."

Name _____   Date _____

Ordinary People, Extraordinary Lives

_____

in _____

lived an extraordinary life because

_____

_____

_____

_____

_____

_____

_____

_____

Name _____   Date _____

"Phillis Wheatley: A Poem to King George"

How would you like to write a poem that would be read by a king and published in a book? This 12-year-old girl did just that!

Vocabulary
You will find these words in today's reading:

crossly: (adv.) in a bad-tempered way
"Stop pulling my ponytail," she said *crossly*, "I don't like it."

repeal: (v.) to undo or unmake a law
President Abraham Lincoln helped *repeal* the laws that allowed slavery in the United States.

seldom: (adj.) rarely, not often
We *seldom* go to the zoo, perhaps only once or twice each year.

feebly: (adv.) weakly
The newborn kitten *feebly* struggled to its feet and took its first steps.

gilded: (adj.) having a thin covering of gold
That picture frame is not solid gold, it is made of wood that has been *gilded*.

meanest: (adj.) having few means; poor
It broke my heart to think of the poor family in the story living in the *meanest* hovel in the village.

clime: (n.) a poetic term meaning climate or region of the earth
Tim enjoys the sun and hot weather, so he chooses to vacation in tropical *climes*.

Think Ahead

Today's reading tells the story of a little girl who faced challenges that most people today cannot begin to understand. Yet, she rose above the difficulties and accomplished great things. As you read her story, think about her circumstances as well as her extraordinary talent.

Read

"Phillis Wheatley: A Poem to King George" in *American Lives and Legends,* pages 13-20

Questions

Answer the following questions in complete sentences in your Reading Notebook.

1. How did Phillis come to live with the Wheatley family?
2. Name two things the Wheatley family taught Phillis how to do.
3. Why did Phillis write the poem to King George?
4. Phillis Wheatley the first African-American to do something. What was it?
5. In the story, Samuel Adams tells Phillis Wheatley, "You have a great gift … a very great gift, and it must be used." What do you think he meant? Do you think Phillis Wheatley used her gift?

Discuss

People can preserve the past by writing biographies or autobiographies. But have you ever sung "The Star-Spangled Banner" or "My Country, Tis of Thee"? Another way to remember an important event in history is to write a song or a poem about it.

Discuss Phillis Wheatley's poem using these questions:
1. Who was the poem for?
2. What important event did Phillis Wheatley write about?
3. How did the colonists feel about the event? How do you know?
4. Why did Phillis Wheatley write the poem?
5. How is the language in the poem different from the language you usually use or see? Why do you think she wrote it that way?

Ordinary People, Extraordinary Lives

Complete an Ordinary People, Extraordinary Lives page for Phillis Wheatley. Write Phillis Wheatley's name and city on the lines. Then write a paragraph that tells one thing she did that was extraordinary. Give at least one reason that explains why it was extraordinary. If you want to, draw a picture of her in the box. Save this page.

Important Places in American History

1. Look at the Important Places in American History map. Write the number of the sentence that describes Phillis Wheatley beside Boston, the city in which she lived.
2. In what colony (now a state) was Boston located?
3. Draw a symbol in the box to represent Phillis Wheatley.

Name _____   Date _____

Ordinary People, Extraordinary Lives

_____

in _____

lived an extraordinary life because

_____

_____

_____

_____

_____

_____

_____

_____

<u>Name</u>   <u>Date</u>

"Paul Revere's Ride"

Read another poem that commemorates an important event in American history.

Vocabulary
You will find these words in today's reading:

belfry: (n.) a room that houses a bell
We climbed a hundred stairs to the *belfry* at the top of the tower to see the ancient bell.

muffled: (adj.) quieted
The sound of her voice was *muffled* by the heavy scarf she wore.

spar: (n.) a strong pole used to hold sails and ropes on ships
The sailor carefully checked the *spar* for cracks that might make it too weak to hold the sails and rigging.

hulk: (n.) a heavy, clumsy ship
The *hulk* rolled and dipped in the water like a lazy whale.

muster: (n.) a group
A *muster* of soldiers gathered at the fort to prepare for battle.

tread: (n.) the sound or act of walking
The puppy sat by the door, listening for the sound of its master's heavy *tread* on the stair.

grenadier: (n.) a soldier who carries or throws grenades
The *grenadier* checked his grenades and tucked them safely into his pack.

impetuous: (adj.) excited, impatient
The *impetuous* young explorer charged into the jungle, leaving the rest of his party far behind.

linger: (v.) to be slow in leaving

The moon seemed to *linger* over the lake, as if gazing upon her reflection in the water.

kindled: (v.) to have started a fire

She *kindled* a fire by rubbing two sticks together.

Think Ahead

1. In the last story you read Phillis Wheatley's poem to King George. Why did Phillis write that poem?
2. Can you think of other famous poems that commemorate important events? In this lesson, you'll read one.

Read

"Paul Revere's Ride" in *American Lives and Legends,* pages 21-26

Questions

Answer the following questions in complete sentences in your Reading Notebook.

1. Why did Paul Revere ride to the villages and farms?
2. Did the British soldiers come by land or by sea?
3. How did Paul Revere know that?
4. On what date did Paul Revere and the two other patriots make their famous ride?
5. To what towns does Paul Revere ride?

Discuss

1. Because Paul Revere warned the colonists, when the British soldiers arrived the colonists were ready to give battle. And that battle, the Battle of Lexington and Concord, began the Revolutionary War. What might have happened if the colonists had not been warned? How might history have been different?

2. Reread the last five lines of the poem. Do you think the poet meant that people can still hear Paul Revere's horse? What do you think he meant?

A Narrative Poem

Henry Wadsworth Longfellow wrote a *narrative poem* about Paul Revere's midnight ride. A narrative poem is a poem that tells a story.

Read aloud the two stanzas below. Summarize what happens in each in your own words.

1. He said to his friend, "If the British march
   By land or sea from the town tonight,
   Hang a lantern aloft in the belfry arch
   Of the North Church as a signal light –
   One if by land, and two if by sea;
   And I on the opposite shore will be,
   Ready to ride and spread the alarm
   Through every Middlesex village and farm,
   For the country folk to be up and to arm.

2. It was twelve by the village clock
   When he crossed the bridge into Medford town.
   He heard the crowing of the cock,
   And the barking of the farmer's dog,
   And felt the damp of the river fog,
   That rises after the sun goes down.

When you finish, complete the "Paul Revere's Ride" Storyboard. Choose six important events that occur in the poem. For example, your first event might be, "Paul Revere and his friend decide on a signal." These events, in the order in which they occurred, will be the captions for your storyboard. Illustrate the events so that your storyboard shows and tells what happens in the poem.

Name _____

Date _____

"Paul Revere's Ride" Storyboard

You read a narrative poem – a poem that tells a story. Now draw and retell in order the main events from the story. Be sure to write a caption under each illustration.

1.

2.

3.

_____

_____

_____

Name _____

Date _____

"Paul Revere's Ride" Storyboard

4.

5.

6.

Name _____ Date _____

Words to Remember: "Paul Revere's Ride"

Review and share the famous tale of Paul Revere.

Think Ahead

Use the Paul Revere's Ride Storyboard to help you complete an Ordinary People, Extraordinary Lives page for Paul Revere.

Write Paul Revere's name and the second city he rode to on the lines. Then write a paragraph that tells one thing he did that was extraordinary. Give two or more reasons that explain why what he did was extraordinary. If you want to, draw a picture of him in the box. Save this page.

Rhythm and Verse

Look back at the poem "Paul Revere's Ride." When Henry Wadsworth Longfellow told his story, he did not only include facts. He also included *imagery*. Imagery is language that appeals to the senses and creates a mental picture. Imagery makes readers see, hear, smell, taste, or feel things in their imagination.

For example, in the third stanza, Longfellow could have only told the fact, "The British ship was called the *Somerset*." Instead, he added the following imagery:

> Where swinging wide at her mooring lay
> The *Somerset,* British man-of-war;
> A phantom ship, with each mast and spar
> Across the moon like a prison bar

Discuss Longfellow's imagery with these questions:

- What do phrases like "phantom ship" and "prison bar" make you think of?

- What words and feelings describe the picture you see when you imagine the *Somerset's* masts and rigging covering the moon like prison bars?

- Think about the imagery Longfellow used to describe the ship. Why do you think he describes the ship this way?

- What different words or feelings might you think of if Longfellow had described the *Somerset* this way:

  > Where swinging wide at her mooring lay
  > The *Somerset,* British man-of-war;
  > A <u>steadfast </u>ship, with each mast and spar
  > <u>Cradling </u>the moon <u>like a mother's arm</u>

Find another example of imagery in the poem. What do you think of or imagine when you read it? (Hint: Look in Stanzas 4 and 5.)

The rhythm of a poem can also add to its imagery. Choose your favorite stanza from the poem. Read it aloud. What does the rhythm remind you of: hoof beats, waves lapping against the side of a boat, or something else? Why do you think Longfellow wrote the poem in this rhythm?

Preserving the Past: Performance

When some people keep history alive, they really keep it *alive*—they act it out or perform for others. They recite poetry, put on plays, or dress up in costumes and pretend to be historical figures. Today, perform a piece of history—read aloud or act out your favorite stanza from "Paul Revere's Ride."

Directions:

1. First, think about what is happening in the stanza. What imagery does the poet use? How can you use your voice to add to the poet's imagery?

2. Rehearse your lines. You don't have to memorize your lines, but you should be able to read them smoothly in a loud, clear voice. Practice some of the gestures you will use. Rehearse in front of a mirror and pretend you are speaking to the audience. Think about where you will stand on the stage as you deliver your lines. If you want to, you may gather props and prepare a costume.

3. Be prepared to give your audience a summary of what happens in the parts of the poem that you do not perform.

4. When you're ready, perform your piece!

Name _____   Date _____

Ordinary People, Extraordinary Lives

_____

in _____

lived an extraordinary life because

_____

_____

_____

_____

_____

_____

_____

_____

Name _____   Date _____

"Sybil Ludington: The Female Paul Revere"

Can you guess why this brave teenager is called one of the heroes of the Revolutionary War?

Vocabulary

You will find these words in today's reading:

tactic: (n.) a way to accomplish something
My little sister seems to have a million *tactics* for staying up past her bedtime.

urgently: (adv.) needing immediate attention
"Doctor, come quickly," he said *urgently*, "my father is very ill."

intently: (adv.) with great concentration
She looked *intently* at the pieces of the jigsaw puzzle, trying to decide how they fit together.

raid: (n.) an attack
The enemy soldiers led a *raid* upon the village, and burned all the buildings and fields to the ground.

muster: (v.) to cause to gather
We're going to play a pick-up game of ball in the park if I can *muster* enough players to form two teams.

brigands: (n.) thieves, highwaymen
The *brigands* hid in the woods and robbed the carriages that passed by.

plunder: (v.) to steal or take something by force
The pirates *plundered* the merchant ship, carrying away everything that wasn't nailed down.

notorious: (adj.) generally known and talked of in an unfavorable way
The group waited impatiently for Martha, who was *notorious* for being late.

Think Ahead
In the last two lessons, you read about Paul Revere's famous midnight ride. In today's lesson, you will read about another Revolutionary-era messenger. Before you do, add Paul Revere to your map.

1. Look at the Important Places in American History map. Write the number of the sentence that describes Paul Revere beside Lexington, one of the cities he rode to.

2. In what colony (now a state) was Lexington located?

3. Draw a symbol in the box to represent Paul Revere.

4. Today's reading begins in the spring of 1777, two years after Paul Revere's famous ride. America has declared its independence from England. The Revolutionary War has begun. General George Washington, the Commander in Chief of the American soldiers, has allowed the men to go home and do their spring planting. But will the British wait? Read on and find out!

Read
"Sybil Ludington: The Female Paul Revere" in *American Lives and Legends,* pages 27-31

Questions

Answer the following questions in complete sentences in your Reading Notebook.

1. Why had many of the American troops gone home from the war?
2. After listening to the messenger, what was Colonel Ludington afraid would happen?
3. Why couldn't the messenger ride to warn the people of the farms and villages?
4. Who rode in the messenger's place?

Discuss

1. Why was Sybil Ludington's ride dangerous? Why do you think she did it?
2. Why was her ride important? Give two or more reasons.

Ordinary People, Extraordinary Lives

Complete an Ordinary People, Extraordinary Lives page for Sybil Ludington. Write Sybil Ludington's name and the place where she lived on the lines. Then write a paragraph that tells one thing she did that was extraordinary. Give at least one reason that explains why it was extraordinary. If you want to, draw a picture of her in the box. Save this page.

Preserving the Past: Monuments and Memorials

A statue of Paul Revere stands in Boston. The Washington Monument towers over Washington, DC. People also remember important events and people in history by creating monuments or memorials.

Research three or more monuments or memorials in the United States. Discuss how they are alike or different. Then create a monument or memorial for Sybil Ludington on the Preserving the Past: Monuments and Memorials page.

Name _____   Date _____

Ordinary People, Extraordinary Lives

_____

in _____

lived an extraordinary life because

_____

_____

_____

_____

_____

_____

_____

_____

```
┌─────────────────────────────┐
│                             │
│                             │
│                             │
│                             │
│                             │
│                             │
│                             │
└─────────────────────────────┘
```

Name _____ Date _____

Preserving the Past: Monuments and Memorials

Draw a monument or memorial for Sybil Ludington. On the lines, explain how your design represents her accomplishment.

_____

_____

_____

_____

_____

_____

Name _____   Date _____

"Sequoyah's Great Invention"

How important is it to remember people and events from the past? Meet one man who dedicated 13 years of his life to creating a new way for his people to preserve their history.

Vocabulary

You will find these words in today's reading:

fascinated: (adj.) very interested, to feel wonder
My brother was so *fascinated* by the space shuttle exhibit at the museum that he stayed there long after the rest of us had gone to look at the other exhibits.

devote: (v.) to give a certain amount of time and effort to accomplishing something
I want to be a ballet dancer when I grow up, so I *devote* at least one hour each day to stretching and practicing.

Think Ahead

1. Look at the Important Places in American History map. Write the number of the sentence that describes Sybil Ludington beside Putnam County, the place where she lived.

2. In what colony (now a state) was Putnam County located?

3. Draw a symbol in the box to represent Sybil Ludington.

4. Today you'll read about a man who was a Cherokee Indian. The Cherokee lived in the southeastern part of the United States, on the land that is now Tennessee, North Carolina, South Carolina, Georgia, and Alabama. Find these states on a map.

Read
"Sequoyah's Great Invention" in *American Lives and Legends,* pages 32-34

Questions
Answer the following questions in complete sentences in your Reading Notebook.

1. What were the "talking leaves" Sequoyah admired?
2. Why did Sequoyah want the Cherokee to learn to put words on "talking leaves"?
3. Describe the system of writing that Sequoyah created.
4. Summarize the test the Cherokee Nation leaders gave Sequoyah and his daughter, Ayoka.

Discuss
1. What were the Cherokee able to do after Sequoyah invented the written language? Why is that important?
2. Inventing the written language was not easy. It took Sequoyah a long time, and he did not know if he would succeed. Why do you think he never gave up?

Ordinary People, Extraordinary Lives
Complete an Ordinary People, Extraordinary Lives page for Sequoyah. Write Sequoyah's name and the area where he lived on the lines. Then write a paragraph that tells one thing he did that was extraordinary. Give at least one reason that explains why it was extraordinary. If you want to, draw a picture of him in the box.

Putting It All Together

Gather all five of your Ordinary People, Extraordinary Lives pages. Put them in order and staple them together to make a book. You may make a cover for the book if you want to.

Review your work, and then discuss these questions:

- What do all five people have in common?
- Why do you think people wrote stories, poems, and biographies about them?
- Which story did you like the best? Why?
- What do you most want to remember about these stories? Why?

Name _____ Date _____

Ordinary People, Extraordinary Lives

_____

in _____

lived an extraordinary life because

_____

_____

_____

_____

_____

_____

_____

Name _____   Date _____

People to Remember

Help keep history alive! Reflect on the biographies you've read and learn about a project that you will complete that involves researching a famous American's life and delivering a multimedia presentation on that person.

Think Ahead

Gather your Important Places in American History page and your Ordinary People, Extraordinary Lives pages. Review all that you have written and learned about these people and their achievements. What was each person's extraordinary accomplishment?

An Extraordinary Life

Choose three of the following: Benjamin Franklin, Phillis Wheatley, Paul Revere, Sybil Ludington, or Sequoyah. For each person, discuss the following questions.

1. Why is each person's accomplishment unusual or extraordinary?
2. Why did the person achieve his or her goals? How did his or her accomplishment affect others?
3. How are their accomplishments alike? How are they different?

Make a chart to find out what these people have in common. Divide a sheet of paper into three columns. At the top of each column, write the name of one of the people you discussed. Underneath each name, list words and phrases that describe the person. You may use the same word for more than one character. For example, under all three, you might write "determined."

When you finish writing your list, review it. Which words and phrases appear most often? Pick two words or phrases that describe the most important traits these people share. Write them here:

1. _____

2. _____

Preserving the Past

You've learned many ways people remember important events in history. They write biographies, autobiographies, songs, and poetry. They put on a performance, build a monument or memorial, or, as in Sequoyah's case, create a written language! In what other ways do people remember the past and keep history alive for others? Why do you think it's important to do so?

You, too, can help keep history alive. In the upcoming lessons, you will create a multimedia presentation about a famous American. You may choose to focus your presentation on one of the people in this unit or on one of these important people from early American history:

    Thomas Jefferson
    Betsy Ross
    Benjamin Banneker
    Abigail Adams

If you choose to do your presentation on one of the people about whom you have already read, you may use some information that you learned from this unit's readings, but you must complete additional research, as well.

Your presentation should include both a speech on the person you've chosen and some piece of media that relates to the content of your speech. Your presentation should contain

- The person's name, the time when he or she lived, and the place(s) where he or she lived
- The person's extraordinary accomplishment(s)
- Why the person is important
- How the person's accomplishment(s) affected others

You will have the opportunity to see and analyze a model presentation in the upcoming lessons. You will need to be online to view the presentation and complete the activities. You will receive documents to help you research and organize your presentation. You will learn how to choose a piece of media to accompany your presentation.

Name _____   Date _____

Analyze a Presentation and Choose a Topic

Watch and explore a model presentation to learn what a presentation should include, how it should be organized, and how to deliver it effectively to an audience. Then choose a topic for your own presentation.

Analyze a Model Presentation for Content

Watch and study one student's presentation about a famous American. Examine the information that the student includes in the presentation, why it is important to include it, and how that information is organized.

Analyze a Model Presentation for Delivery

Watch and study one student's presentation on a famous American again. This time examine how the student's delivery affects the presentation and the audience's experience.

Choose a Topic for Your Presentation

Now it's time to choose a topic for your presentation. Your presentation will be about a famous American, too. Read over the choices before choosing the figure who most interests you. Write the name of the person on the line.

Possible Topics

Benjamin Franklin   Phillis Wheatley
Paul Revere   Sybil Luddington
Sequoyah   Thomas Jefferson
Betsy Ross   Benjamin Banneker
Abigail Adams

My Topic: _____

Name _____   Date _____

Research a Topic and Organize a Presentation

Examine the steps one student took to research a topic and organize information for a presentation. Then begin to research the famous American you selected and organize the information you find.

Analyze the First Steps of Creating a Model Presentation

Explore how one student developed a plan for a presentation by doing research, filling out a graphic organizer, and completing an outline. These tools—a graphic organizer and an outline—can help you take notes and organize your thoughts.

Research a Topic and Organize Information

Now it's time to begin to research the topic of your presentation.

First, find at least two trustworthy sources of information on your topic. Remember that trustworthy sources are ones whose information can be proven to be true and accurate.

Offline, some trustworthy sources are

- Books
- Newspaper and magazine articles
- Encyclopedia entries

Online, some trustworthy sources are
- Websites created by people and organizations with recognized expertise on the subject
- Websites with URLs that end in .gov, .edu, or .org.

NOTE: Wikipedia.org and other websites that allow users to freely add information are not trustworthy.

When it comes to learning about the famous Americans that you had to choose from, some useful offline resources are books written about the person and magazines, such as *American History* and *Smithsonian*.

Online, look for websites maintained by historical societies, museums, and universities.

Once you have found <u>two</u> trustworthy sources of information, use them to learn the answers the following questions about your topic. You will need to answer all of these questions for your presentation.

- Which famous American will your presentation be about?

- Where and when did this person live?

- What important accomplishment(s) did this person achieve?

- How did this person's achievements affect others?

- What is this person most remembered for today?

- What other interesting facts did you learn about this person? Next, write the name of the person you've chosen in the center circle below and in the surrounding circles fill in the most important information you found during your research. Remember that you do not have to write in complete sentences. List your sources at the bottom.

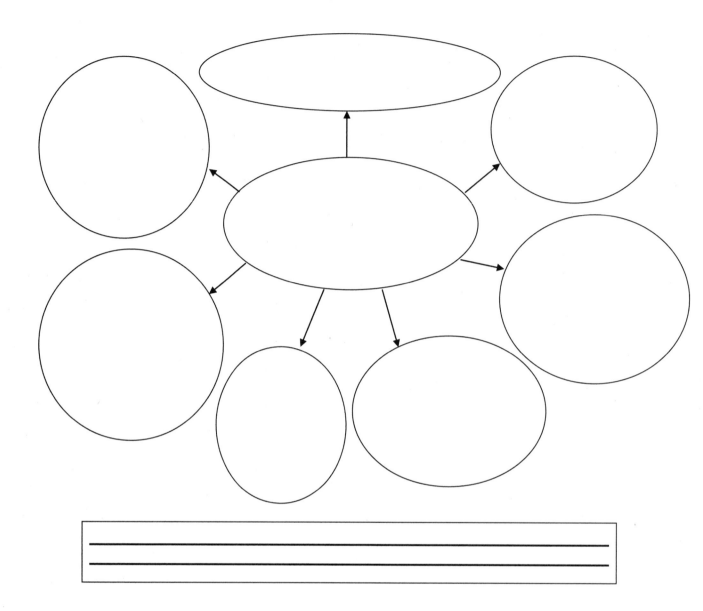

After you have completed your research and filled in the graphic organizer, organize the information into an outline. Complete the outline below. Remember that the hook should contain information that will interest an audience or capture their attention and that the supporting information and details should help prove or explain the main idea.

I. Introduction

    A. Hook:

    _____

    _____

    B. Statement of topic and main idea:

    _____

    _____

II. Body

    A. Supporting information/detail:

    _____

    _____

    B. Supporting information/detail:

    _____

    _____

C. Supporting information/detail:

_____

_____

D. Supporting information/detail:

_____

_____

III. Conclusion

A. Wrap-up:

_____

_____

B. Restatement of main idea:

_____

_____

Name _____   Date _____

Create a Presentation

See how one student prepared for a presentation by creating note cards and selecting appropriate media to accompany the information in the presentation. Then prepare for your own presentation by creating note cards and selecting appropriate media.

Analyze the Creation of a Model Presentation

Explore the steps one student took when transferring information from an outline to note cards to create a presentation. Remember that the order of the facts and the way the ideas fit together is important.

Analyze How Media Is Chosen for a Model Presentation

Appropriate media—sound, visuals, and videos—can make a presentation much better. Learn how to choose media that is appropriate to a topic by examining how one student chose media for the model presentation.

Create Your Presentation and Choose Media

Fill out note cards to use during your presentation and choose media that is appropriate for your presentation. You might consider an important American symbol, a map, or a meaningful American song as part of the media for your presentation.

Create Notecards

First, gather the outline you created and several note cards.

On the top of each note card, write a heading—Introduction, Body, Conclusion—to match a heading from the outline. Note that you may wish to make more than one Body note card.

In the middle of each note card, write in the proper subheadings from your outline. For example, the Introduction note card should have these subheadings: Hook, Statement of Topic, and Main Idea.

Finally, fill the note cards with information from the outline. It is not necessary to write in complete sentences. But, you may wish to expand on some details or change the language to make it easier for you to say. Remember that you will use the note cards when you are giving your presentation, so be sure that what you write is clear to *you*.

When you have finished creating your note cards, put them in order with the same pattern of organization as your outline.

Choose Media

There are many different kinds of media. Pictures, videos, maps, diagrams, charts, graphs, models, and audio recordings are just a few. To choose the right media to go with your presentation, first answer the following questions:

1. What key point or idea do you want the audience to understand or imagine more clearly?

    _____

    _____

2. What type of media will best convey that point?

    _____

    _____

Remember that different types of media are best suited to go with different types of ideas or points.

For instance, if you want to make it clear to audience members what a person looks like or how something changed over time, you may want to show a picture or video during your presentation. If the key point relates to an invention, a diagram may be the more appropriate media. If the key idea relates to sound, you may wish to play audio during your presentation.

Once you have chosen media that fits with the point or idea you want to make clear to the audience, it's time to find or create that media.

In many cases, you may be able to find the media you need in one of your sources. If you choose to show media from a source, be sure to give credit to that source.

Whether you find media or create it yourself, be sure that the media you include in your presentation is large enough or loud enough to be seen or heard by audience members.

After you have found or created the media for your presentation, decide when and how you will refer to it during your presentation. Consider leaving a note on one of your note cards to remind you to refer to your media at that point.

Now that you have found or created the media for your presentation, you are ready to practice delivering it.

Name _____   Date _____

Practice a Presentation

Examine how one student practiced delivering a presentation before using a checklist to help you practice delivering your own presentation.

Review Presentation Techniques
Examine how one student practiced delivering a presentation with the help of a checklist.

Practice Your Presentation
Use the checklist to help you as you practice delivering your own presentation several times. If possible, deliver your presentation in front of a peer and/or your Learning Coach in order to get feedback. You may even wish to videotape yourself and watch.

Presentation Checklist

Use this checklist as you practice your presentation.

- Present your points in the proper order.

- Use your note cards to help you remember what points to make, but do not read directly from the note cards.

- Pronounce each word clearly as you speak.

- Speak with enthusiasm and expression.

- Speak at an appropriate pace: not too fast or too slow.

- Speak with a pleasing volume: not too loud or too soft.

- Show confidence in your knowledge of your topic.

- Stand up straight. Don't fidget.

- Look at your audience as much as possible.

- Direct your audience's attention to the media you have chosen at the right time.

- Practice the presentation so you know what to say.

- Use standard, formal English when you speak. Do not make grammatical or usage errors.

Also consider videotaping one of your practice presentations. Watching yourself is a great way to notice your own strengths and spot weaknesses in the presentation that you can then work to improve.

Peer Feedback: Tell Me About My Presentation

Have another person watch and listen to your presentation and answer the questions as you practice.

1. What topic is the presentation about?

2. What is the thesis statement, or the most important point, that the speaker makes about the topic?

3. Does the speaker include both interesting facts or details (a hook) and the thesis statement of the presentation at the start of the presentation? If not, when is the thesis statement included?

4. Does the speaker support the thesis statement with evidence and reasons? If not, how might the speaker do so?

5. Does the speaker conclude the presentation with a suitable wrap-up conclusion and by restating the thesis statement? If not, how might the speaker do so?

6. What media does the speaker include in the presentation? How does the media relate to the points being made? Is the connection between the media and the content of the presentation clear? If not, how might the speaker make it clearer?

7. At what points in the presentation does the speaker speak too quickly or too slowly? Too loudly or too softly? At what points does the speaker mumble?

8. Does the speaker make eye contact often with the audience? Does the speaker maintain good posture while speaking? If not, at what points should the speaker have looked at the audience and stood up straighter?

9. Describe the tone of the speaker's voice? Does the speaker sound confident in his or her knowledge of the topic and enthusiastic about speaking to the audience? If not, how might the speaker improve his or her tone?

10. After watching the presentation, do you feel as if you learned important and interesting information about the speaker's topic? Do you feel as if you understand the speaker's position? Do you agree with the speaker's position? If not, what could the speaker do to make the presentation better?

Name _____   Date _____

Deliver Your Presentation

Make a presentation on the famous American you chose.
Remember to include media and to deliver the presentation
as you practiced it. Good luck!

Presentation Assessment

Deliver your presentation in front of an audience. Show confidence and do your
best job.

Name _____   Date _____

"Rip Van Winkle": Session 1

What might happen if a person took one of the longest naps in history? Find out what happens when Rip Van Winkle does just that.

Vocabulary
You will find these words in today's reading.

clambered: (v.) to climb with great effort
The little boy *clambered* up his father's back and asked for a piggy-back ride.

gable: (n.) the triangular meeting point of a wall and the sloping ends of the roof
Just below the roof of the house, right underneath the *gable*, there was a small window which we assumed was inside the attic.

hues: (n.) shades of color
In the autumn, the leaves turn beautiful *hues* of red and gold.

incessantly: (adv.) without stopping or being interrupted
In the background, the children chattered *incessantly*, so I strained to hear my telephone conversation.

jerkin: (n.) a snug jacket that comes to the top of the hips
For his costume, the boy wore his regular pants, a shirt with a ruffled front, and a *jerkin* on top of his shirt.

latticed: (adj.) covered with wood in a criss-cross design
The criss-cross design on the *latticed* windows reminded me of a gingerbread house.

peals: (n.) loud, echoing sounds
The joke was so funny that we burst into *peals* of laughter and just couldn't stop giggling.

quaff: (v.) to drink deeply
I *quaffed* my lemonade quickly because I was very thirsty.

rubicund: (adj.) with a reddish skin tone
After being out in the sun and fresh air all day, her cheeks had
a *rubicund* glow.

termagant: (adj.) quarrelsome, abusive, or shrewish
My *termagant* neighbor creates difficulties over the smallest issues;
he even yells at my children if they bounce their ball too loudly.

vehemently: (adv.) forcefully
She *vehemently* disagreed with his opinion, and the angry look
on her face clearly demonstrated her feelings.

ninepins (n.) a form of bowling that was popular in the colonies
Just as some people today enjoy the modern game of bowling, some
colonists enjoyed playing *ninepins.*

weathercock: (n.) a figure that turns in the wind to show wind direction
Check the *weathercock* to determine which way the wind is blowing.

Think Ahead

1. "Rip Van Winkle" is a legend by American author Washington
   Irving. A *legend* is a story that is handed down from the past.
   Legends often contain historical facts, but sometimes the facts
   change over time and the legend becomes fiction. Legends
   may even contain historical characters; however, the facts
   about these real people may not be true. For example, the story
   of George Washington chopping down the cherry tree is a
   legend. What are some other legends you have read?

2. "Rip Van Winkle" is set in the Catskill Mountains in the New
   York colony. The legend begins before the Revolutionary War.

Read
"Rip Van Winkle" in *American Lives and Legends*, pages 36-43

Questions
Answer the following questions in complete sentences in your Reading Notebook.

1. Describe the setting of this legend.
2. How does Rip Van Winkle get along with the people in town?
3. Describe the relationship between Rip and his wife.
4. Describe the stranger Rip meets in the mountains.
5. Where does the stranger lead Rip? Whom does he see?
6. How does Rip feel among the group of men? What does he do?
7. Why is Rip concerned when he awakens from his sleep?

Discuss
1. Why do you think the stranger approaches Rip Van Winkle?

2. *Foreshadowing* is a literary technique of using clues that suggest what is going to happen. Writers use foreshadowing to create suspense, alert their readers to important ideas, or build their readers' expectations. Reread Irving's description of the men (p. 41) whom Rip meets in the mountains. Does the author's language give you any clues about these men? How does Rip Van Winkle feel about them? What do you think Irving is foreshadowing?

3. What differences does Rip notice when he awakens from his sleep? What do you think might happen next?

Figures of Speech
Washington Irving uses *figurative language* to describe the setting, characters, and action in this story. Figurative language uses figures of speech such as metaphor, simile, and personification, for poetic effect rather than for precise, factual meaning. For example, "Her eyes are stars" is figurative language, whereas "the stars are shining brightly tonight" is literal language.

For example, "When the sky is fair, the mountains are clothed in blue and purple" (p. 36) is an example of figurative language. The author uses personification to describe the way the mountains look. The mountains aren't really clothed.

This poetic language helps create the mood of the story. How would you restate Irving's language in your own words? Complete the Figures of Speech page. Rewrite the phrases to explain what they mean. Then create some figurative language of your own. If you wish, you may illustrate the *literal* meaning of one of the sentences.

Character Foreshadowing

Does Rip Van Winkle's own character give readers clues about what is going to happen in the story? Reread Irving's description of Rip on page 37 in your book. What might the author be foreshadowing?

Answer the questions below in your Reading Notebook. Read the first full three paragraphs on page 37. The author uses these paragraphs to foreshadow later events in the story.

- After you read these paragraphs, choose an adjective to describe Rip Van Winkle.
- List specific examples to support the adjective you have chosen.
- The author could just have chosen an adjective or two to describe the character. Why do you think the author went into such great detail about the character's actions?

Using your answers to the questions above, explain how the author might be foreshadowing what happens to Rip Van Winkle in Part 2. Predict what might happen in Part 2.

Name _____ Date _____

Figures of Speech

Explain the meaning of the figurative language in these phrases from "Rip Van Winkle." It may help you to reread the sentences in context. Refer to the page numbers at the end of each example. Then restate the phrases in your own words.

1.   When the sky is fair, the mountains are clothed in blue or purple. (p. 36)

_____

2.   They would rather starve on a penny than work for a pound. (p. 37)

_____

3.   He would have been perfectly content to whistle his life away. (p. 37)

_____

4.   . . . a sharp tongue is the only edged tool that grows keener with use. (p. 37)

_____

5.   The neighbors could tell the hour by his movements as accurately as by a sundial. (p. 38)

_____

6.   . . . his eyes swam in his head. . . .(p. 42)

_____

Figures of Speech

Now try writing some figurative language of your own. Select one one of the following or think of your own situation and describe it with figurative language.

- A starry night
- The sun reflecting on the water
- A person who walks with very straight posture
- A field that is covered with snow

_____

_____

_____

_____

_____

_____

_____

_____

Guidelines for Peer Discussion

Share your thoughts, ideas, questions, and feelings about a text with a peer or others. Listen carefully to what everyone has to say about the text. During your discussion, follow these guidelines.

1. Be prepared to discuss what you think about the text. You should have already read the assignment. Come prepared to discuss your ideas and use examples from the text to support your thoughts and answers.

2. You will be asked questions about the text. Be ready to answer them, and bring some questions of your own to ask others, such as:

   "Who was your favorite character? Why?"

   "What was your favorite part of the text? Why?"

   "What fact did you enjoy learning? Why do you find this fact interesting?"

   "What question would you ask if you had the chance to meet the author?"

3. Listen if it's not your turn to speak. Pay attention to what others say so that you can add your ideas. Speak clearly and in complete sentences.

4. If you don't understand what someone says, ask a question.

   "What do you mean when you say . . . ?"

   "Can you give an example of . . . ?"

5. If you don't agree with what someone says, explain why.

   "I don't agree with that because . . . "

6. Keep discussions positive! You can disagree, but don't argue. Be respectful.

Name _____   Date _____

"Rip Van Winkle": Session 2

Rip Van Winkle goes back home. How will he figure out what has happened to him? How is Rip different? How is the town different? What surprises await Rip Van Winkle?

Vocabulary
You will find these words in today's reading.

addled: (v.) confused
I am feeling dizzy and rather *addled*; I think I should sit down.

cur: (n.) a mutt
That dog isn't a purebred; he's a *cur*.

piping: (adj.) high-pitched and loud
The little girl threw a tantrum in the store and everyone could hear her *piping* voice and her screaming.

riot: (n.) an outburst of disorder by a group of people
The police were afraid that there might be a *riot* because people were so upset; however, everyone remained calm and orderly.

Tory: (n): an American who upheld the cause of the British Crown, instead of colonial independence
During the Revolutionary War era, colonists who did not want independence from Britain identified themselves as *Tories*.

scepter: (n.) a royal staff, or baton, that shows authority
The king sat on his throne wearing his crown and holding his *scepter*.

tavern: (n.) an inn
We stopped at the *tavern* for food, drink, and rest.

Think Ahead

1. Summarize Parts 1 and 2 of "Rip Van Winkle." In your summary, tell :
   - Where the story takes place
   - How Rip gets along with others in the village
   - Where Rip goes when he leaves the village
   - What happens to Rip on the mountain

2. Describe how Rip feels when he wakes up. What changes does he notice? What do you think he will find when he reaches the village?

Read

"Rip Van Winkle" in *American Lives and Legends*, pages 43-47 from the beginning of Part 3 to the end of Part 3

Questions

Answer the following questions in complete sentences in your Reading Notebook.

1. What surprises Rip when he nears the village?
2. How have the people in the village changed?
3. How do the people and dogs react to Rip as he enters the village?
4. Give at least three examples of how the village has changed.
5. Why does the man in the cocked hat accuse Rip of being a Tory? What does this accusation mean?
6. Who might the person leaning against the tree be? Support your prediction with details from the story.

Discuss

1. How does the landscape tell Rip that he is in the same place?
2. Why is the man with the cocked hat angry at Rip for being a loyal subject of the king?
3. What other changes in the village show that there has been a change in the political situation?
4. Based on the story events to this point, what do you think happened to Rip?

Comparing and Contrasting

By comparing and contrasting, authors can make events and characters stronger and more interesting. Sometimes, the author tells you that a comparison or contrast is being made. The author might use words such as *like, as, same, different, unlike,* and *however.* Sometimes, though, the author leaves it up to the reader to compare and contrast. You can compare events and characters in "Rip Van Winkle" by noticing how Rip has changed. You can see how people and animals in the town treat him differently.

Complete the Rip Van Winkle: Before and After page. You may illustrate your work on the back of the page or on separate paper if you wish.

- List at least three ways in which Rip has changed. Look at the descriptions of Rip from before he went up to the mountain and compare them with how he looks upon his return.
- List at least three ways in which Rip is treated differently in the town. Look back to how Rip is treated before he went up to the mountain and contrast these descriptions with how he is treated upon his return.

You will want to look back to Parts 1 and 2 of the story to complete this activity.

Rip's Journal

Imagine that you are Rip Van Winkle. How would you feel about what has happened to you? Using your answers to the questions above, write a journal entry explaining what has happened to you, how your town has changed, and how you feel about your experiences. Use examples from the story to support your feelings. Complete this activity in your Reading Notebook.

Name _____   Date _____

Rip Van Winkle: Before and After

Fill in the chart by writing detailed descriptions that compare and contrast Rip before he went to the mountain and after he came home.

Rip Before	Rip After
How Rip is Treated Before	How Rip is Treated After

Name _____   Date _____

"Rip Van Winkle": Session 3

Rip Van Winkle meets his relatives. He realizes what has happened to him. What will his life be like now?

Vocabulary
You will find these words in today's reading.

inhabitants: (n.) people who live in a specific place
The *inhabitants* of the town were extremely welcoming to our tour group.

totter: (v.) to move unsteadily
When my baby sister was first learning to walk, my parents took a lot of video of her *tottering* around our house.

yoke of England: (n.) a figure of speech referring to British rule
The colonists' desire to be free of the *yoke of England* led to the American Revolution.

Think Ahead
1. Summarize Parts 1-3 of "Rip Van Winkle." In your summary, tell:
   - How Rip has changed since the beginning of the story
   - How people and animals treat him differently when he returns
   - How the town has changed while Rip was sleeping
   - How Rip feels when he returns

2. At the end of Part 3, Rip says, "I can't tell what's my name . . ." Why does he say this?

3. What kind of a life do you think that Rip will have in the village? What can he do that will be helpful and useful to the people?

Read

"Rip Van Winkle" in *American Lives and Legends*, pages 47-51

Questions

Answer the following questions in complete sentences in your Reading Notebook.

1. Who is the man leaning against the tree, the one who looks just like Rip Van Winkle did when he was young?

2. Who is the woman who walks up to Rip Van Winkle with the baby in her arms?

3. How is Peter Vanderdonk helpful to Rip?

4. The author uses figurative language when he describes how people in the village reacted to Rip's story: "The neighbors stared when they heard it. Some winked at each other, and put their tongues in their cheeks." (p. 48) What does this mean and why do the people react this way?

5. Why does Rip prefer making friends among the younger people?

6. How does Rip live out his days?

7. At the end of the story, the author explains that people say they hear Henry Hudson and his crew playing ninepins during a thunderstorm. What does the author mean?

Discuss

1. How does "Rip Van Winkle" fit the description of a legend?
2. How can a legend help history come to life?
3. Why do you think the author writes that Rip varied his story each time he told it?
4. Did your predictions about this legend come to pass? Support your answer with story details.

Becoming a Historian

As you know, a legend has historical elements. "Rip Van Winkle" is a legend. Within the legend, Rip himself becomes a historian of sorts. How does he do this? How does this element make the story more interesting?

- Explain how Rip becomes a historian.
- Why is Rip more valuable as a historian than most of the other people in the village?

Using your answers to the questions above, create a short history book of Rip and his village. You may draw or trace illustrations of historical events that are part of the legend. Below each illustration, write a brief explanation of what happened as Rip would have written it. Consider the following in creating your book:

1. What happens before Rip is born? How is the village settled?
2. What is the village like when Rip is a young man? Who lives there? Who are the rulers?
3. What happens while Rip is asleep?
4. What is the village like upon Rip's return?

Name _____   Date _____

"The Legend of Sleepy Hollow": Session 1

What happens when a teacher's imagination is lit by images of the Headless Horseman? You'll find the answer in this legend.

Vocabulary

You will find these words in today's reading.

anaconda: (n.) a type of snake
Of all of the snakes in the jungle, I am most afraid of the *anaconda.*

apparition: (n.) a ghost-like figure
When I peered through the dusty basement window, I saw an *apparition* and was terrified, but it was only a dusty sheet.

drowsy: (adj.) sleepy
The *drowsy* toddler was rubbing her eyes and really needed to nap.

gazette: (n.) newspaper
The town's local newspaper is called the Village *Gazette.*

glen: (n.) a small valley
This quiet *glen* is the perfect place for our picnic; it has grassy banks and shady trees.

Hessian: (n.) a German soldier in the British forces during the American Revolution
German soldiers who fought in the British forces during the American Revolutionary War were called *Hessians.*

quavers: (n.) trembles in the voice
The candidate's speech was very strong and she delivered it well; there were no *quavers* in her voice when she spoke in front of the large audience.

shillings: (n.) British coins
When I was in London, I changed my money for British currency, and I had *shillings* jingling in my pockets.

Think Ahead

1. Like "Rip Van Winkle," "The Legend of Sleepy Hollow" is a legend by American author Washington Irving. What is a legend?

2. You may remember that Irving heard stories from the Dutch in New York when he was growing up. He wrote about these stories and included the countryside he knew so well.

Read

"The Legend of Sleepy Hollow" in *American Lives and Legends*, pages 52-55

Questions

Answer the following questions in complete sentences in your Reading Notebook.

1. What is the setting of this legend? How is it like the setting of "Rip Van Winkle"?

2. Describe Sleepy Hollow. Find details in the text to support your description.

3. Remember that *figurative language* is poetic language and figures of speech such as metaphor, simile, and personification. Just as he did in "Rip Van Winkle," author Washington Irving uses figurative language to describe the setting of this legend. List at least two examples of figurative language.

4. Who is the most famous character in Sleepy Hollow and what is the legend about him?

5. Ichabod Crane is compared to a "traveling gazette." What does this mean?

6. What are three things Ichabod Crane enjoys doing in his spare time?

7. What price does Ichabod Crane pay for listening to the frightening stories?

Discuss

1. The author says that the "hollow has a strange, dreamy effect on its residents and on visitors to its valley." What do you think this effect is, and why do you think it might be important?

2. The author writes that Ichabod Crane's name suited him well. Why does he say this?

3. What kinds of stories do people in Sleepy Hollow tell? Do you think that these stories seem out of place in this quiet town? Why or why not?

Character Sketch

We learn about characters by paying attention to what they say and do, and what others say about them. And sometimes, to understand a character, we go beyond the words in the story. We *make inferences.* To make an inference, or *infer,* means to think about the evidence in the story, and then draw conclusions based on that evidence.

To make inferences about Ichabod Crane, begin by discussing these questions. Look back to the story for specific evidence.

- What does Ichabod Crane look like?
- Describe Ichabod Crane's relationship with his students.
- How does Ichabod Crane interact with other people in the town?
- Is Ichabod Crane a brave man or a fearful man? How do you know?

Using your answers to the questions above, draw conclusions about Ichabod Crane. In your Reading Notebook, write a paragraph describing the kind of person he is. Then draw a picture of Crane as you see him and write three important adjectives underneath it. Use evidence from the story to support your ideas.

Name _____   Date _____

"The Legend of Sleepy Hollow": Session 2

Ichabod Crane has a girlfriend and a rival. Who will win the love of Katrina Van Tassel?

Vocabulary

You will find these words in today's reading.

burly: (adj.) large and strong
The weightlifters were big, *burly* men with huge muscles.

feud: (n.) a serious quarrel that goes on for a long period of time
Romeo and Juliet is a famous love story of a couple that is kept apart by their parents' *feud*.

formidable: (adj.) having qualities that discourage other people from attacking
The dog certainly looked *formidable*, so it was a good thing that there was a fence with a sign that said, "Beware of Dog."

madcap: (adj.) crazy
My uncle is a real practical joker; he is always pulling a *madcap* stunt or trick on someone in the family.

mettle: (n.) courage
The fighter pilots were full of bravery, courage, and *mettle*.

pewter: (adj.) a metal that looks like silver
Is that tea set made of silver or *pewter*?

ruddy: (adj.) of a healthy red color
The healthy lifestyle and time spent outdoors must agree with Joan because her cheeks have turned a *ruddy* color.

smitten: (adj.) taken with or captured by

The new mother is so *smitten* with love for her new baby that she can't focus on anything else.

steed: (n.) horse

If you are going to journey on horseback, you will want to make certain that your *steed* is strong and trustworthy.

Think Ahead

1. Summarize Parts 1 and 2 of "The Legend of Sleepy Hollow." In your summary, tell:
   - Where the story takes place
   - What Ichabod Crane is like
   - What frightens Ichabod Crane

2. Describe how Ichabod Crane feels when he walks home.

Read

"The Legend of Sleepy Hollow" in *American Lives and Legends*, pages 56-59, from the beginning of Part 3 to the end of Part 3

Questions

Answer the following questions in complete sentences in your Reading Notebook.

1. Describe Katrina Van Tassel.
2. Why does Ichabod like Katrina? How does he imagine his life with her?
3. Who is Ichabod's chief rival for Katrina?
4. Why do the people in town give Abraham Van Brunt the nickname Brom Bones?
5. What are the names of Brom's and Ichabod's horses?
6. How does Brom treat Ichabod?
7. What happens during the party at the Van Tassels home?

Discuss
Discuss today's reading. Write a paragraph in response to one of the questions.

1. Summarize the relationships between the main characters: Crane, Bones, and Katrina van Tassel.
2. Do you think the author has foreshadowed later events through these relationships? Why or why not?

Character Sketch
You completed a character sketch of Ichabod Crane in the last lesson. Now complete a character sketch of Brom Bones.

To make inferences about Brom Bones, begin by discussing these questions. Look back to the story for specific evidence.

- What does Brom Bones look like?
- What is Brom Bones famous for?
- How do people in the town react to Brom Bones?
- Why does Brom Bones play pranks?
- Why doesn't Brom Bones fight Ichabod Crane for Katrina's love?
- Is Brom Bones a brave man or a fearful man? How do you know?

Using your answers to the questions above, draw conclusions about Brom Bones. In your Reading Notebook, write a paragraph describing the kind of person he is. Then draw a picture of Brom as you imagine him and write three important adjectives underneath it. Use evidence from the story to support your ideas. Save your character sketch for a future lesson.

Name _____   Date _____

"The Legend of Sleepy Hollow": Session 3

The party ends, and Ichabod Crane heads home at a very late hour. What will happen to him on the way? Will he meet the Headless Horseman?

Vocabulary

You will find these words in today's reading.

ado: (n.) trouble
William Shakespeare wrote a play entitled *Much Ado About Nothing,* which means a lot of trouble over nothing.

crestfallen: (adj.) sad and disappointed
The little boy was *crestfallen* when he didn't win the contest.

dismal: (adj.) gloomy
The clouds were gray, the sky was stormy, and the whole day was *dismal* and gloomy.

jilted: (v.) harshly broke up with someone
Doris *jilted* Sam and she is now dating Robert.

melancholy: (adj.) very sad
The song was so *melancholy* that the choir's singing brought tears to every member of the audience's eyes.

parched: (adj.) extremely dry
The *parched* ground gratefully absorbed the rainfall after the long drought.

pommel: (n.) a knob-shaped piece the rider holds onto at the front of a saddle

Sarah sat astride the horse and held onto the *pommel* on the saddle in order to learn to ride.

supernatural: (adj.) beyond known forces of nature

We sat by the campfire and told scary stories of *supernatural* events.

Think Ahead

1. Summarize Parts 1-3 of "The Legend of Sleepy Hollow." In your summary, tell:
   - Where the story takes place
   - What Ichabod Crane is like
   - What frightens Ichabod Crane
   - What Brom Bones is like
   - What Katrina van Tassel is like
   - What the relationships between Crane, Bones, and Katrina van Tassel are like
   - What happens at the party

2. At the end of Part 3, Bones is brooding by himself in a corner. Why?

Read

"The Legend of Sleepy Hollow" Parts 4-5 in *American Lives and Legends*, pages 60-64

Questions

Answer the following questions in complete sentences in your Reading Notebook.

1. What kinds of stories were people telling at the party?
2. Why is Ichabod Crane sad when he leaves the party?
3. What happens after Ichabod Crane leaves the party?

4. Why does Ichabod Crane think he'll be safe after he crosses the bridge?
5. What happens after Ichabod Crane crosses the bridge?
6. There are two opinions about why Ichabod Crane disappeared. What are they?
7. Why do you think Brom Bones laughs at the mention of the pumpkin? Give at least one reason to support your answer.

Discuss

1. Do you believe that Brom Bones really does see the Headless Horseman one night and dares him to race? Why or why not? Support your answer with details from the text.
2. Explain how Ichabod Crane tries to escape the Headless Horseman.
3. What do you think happened to Ichabod Crane after he was hit in the head? Support your answer with details about Ichabod from the story.
4. Why do you think Washington Irving leaves the end of the story a little mysterious?

Compare and Contrast Characters

Washington Irving shows his reader two very different characters in Ichabod Crane and Brom Bones. How would you compare and contrast these characters? Think about their appearances, their actions, and their relationship with other people in the town. Complete the Compare and Contrast Characters page using examples from the story that show how these characters compare with one another. Use your two character sketches as guides.

Why do you think Irving made these characters so different?

Name

Date

Compare and Contrast Characters

	Character's name:	Character's name:
Three important adjectives that describe the character		
A description of what each character looks like		
A description of how the character gets along with other people in town		

Compare and Contrast Characters

	Character's name:	Character's name:
A description of how each character feels about Katrina		
A description of how each character reacts to the Headless Horseman		
A description of each character's strengths		
A description of each character's weaknesses		

Name _____   Date _____

Incidents and Messages

A glimpse of a face as you look out a car window, a scrap of a note that drops to the floor, a familiar line of a song as you switch from one station to another on the radio—all of these can make you stop and think. In the eyes of a poet, such passing moments can be full of meaning.

First Reading: "The White Horse"

Vocabulary
You will find this word in today's first reading.

halter: (n.) straps put on a horse's head and used to lead the horse
After putting a *halter* on the pony, the girl led him out of the stable.

Read
Read "The White Horse" (page 146) once silently and a second time aloud.

Discuss
1. What happens in the poem?
2. What do you think it means that "they are in another world"?

Second Reading: "Incident"

Vocabulary
You will find these words in today's second reading.

incident: (n.) a brief event; an event that causes trouble
When the policeman caught the boy lighting firecrackers, he said, "Young man, let's go see your parents and discuss this *incident*."

whit: (n.) a very small amount
My uncle Charley is so absent-minded that most people think he hasn't got a *whit* of sense.

Think Ahead

Do you remember the children's rhyme, "Sticks and stones may break my bones, but names can never hurt me"? As you will see in the next poem, some names *can* hurt, almost as much as sticks and stones.

Read

Read "Incident" (page 145) once silently and a second time aloud.

Discuss

1. Who is the speaker of the poem?
2. In the first stanza, how does the speaker feel? Which words show you this?
3. What is the "incident" the title refers to?
4. The poem says that after the incident the speaker stayed in Baltimore for several months, "from May until December." Why do you think this incident is all that the speaker remembers of Baltimore?
5. Why does the other child act in such an ugly manner?

Third Reading: "This Is Just to Say"

Vocabulary

You will find this word in today's third reading.

icebox: (n.) refrigerator
Always put the milk back in the *icebox* or it will spoil.

Think Ahead

When you think of *poems,* what do you think of? Do you think of words that rhyme? Or similes and metaphors? As you read, think about how the next poem does or does not fit your expectations of what a poem should be.

Read

Read "This Is Just to Say" (page 146) once silently and a second time aloud.

Discuss

1. In your own words describe what is happening in this poem.
2. To whom do you think the speaker is talking or writing in this poem? What words make you think this?
3. Did the speaker enjoy eating the plums? What specific words let you know?
4. Look at the title of the poem. How does the title connect with the poem itself? What does the "This" in the title refer to?
5. Can you imagine a situation in which someone might speak or write these words? Describe the situation.
6. On a sheet of paper, write the poem, including the title, as two or three sentences. How does it change the poem to write it this way?
7. Do you think "This Is Just to Say" is a poem at all? What makes it a poem?

Activity

William Carlos Williams, who wrote "This Is Just to Say," was not only a poet but also a doctor who lived in New Jersey. In his poems, he often paid attention to common everyday objects and everyday speech.

When you take everyday language and break the words into stanzas and lines, you give it the form of a poem. And when you do this, you see and hear the words in a new way.

Choose one of the activities on the Everyday Poetry page.

Name _____   Date _____

Everyday Poetry

"This Is Just to Say" takes everyday language and turns it into a poem. You can do the same. Choose one of the following three activities.

A. Found Poetry

You can find poetry in the most unexpected places. All around you there are words that might not seem like poetry until they are shaped into a poem.

For example, look at the words on packages, clothing labels, and food boxes. Look at ads and articles in newspapers and magazines. Look on the back covers of books. Select some of these words and arrange them into lines and stanzas.

Think about how you will arrange the words in lines. Try breaking the lines in different places to see what difference it makes. Don't forget to give your "found poem" a title.

Here are two examples, one from a box of pancake mix, and the other from a label on a tee shirt.

What I Want for Breakfast

Fluffy
golden brown
pancakes

Steaming
from the griddle
and drizzled
with syrup

That's how you make them—
perfect
every time.

Tee-Shirt

100% cotton

Machine wash
warm

Tumble dry
medium

100% USA
materials

Assembled in
Dominican Republic

Everyday Poetry

B. This Is Just for *You* to Say

Imagine a situation in which you might leave a poetic message, as William Carlos Williams did in "This Is Just to Say." Use his poem as a model to write your own, with the same number of stanzas and lines.

This Is Just to Say

I have_____

_____

_____

_____

_____

_____

_____

_____

_____

_____

_____

Everyday Poetry

C. This Is Just to Say to You

Reread "This Is Just to Say." Now pretend you are the person who discovers at breakfast that the plums are no longer in the icebox. Write a response in your own "This Is Just to Say *to You*" poem. How will you respond? Will you be upset? Will you be forgiving?

This Is Just to Say to You

I have_____

_____

_____

_____

_____

_____

_____

_____

_____

_____

Guidelines for Peer Discussion

Share your thoughts, ideas, questions, and feelings about a text with a peer or others. Listen carefully to what everyone has to say about the text. During your discussion, follow these guidelines.

1. Be prepared to discuss what you think about the text. You should have already read the assignment. Come prepared to discuss your ideas and use examples from the text to support your thoughts and answers.

2. You will be asked questions about the text. Be ready to answer them, and bring some questions of your own to ask others, such as:

   "Who was your favorite character? Why?"

   "What was your favorite part of the text? Why?"

   "What fact did you enjoy learning? Why do you find this fact interesting?"

   "What question would you ask if you had the chance to meet the author?"

3. Listen if it's not your turn to speak. Pay attention to what others say so that you can add your ideas. Speak clearly and in complete sentences.

4. If you don't understand what someone says, ask a question.

   "What do you mean when you say . . . ?"

   "Can you give an example of . . . ?"

5. If you don't agree with what someone says, explain why.

   "I don't agree with that because . . . "

6. Keep discussions positive! You can disagree, but don't argue. Be respectful.

Name _____   Date _____

Child's Play

Riding a skateboard, skating, and stealing a base in baseball—in today's poems, see how the poets bring these actions to life through their language, including metaphors, similes, and vivid verbs.

First Reading: "The Sidewalk Racer (or On a Skateboard)"

Vocabulary
You will find this word in the first poem you will read today.

> **asphalt:** (n.) a mixture of tar, gravel, and other materials used for paving roads; (adj.) made from asphalt
> On hot summer days, the *asphalt* road is too hot to cross with bare feet.

Think Ahead
Think about some physical activity you really enjoy, such as swimming, riding a bike, dancing, running, or playing basketball. When you are completely absorbed in the activity, how does it feel? Can you put the sensation you experience into words?

Read
Read "The Sidewalk Racer" (page 147) once silently and a second time aloud.

Discuss
1. What is the speaker doing in the poem?

2. The first half of the poem is full of action, beginning with the first word, *skimming.* Identify four action verbs in the first half of the poem and write them here:

_____ _____ _____ _____

3. The poet uses *metaphor* to describe the experience of riding a skateboard. Remember, a metaphor suggests or states a comparison between two unlike things without using the words "like" or "as." In the metaphor in the second line of the poem, what is being compared to "an asphalt sea"? How is riding a skateboard like "skimming an asphalt sea"?

4. The next two metaphors compare the skater to different things. (See lines 6-8.) Write the metaphors here:

   I'm _____

   I'm _____

   Why does the speaker say that she is both "the sailor *and* the sail," and both "the driver *and* the wheel"? What does this tell us about the experience of riding a skateboard?

5. In the final metaphor of the poem (lines 9-12), to what does the speaker compare herself?

6. There are rhymes in this poem, but not always at the ends of the lines, where you usually find rhyming words in poetry. Read the poem aloud again and identify three pairs of rhyming words.

7. Look at the shape of the poem on the page. The lines do not start evenly along the left margin, and some of the lines break in unexpected places. Why do you think the poet wrote the lines in the way she did?

Second Reading: "Song Form"

Vocabulary
You will find this word in today's second reading.

distinctions: (n.) differences
There seemed to be no *distinctions* between the twins—they looked the same, talked the same, and even smiled the same!

Think Ahead
Imagine: You lie back on the grass and look up at the sky and feel all your thoughts and cares just melt away. You feel a calm, pleasant warmth, and the joy of just being alive. Have you ever felt that way?

Read
Read "Song Form" (page 148) once silently and a second time aloud. (Note: The last line of the poem might look odd, but it is printed correctly in your book, just as the poet wrote it.)

Discuss
1. There are two people in the poem. Who are they and what are they doing?

2. What is the *setting* of the poem? What time of day is it, and where are these people? Point to specific words and phrases that describe the setting.

3. What happens in this passing moment between the speaker and the kid? Why does it matter that they do not have "to smile too tough" or "be very pleasant even to each other"?

4. What kind of pleasure does the speaker in this poem get from skating? In particular, what do you think he means by "merely to be"?

5. Compare and contrast the experience of riding a skateboard in "The Sidewalk Racer" to skating in "Song Form." Which is more active?

Third Reading: "The Base Stealer"

Vocabulary

You will find these words in today's third reading.

poise: (v.) to balance; to hold in a steady position
The ballerina stood *poised* on one toe.

taut: (adj.) tight
When the line went *taut*, we knew a fish was on the hook.

scattering: (n.) a small amount of something
The man threw a *scattering* of crumbs on the ground for the pigeons.

teeter: (v.) to wobble; to move unsteadily
As I crossed the narrow log over the stream, I *teetered* and shook, but I didn't fall in!

skitter: (v.) to move in a fast, light way
I like to watch the water bugs *skitter* across the lake.

taunt: (v.) to tease; to mock; to provoke with insulting words
Sir Galahad remained calm even though the cruel knight *taunted* him by shouting, "You have the strength of a flea and the courage of a mouse!"

ecstatic: (adj.) extremely joyful; wildly delighted
When Melinda learned she had been given the lead role in the play, she was more than happy—she was *ecstatic*.

Think Ahead

Have you ever watched a baseball game or been a player on the field? See if you can picture the scene described in the next poem.

Read
Read "The Base Stealer" (page 148) once silently and a second time aloud.

Discuss
1. In your own words, describe what is happening in the poem. Where is the base stealer? What is he doing?

2. The poet describes this moment with *similes*. A simile compares two things using *like* or *as.* In the second line, the base stealer is "pulled . . . taut like a tightrope-walker" between the bases. Find two other similes in the poem and write them below:

   _____

   _____

3. Identify the six vivid verbs in lines 7 and 8, and write them here:

   _____   _____   _____

   _____   _____   _____

4. Reread the last two lines of the poem. What is happening at the very end (when the poet writes, "—now!")? Read aloud the last line with expression. How will you vary the way you say "delicate," which is repeated four times? How will you say "now"?

Optional Activity

Act It Out
While a friend or family member reads aloud "The Base Stealer," act out the movements in the poem—balancing with your arms out and fingers pointed, bouncing in place, teetering back and forth, delicately leaning or inching forward, then bursting into a full-speed run!

Name _____   Date _____

Moments in Nature

Today's poems depict passing moments in the natural world.

First Readings: "The Tide in the River" and "The River Is a Piece of Sky"

Vocabulary

You will find these words in the first poems you will read today.

cockleshell: (n.) the wavy, rounded shell of a small water creature
The children found *cockleshells* in the tide pools.

cobblestone: (n.) a stone used to pave streets in former times
The horse's hooves clattered on the *cobblestones* as it pulled the wagon through the streets of old London.

Think Ahead

Close your eyes and think of a river. Imagine the water running by. Imagine standing on a bridge over the river and looking down into the water. In your mind's eye, what do you see?

Read

Read "The Tide in the River" (page 150) once silently and a second time aloud. Then read "The River Is a Piece of Sky" (page 149) once silently and a second time aloud.

Discuss

1. In the last three lines of "The Tide in the River," the poet imagines the tide in the river as almost human. Explain how she *personifies* the tide.

2. How would you describe the *mood* of this poem? What effect does the repetition in the first three lines have on the mood?

3. Describe the perspective in "The River Is a Piece of Sky." Where exactly does the poet want you to imagine you are standing?

4. How can a river be "a piece of sky"? What is the poet describing?

5. When you throw things in, why do you know that the river is a river and not "a piece of sky"?

6. The title of the poem is a figure of speech. What kind of figure of speech is it? (Hint: Is it a simile or metaphor?)

Second Reading: "Snow Toward Evening"

Vocabulary
You will find this word in the next poem you will read today.

intensely: (adv.) very; extremely
The heat from the fireplace was *intensely* hot.

Think Ahead
Sometimes a title can be very important for the understanding of a poem or story. This is the case in the poem you are about to read.

Read
Read "Snow Toward Evening" once silently and a second time aloud.

Discuss

1. In this poem there is an "invisible blossoming tree" from which "millions of petals" are falling. This tree with its petals is a *metaphor*. What is the poet really describing?

2. If you did not know the title of the poem, which words would suggest that the "petals" are not really petals but snow?

3. Identify five verbs that describes the action of the "petals":

   _____   _____   _____

   _____   _____

4. Did you notice that the verbs in lines 8 and 9 rhyme? Identify the rhyming pairs.

5. *Alliteration* is the use of words with the same or similar beginning sounds, as in "Peter Piper picked a peck of pickled peppers." Read aloud this line from "Snow Toward Evening" and notice the repeated *s* sound:

   Grew intensely **s**oft and **s**till.

   Identify the alliteration in the last line of the poem. Read it aloud and underline the letter of the repeated sound:

   Fell with the falling night.

Activity

Rhyme Schemes

Complete the activity on the Rhyme Schemes page.

Name _____   Date _____

Rhyme Schemes

What Is a Rhyme Scheme?

A *rhyme scheme* is the pattern of rhymes made by the final words or sounds in the lines of a poem. You use a different letter of the alphabet to stand for each new rhyme.

For example, here is how you mark the rhyme scheme of a familiar childhood poem. The rhyming words or syllables are underlined.

Sing a song of sixpence,	**a**
A pocket full of <u>rye</u>;	**b**
Four and twenty blackbirds	**c**
Baked in a <u>pie</u>.	**b**
When the pie was opened,	**a**
The birds began to <u>sing</u>;	**b**
Wasn't that a dainty dish	**c**
To set before a <u>king</u>?	**b**

Notice that with each new stanza, you start again with **a**. You can write the rhyme scheme of this poem as **a b c b**.

For practice, identify the rhyme scheme of another familiar childhood poem. You will find the answer at the end of this activity.

Little Jack <u>Horner</u>	_____
Sat in a <u>corner</u>	_____
Eating his Christmas <u>pie</u>.	_____
He put in his <u>thumb</u>	_____
and pulled out a <u>plum</u>	_____
and said, "What a good boy am <u>I</u>."	_____

Write the rhyme scheme of the poem here, then look to the end of this activity to check your answer: _____

Rhyme Schemes

Try It!

1. Fill in the rhyme scheme of "The Tide in the River," reprinted for you below:

The tide in the river,	_____
The tide in the river,	_____
The tide in the river runs deep.	_____
I saw a shiver	_____
Pass over the river	_____
As the tide turned in its sleep.	_____

How would you write the rhyme scheme of "The Tide in the River"?

_____

2. Identify the rhyme scheme of "Snow Toward Evening" (see page 150 of your book) and write it in the blank below. (Note that you only identify the rhymes at the ends of the lines. For example, in lines 8 and 9, "drifted" and "lifted" are *not* part of the rhyme scheme.)

_____

Answer: The rhyme scheme of "Little Jack Horner" is **a a b c c b**.

Name _____   Date _____

Of Children on Rooftops, and Birds Big and Small

In the first poem, you'll find a child where he probably should not be. The next two poems capture passing moments in the lives of two very different kinds of birds.

First Reading: "Child on Top of a Greenhouse"

Vocabulary

You will find these words in today's first reading.

billow: (v.) to rise in waves; to puff out or swell
When the wind *billowed* the sails, the sailboat began to speed through the water.

putty: (n.) a gooey mixture used to hold glass in window frames and fill cracks in wood
We put extra *putty* around the glass to help keep out the winter wind.

Think Ahead

Picture a greenhouse in your mind. What is the greenhouse made of? What do you see inside the greenhouse? Would you normally expect to find anyone *on top of* a greenhouse?

Read

Read "Child on Top of a Greenhouse" (page 147) once silently and a second time aloud.

Discuss

1. The title tells you that the child is "on top of a greenhouse." What position is he in? Is he looking up or down? Find specific words in the poem that help you imagine exactly where the child is.

2. Why do you think there are "splinters of glass and dried putty"?

3. In line 3, the poet *personifies* the chrysanthemums. He gives the flowers human qualities: "the half-grown chrysanthemums staring up like accusers." What does this personification tell us about the speaker's state of mind?

4. Many words in the poem express the action going on around the child, such as the wind "billowing" in the first line. Identify and list more of these "-ing" words that convey the action surrounding the boy:

_____   _____   _____

_____   _____   _____

5. The last line of the poem describes "everyone pointing up and shouting!" What do you think they might be saying?

Second Reading: "The Eagle"

Vocabulary

You will find these words in the second poem you will read today. Study each word and how it is used in the sentence.

crag: (n.) a rough, sharp, steep rock or cliff
The mountain climber struggled to pull himself up the rocky *crag*.

azure: (n. or adj.) a sky-blue color
There was not a cloud to be seen as the sun shone brightly in the clear *azure* sky.

Think Ahead

The short poem you're about to read is packed with powerful descriptive language. Before you begin, make sure you understand each of the following terms by matching the term with its definition.

1. alliteration   _____
2. simile   _____
3. personification   _____

a. a figure of speech that compares two things, using the words *like* or *as*
b. giving human qualities to a thing or abstraction
c. use of words with the same or similar beginning sounds

Read

Read "The Eagle" (page 151) once silently and a second time aloud.

Discuss

1. Describe the setting of the poem. Where is this eagle?

2. Identify the four verbs that tell what the eagle is doing and list them in the blanks below. What picture of the eagle is suggested by the first three verbs? How does the last verb change this picture?

   Line 1: he _____

   Line 3: he _____

   Line 5: he _____

   Line 6: he _____

3. How is the eagle personified in line 1?

4. Identify the simile the poet uses to describe the eagle and write it here:

   _____

   What two things does the simile compare? What does the simile tell you about the movement of the eagle?

5. Read aloud the first line of the poem and listen for the alliteration. Underline the first letters of the words that have the same beginning sounds:

   He clasps the crag with crooked hands.

Third Reading: "A Bird Came Down the Walk"

Vocabulary
You will find these words in the third poem you will read today. Study each word and how it is used in the sentence.

convenient: (adj.) handy; easy to get to or use; just right for the situation
When I want to see a movie, I can walk to a *convenient* theater just two blocks from our apartment.

plash: (v.) to splash
My baby sister loves to *plash* around in the bathtub.

seam: (n.) a line where two things (usually cloth) come together
The *seam* of Margaret's shirt tore while she was climbing the ladder.

stir: (v.) to move or cause to move slightly
When a bee landed on my nose, I didn't *stir* at all, not even an eyelash, until it flew away.

Think Ahead

The next poem is by Emily Dickinson, one of the greatest American poets. She was born in Amherst, Massachusetts in 1830. She wrote her poems and tucked them away in boxes, or sent some to her friends. Only after her death were her poems collected and published in a book.

In her poems, Emily Dickinson had her own unusual way of capitalizing words, and she followed her own ideas about punctuation. (Don't try this when you write a research paper!)

Read

Read "A Bird Came Down the Walk" once silently and a second time aloud.

Discuss

1. In line 2, the speaker says of the bird, "He did not know I saw." Imagine the scene in your mind. Where might the speaker be?

2. Tell in your own words what the bird does in the first two stanzas of the poem. (Note: An "angleworm" is an earthworm.)

3. Look at the language used to describe the bird in the first two stanzas. Some of it is odd and playful. For example, is there any other way for a bird to eat a worm than "raw"? When the bird drinks "a Dew from a convenient Grass," can you almost imagine him washing down his meal with a refreshing beverage? And what does it suggest about the bird that he "hopped sideways . . . to let a Beetle pass"?

4. Identify a simile in the third stanza, and explain what two things the simile is comparing.

5. In the fourth stanza, when the speaker offers the bird a crumb, the bird flies away. But the speaker doesn't say that the bird *flew* home. She says he "unrolled his feathers and rowed" home. The poet is using a surprising metaphor here. To what is the poet comparing the bird?

Optional Activities

Close Reading

If you would like to dig deeper into the last two stanzas of "A Bird Came Down the Walk," read the Close Reading page.

Picture This

Draw or paint a picture that shows a particular moment in either "The Eagle" or "A Bird Came Down the Walk." Pick a line or two from the poem to serve as a caption for your picture, for example:

He clasps the crag with crooked hands

or

And then hopped sideways to the Wall
To let a Beetle pass—

Name _____   Date _____

Close Reading

Sometimes you can look at literature in much the same way a detective examines evidence through a magnifying glass, or a scientist studies a specimen under a microscope. When you look patiently and carefully at a work of literature, and try to understand how it works and what it means, you are doing a close reading. Let's do a close reading of the last seven lines of "A Bird Came Down the Walk."

First, read the lines aloud again:

> I offered him a Crumb
> And he unrolled his feathers
> And rowed him softer home—
>
> Than Oars divide the Ocean,
> Too silver for a seam—
> Or Butterflies, off Banks of Noon,
> Leap, plashless, as they swim.

- Emily Dickinson is using a metaphor here. She is comparing the flight of the bird through the air to the way a boat travels on water (the "Ocean"). The bird "rowed" himself home through the "Ocean" of air.

- When you pull an oar through water, you make a ripple that looks like a line or "seam." But the bird's rowing was even "softer" than that. When the bird "rowed" through the "Ocean" of air, his movement was so soft that it was "too silver for a seam."

- Why do you think Emily Dickinson used the word "silver"? Perhaps because silver is bright, shiny, gleaming? There's no single right answer. Read the line aloud again: "Too silver for a seam." Do you hear the alliteration?

- When the bird "rowed," it was even softer than the "Butterflies." What are the two verbs that tell what the butterflies are doing? Write them here:

_____   _____

Close Reading

- Do butterflies "swim"? No, they fly. Emily Dickinson is extending the metaphor here. Just as the bird "rows" through the "Ocean" of air, so the butterflies "swim" through it.

- Now, imagine children on a riverbank, leaping into the water. A riverbank is made of dirt and grass. But the butterflies in this poem leap from "Banks of Noon." Is "Noon" something solid, something you can touch or step on? No— noon is a time of day, when the sun is at or near its highest point in the sky. So, what do you think "Banks of Noon" are? There is no single right answer to that question. In the end, "Banks of Noon" are whatever your imagination makes of them.

- When children leap into a river, you can bet they make a splash. As the butterflies in this poem leap "off Banks of Noon," they are "plashless"—in other words, they do not disturb the "Ocean" of air at all. But the bird "rows" even "softer" than the butterflies "leap." If the butterflies are "plashless" when they "leap," then the bird, when it flies, must move in an almost impossibly delicate and graceful way. At least, that is one way to understand the amazing picture that Emily Dickinson paints with her beautiful words.

Name _____ Date _____

Semester Review

Review the skills you've learned and the stories and poems you've read this semester.

Poetry Detective

Choose one or more of the poems below to read aloud or act out.

Poems:
"Spring"
"Winter the Huntsman"
"On a Snowy Day"
"The Leaves Do Not Mind at All"
"The Eagle"
"Snow Toward Evening"
"The Arrow and the Song"

After you finish:

- Describe the setting and tone of the poem.

- Give one example of literal language in the poem. If there isn't one, write your own literal language that fits the subject matter of the poem.

- Give one example of figurative language in the poem. If there isn't one, write your own figurative language that fits the subject matter of the poem.

- Show where there is alliteration in the poem. If there is no alliteration, write your own alliteration that fits the subject matter of the poem.

- Use letters to write the poem's rhyme scheme.

Author's Purpose
An author has many ways to present information. Review your *Curious Creatures* projects. Then write four ways an author can present nonfiction information on the lines below.

_____   _____

_____   _____

Read the beginnings of "Eating Like a Bird," "Stormflight," and "Lingering Leeches" in *Curious Creatures*. Remember that these authors each used a hook to begin their articles.

- Describe each hook. Does it ask a question, tell a story, or present the information as if the reader were there?
- Authors use hooks to catch a reader's attention and to give information about the main idea. Choose one article from the *Curious Creatures* unit. Describe the hook, then give the main idea of the article. What does the hook tell you about the main idea?

Another way an author may present nonfiction information is to write a poem. You have read two such poems this semester. Henry Wadsworth Longfellow wrote a narrative poem that told the story of Paul Revere's ride, and Phillis Wheatley wrote a poem to King George III that explained how people felt when the Stamp Act was repealed. Write a poem about one of the subjects from the *Curious Creatures* unit. Include two or more facts from the article and one or more examples of figurative language. Your poem does not have to rhyme. If you want to, you may illustrate your poem.

All About Genre
This semester, you have read works in different genres. A genre is a category of literature. You have read biographies, autobiographies, legends, hero tales, narrative poetry, short stories, and others. Some of the genres share characteristics. Use what you know to complete the All About Genre chart.

Name That Character!

Name the character identified in each quotation. Summarize the story and name the author.

1. "Oh, he would sit on a wet rock and fish all day even if he didn't get a single nibble. He would carry a fowling-piece on his shoulder for hours, trudging through woods and swamps, up hill and down dale, to shoot a few squirrels or wild pigeons. And he would never refuse to help a neighbor. But as to doing his family duty, and keeping his farm in order, he found it impossible. In a word, he was ready to attend to everybody's business except his own."

2. "So the Prince had a special saddle made for it—very long it was— and one hundred and fifty seats were fitted to this. Its greatest pleasure was now to give pleasure to others, and it delighted in taking parties of children to the seaside. It flew through the air quite easily with its hundred and fifty little passengers, and would lie on the sand patiently waiting till they were ready to return. The children were very fond of it and used to call it 'dear,' a word which never failed to bring tears of affection and gratitude to its eyes."

3. "His head was small, and flat at top, with huge ears, and large green glassy eyes. He had a long snipe nose. It looked like a weathercock perched upon his skinny neck to tell which way the wind blew. To see him striding over a hill on a windy day, with his clothes bagging and fluttering about him, one might have mistaken him for a scarecrow escaping from a cornfield."

4. "He often read the priest's old books and got him to explain them. His dreamings and readings changed him. His dream-people were so fine that he began to feel sad about his shabby clothing, and to wish to be clean and better clothed.

   By and by, he began to act like a prince. His speech and manners became ceremonious and courtly. In time, the other boys of Offal Court looked up to him with a wondering awe. He seemed to know so much! And he could do and say such marvelous things!"

Real Life Heroes

In the Early American Lives unit, you read about real people who made a difference in American history. Choose two people from the unit and do the following things:

- Tell three important facts from each story.
- Describe an important choice the person made, why he or she made it, and the consequences of the choice.
- Explain one way the characters are alike and one way they are different.
- Give your opinion about each person. What advice do you think each person might give people today?

Conflict, Resolution, and Theme

In almost every story, a character faces a *conflict*—a clash or struggle between people, ideas, or feelings. Describe the conflict two of the following characters face. Is it a conflict with another character or group of characters, his or her own thoughts and feelings, or his or her society?

- The king in "Salt and Bread"
- Ali in "Ali and the Magic Stew"
- Damocles in "The Sword of Damocles"
- Mulan in "The Story of Mulan"
- St. George or the princess in "St. George and the Dragon"
- Tom Canty in "The Prince and the Pauper"
- Ruth in "The Story of Ruth"
- David in "The Story of David"
- Daniel in "The Story of Daniel"

In a story, characters usually need to *resolve*, or work out, their conflicts. How does each character you chose resolve his or her conflicts?

The *theme* of a story is the author's main message or big idea. Readers can discover the theme by paying attention to the way characters resolve their conflicts. Discuss these questions about theme and the characters you chose:

- Describe each character at the beginning and end of the story. How does the character change?

- What do you think the character learns? If the story were to continue, do you think the character would behave differently in the future? Why or why not?

- What do you think a reader can learn from the character's actions? What do you think the author wants readers to think about after reading the story?

- Look back to the list. Do any of the other stories have a theme that is similar to the story you chose?

Name _____   Date _____

All About Genre

Write each phrase under the correct genre. You will use some phrases more than once. At the bottom of each column, write an example story or poem that you have read that is from the genre.

Phrase Bank

handed down from the past

includes historical events or characters

tells about a person's life

main character defeats a terrible enemy

includes facts and information

includes fictional events

story is about the author

Legend	Hero Tale	Biography	Autobiography

Name _____ Date _____

"Your Fingerprints"

Notice the bumps, ridges, and swirls on your fingers. Those patterns are called *fingerprints.* Does anyone else in the world have fingerprints like yours? Read on and find out!

Pronunciation
Alphonse Bertillon (AL-fahns ber-TEE-yohn)

Vocabulary
You will find these words in today's reading.

secrete: (v.) to release through the pores
When we exercise, we *secrete* sweat through our pores and our skin becomes damp.

friction: (n.) a force that slows down the motion of an object that is touching something else as it moves
The ball was rolling quickly down the street, but as *friction* acted on it, it began to slow down and finally stopped.

investigator: (n.) a detective
The *investigators* searched the building looking for clues that would help them catch the thief.

minute: (adj.) tiny
We paid such close attention to the *minute* details of setting the table that even the beaks of the napkin-swans all pointed the same way.

distinction: (n.) difference
My dog makes a *distinction* between the sound of a box of dog biscuits being opened and the sound of a box of cereal being opened—guess which one he comes running for!

coincidental: (adj.) by chance

My friend and I had a *coincidental* meeting at the grocery store; our parents had both decided to go shopping at the same time.

resemble: (v.) to look like

My brother and I *resemble* each other so closely, people think we are twins.

Think Ahead

1. Look through the magazine. Are the articles fiction or nonfiction? How do you know?
2. Find the table of contents, the glossary, and the index. Explain how a reader can use each part.
3. Look carefully at your fingerprints. Describe the patterns you see.

Read

"Your Fingerprints" in *I Didn't Know That!,* pages 3-5

Questions

Answer the following questions in complete sentences in your Reading Notebook.

1. Write the three basic fingerprint patterns.
2. What is the purpose of fingerprints?
3. List three ways a person's fingerprints can change.
4. What are latent fingerprints and why are they useful?
5. What do experts look for when they compare latent and inked fingerprints?
6. Describe Alphonse Bertillon's system of identification. Was it reliable? Why or why not?
7. Why did the Bertillon system fail in 1903?

Discuss

1. Do you know the saying, "A picture is worth a thousand words"? Explain what this saying means. Look at the picture on page 5. Even though this picture is not realistic, it provides information. How does the picture show one of the problems with the Bertillon system?

2. How did Francis Galton convince scientists and legal experts that fingerprints are a positive proof of a person's identity? Do you think that was difficult? Why?

3. Do you think all people should be fingerprinted? What are the advantages and disadvantages of such an idea?

What Do You Know?

You will make a booklet to help you remember information from the articles in this magazine. Complete the What Do You Know? page. Draw and label each kind of fingerprint in the boxes. On the lines, write the following things:

- The title of the article
- The main idea
- Two details
- Why the discovery was useful

When you are finished, return to the article. Find the *conclusion* of the article. Which sentence in the conclusion restates the main idea? A conclusion frequently restates the main idea of an article to emphasize the point and make the reader feel that the article has said something important.

Name _____ Date _____

What Do You Know?

Draw and label each kind of fingerprint in the boxes. On the lines, write the title of the article, the main idea, two details, and why this discovery was useful.

_____   _____   _____

Title: _____

Main Idea: _____

_____

Detail 1: _____

_____

Detail 2: _____

_____

Why was this discovery useful? _____

_____

_____

_____

Guidelines for Peer Discussion

Share your thoughts, ideas, questions, and feelings about a text with a peer or others. Listen carefully to what everyone has to say about the text. During your discussion, follow these guidelines.

1. Be prepared to discuss what you think about the text. You should have already read the assignment. Come prepared to discuss your ideas and use examples from the text to support your thoughts and answers.

2. You will be asked questions about the text. Be ready to answer them, and bring some questions of your own to ask others, such as:

   "Who was your favorite character? Why?"

   "What was your favorite part of the text? Why?"

   "What fact did you enjoy learning? Why do you find this fact interesting?"

   "What question would you ask if you had the chance to meet the author?"

3. Listen if it's not your turn to speak. Pay attention to what others say so that you can add your ideas. Speak clearly and in complete sentences.

4. If you don't understand what someone says, ask a question.

   "What do you mean when you say . . . ?"

   "Can you give an example of . . . ?"

5. If you don't agree with what someone says, explain why.

   "I don't agree with that because . . . "

6. Keep discussions positive! You can disagree, but don't argue. Be respectful.

Name _____   Date _____

"The Discovery of X-Rays"

Read about how one unusual scientist changed the way we look at the world.

Pronunciation

Wilhelm Conrad Roentgen (VIL-helm KAHN-rad ROUNT-guhn)
Utrecht (YOO-trekt)
Zurich (ZUHR-ick)
W_ürzburg (VOURTS-buhrk)

Vocabulary

You will find these words in today's reading. If the definition is missing, look it up in the magazine's glossary.

reputation: (n.) the way others see a person's character or qualities
Since he has a *reputation* for being fair, many people ask him to help settle their arguments.

caricature: (n.)
She drew a *caricature* of me that made my eyes look tiny and my nose look twice as big as it really is!

culprit: (n.)
I looked at the torn pillow and then at the four kittens, wondering which of them was the *culprit.*

expel: (v.) to force out; to dismiss
The dean *expelled* the student from college because he had turned in a paper that he didn't write.

emanate: (v.)
Now that my brother is part of a band, loud music always seems to *emanate* from his room.

hypothesize: (v.)

When my petunias didn't bloom even though I watered them, I *hypothesized* that they were not getting enough sun.

properties: (n.) characteristics or traits

Gold has three *properties:* it is easy to shape, it does not rust, and it is one of the heaviest of all metals.

exploit: (v.) to use unfairly

She *exploited* the fact that she was the tallest; she put the paints on the highest shelf so that only she could use them.

emission: (n.) something sent out

The factory's steam *emissions* hung in the sky like huge, white towers.

Think Ahead

If you've ever had a broken bone fixed, had your teeth x-rayed, or walked through an airport security check, you've experienced x-rays at work. Describe what you remember. Were you given something unusual to wear? What did you see?

Read

"The Discovery of X-Rays" in *I Didn't Know That!*, pages 6-9

Questions

Answer the following questions in complete sentences in your Reading Notebook.

1. Summarize how Wilhelm Roentgen discovered x-rays.
2. Why did Wilhelm Roentgen choose the letter *x* to describe the rays?
3. Why did Wilhelm Roentgen refuse to patent his discovery?

Discuss

Reread the paragraph on page 8 that describes how Wilhelm Roentgen reacted to the fame and fortune that came to him after his discovery. Was his reaction unusual? What conclusions can you draw about Wilhelm Roentgen from his reaction?

A Picture Worth a Thousand Words

Drawings and photographs in a nonfiction article often give more details about the subject of an article. *Captions* are words, phrases, or sentences that tell more information about a drawing or photograph. Captions are usually written under or beside the image.

Discuss:
- Find a caption in the article. What does it tell you about how x-rays are or were used?
- Find a caption that is just a descriptive phrase. What other information about the image would you have liked the caption to include?
- Find a caption written in sentences. How could you shorten it and keep the most important information?

Look at the picture on page 7. Draw it in the box on the What Do You Know? page. Then write two captions for the drawing on the lines. For the first caption, write one or two sentences. For the second caption, write one descriptive phrase.

What Do You Know?

Complete the What Do You Know? page. Draw the picture on page 7 in the box and include two captions. On the lines, write:
- The title of the article
- The main idea
- Three details

Identify the conclusion of the article. What do you notice about the main idea and the conclusion of the article?

Name _____   Date _____

What Do You Know?

Draw the picture from page 7 in the box and write two captions. On the lines, write the title of the article, the main idea, and three details.

Sentence Caption:_____

_____

_____

Descriptive Phrase Caption: _____

_____

_____

Title: _____

Main Idea: _____

_____

Detail 1:_____

_____

Detail 2:_____

_____

Detail 3: _____

_____

Name _____ Date _____

"From Pygg Jars to Piggy Banks"

Why are coin banks called "piggy banks" instead of "kitty banks" or even "aardvark banks"?

Vocabulary

You will find these words in today's reading. If the definition is not written, look it up in the magazine's glossary.

thrifty: (adj.) being careful with money

If you are *thrifty* with your savings, they will grow and grow.

penchant: (n.)

I have such a *penchant* for cherries that when they come into season, they are the only fruit I eat.

Think Ahead

1. What is a "piggy bank"? What do people put in piggy banks?
2. Are all piggy banks shaped like pigs?
3. Where do you think the name piggy bank comes from?

Take Note!

Take notes on "From Pygg Jars to Piggy Banks." When you *take notes*, you write down the most important pieces of information from something you read or hear.

Listen as the article is read to you. You will hear the article twice. Write down your notes on the Take Note! page. You do *not* have to write in complete sentences.

Questions

Answer the following questions in complete sentences in your
Reading Notebook. Use your notes to help you.

1. What was *pygg?*
2. In your own words, summarize why pygg banks may have been shaped
   like pigs and why people began to use iron, copper, pewter, and silver
   instead of pygg clay to make things.

Discuss

In your own words, explain the saying "A penny saved is a penny
earned." Why is it good advice to give someone with his or her first
piggy bank?

Creative Captions

You have learned about captions and the information they provide
for the reader. What information would you add to the caption on
page 10 to make the connection clear between this photograph
and modern piggy banks?

Now create your own caption for the illustration on page 10. Your
caption should reflect the main idea of this article.

Draw your pictures and write the captions on the What Do You
Know? page.

What Do You Know?

To complete the What Do You Know? page, write the title and the
main idea.

Sometimes finding the main idea requires a little detective work. In
many articles, the main idea is stated in the first or last paragraph.
But in other articles, it is *unstated*. *Unstated* means "not said."
When the main idea is *unstated,* no one sentence in the paragraph
tells the main idea.

To find the unstated main idea of "From Pygg Jars to Piggy Banks," look back over your notes about the details in the text, and then discuss the questions below.

- What two reasons does the author give to explain how coin banks might have come to be shaped like pigs?
- Does the author give one definite answer to the question: Why are so many coin banks shaped like pigs?
- What conclusion can you draw from that information? Write the unstated main idea of the article on the What Do You Know? page.

Name _____   Date _____

What Do You Know?

Draw or trace the picture of the bank from Pompeii in the box on the left. On the right, draw a picture of a pygg bank from the Middle Ages. Write a caption for each.

Coin Bank from Pompeii   Pygg Bank from the Middle Ages

_____   _____

_____   _____

_____   _____

Title: _____

Main Idea: _____

_____

_____

Name _____   Date _____

Take Note!

Listen as "From Pygg Jars to Piggy Banks" is read to you. Write the important information from the section. You do not have to write in complete sentences.

What *pygg* was: _____

_____

How pygg was used: _____

_____

When it was used: _____

_____

One reason why coin banks might have been shaped like pigs: _____

_____

_____

A second reason why coin banks might have been shaped like pigs: _____

_____

_____

Why pygg clay was replaced: _____

_____

_____

Other important information: _____

_____

_____

Name _____   Date _____

"Sweeter than Sugar, Black as Night"

Can you guess what ancient food we use to make candies, boxes, *and* fire extinguishers?

Pronunciation
Glycyrrhiza (gliy-kiy-RIY-zuh)

Vocabulary
You will find these words in today's reading. If the definition is missing, look it up in the magazine's glossary.

acrid: (adj.)
I meant to take a chewable aspirin, but I accidentally chewed a nonchewable tablet, and I still have an *acrid* aftertaste in my mouth.

abundantly: (adv.) in great plenty
Daffodils bloom *abundantly* in that meadow; there must be a thousand of them out there every year.

guild: (n.) an organization made up of people in the same profession
In the 1500s, actors' *guilds* would tour the countryside and perform in different towns.

Think Ahead
1. What is the sweetest food you can think of?
2. There is a food that is *fifty* times sweeter than sugar that we use today in candies. And it has other uses, too. What do you think the food is?

Read

"Sweeter than Sugar, Black as Night" in *I Didn't Know That!*, pages 12–15

Questions

Answer the following questions in complete sentences in your Reading Notebook.

1. Describe two ways licorice was used in ancient times.
2. According to the article, what can happen if you eat too much licorice?
3. Describe the two processes for making licorice candy.
4. Describe three things made from licorice today.

Discuss

1. Summarize how people's use of licorice has changed since ancient times and how it has stayed the same. Give facts from the story to support your opinion.
2. Do you think candy should be called licorice if it does not really contain licorice, but fennel or anise instead? Why or why not?

What Do You Know?

Drawings and photographs in an article can make information easier to understand. A *diagram* is a drawing that identifies an object's parts and explains how the object works.

Look at the drawing of the licorice plant on page 13. Turn the drawing into a diagram on the What Do You Know? page.

Finish the page by writing the following things:
- The title
- The unstated main idea
- Two details

Name _____   Date _____

What Do You Know?

Draw and color a licorice plant in the box. Identify the flowers, stems, leaves, and roots. Include one descriptive fact from the article about each part of the licorice plant. Then identify the title, main idea, and two details.

Flowers: _____

_____

Stems: _____

_____

Leaves:_____

_____

Roots: _____

_____

_____

_____

Title: _____

Main Idea: _____

_____

Detail 1: _____

_____

Detail 2: _____

_____

Name _____   Date _____

"The Lady with the Green Skin" and "Do You Know Your Uncle Sam?"

Learn about the history of two famous American figures: Lady Liberty and Uncle Sam.

Pronunciation

Frédéric Auguste Bartholdi (fray-day-reek aw-goost bahr-tohl-dee)
Alexandre Gustave Eiffel (ah-lek-SAHN-druh goo-STAHV ee-FEL)

Vocabulary

You will find these words in today's reading. If the definition is missing, look it up in the magazine's glossary.

commemorate: (v.)
Many people *commemorate* important events with a yearly holiday.

engineer: (v.) to design or plan
I *engineered* our clubhouse, then all of us and our parents helped build it.

colossal: (adj.) giant, of stupendous size
When I was little, the fair's Ferris Wheel seemed *colossal;* I believed the highest seats must brush the clouds.

asbestos: (n.)
Long ago, builders used *asbestos* to try to keep buildings from burning down.

envision: (v.) to plan or see as if in a dream
Though the pioneer families looked out over a sea of grass, they *envisioned* a busy town, with homes, farms, and a market.

insist: (v.) to demand

My cousin *insists* upon having her stuffed bear in bed with her at night; she simply will not go to sleep without it.

repeal: (v.) to take back or unmake a law

If an unfair law is made, it does not have to be permanent, it can be *repealed.*

erratic: (adj.) not coming and going regularly

The trains were *erratic* for two weeks until the men cleared all the snow and ice from the tracks.

Think Ahead

1. What is a *symbol?*
2. A dove is a symbol for peace. A four-leaf clover is a symbol for luck. Can you think of other symbols?
3. Today you are going to read about two symbols from American history: the Statue of Liberty and Uncle Sam. What do you know about one or both of these American symbols?

Read

"The Lady with the Green Skin" and "Do You Know Your Uncle Sam?" in *I Didn't Know That!,* pages 16-21

Questions

Answer the following questions in complete sentences in your Reading Notebook.

1. What did Frédéric Bartholdi and other French citizens admire about the United States?
2. What was Bartholdi's gift, and what was it celebrating?
3. Why did people call Samuel Wilson "Uncle Sam"?
4. How did Samuel Wilson inspire the national symbol "Uncle Sam"?

Discuss

1. Describe Bartholdi's vision when he entered New York Harbor. What do you think he wanted the statue to stand for?
2. Why did the Statue of Liberty's copper skin turn green? Why didn't the restorers polish her skin back to its original bright copper?
3. How did "Uncle Sam" come to be a symbol for the United States?

Political Cartoons

In today's reading, you saw a new kind of drawing in the lower right-hand corner of page 21. It is called a *political cartoon.* A political cartoon is a drawing that comments on current events. Sometimes political cartoons are complimentary. Other times, they criticize.

Look at the political cartoon and read the caption. Then discuss the following questions:

- Is the smaller man standing on the East or West Coast of the United States? How do you know?
- How is the man with the 1776 on his hat dressed? Whom does he look like? Why is he smaller than Uncle Sam?
- Why is Uncle Sam wearing striped pants? Why does he have one foot in California and one foot in New York?
- What do you think is the artist's *main idea?* Do you think he is being critical or complimentary? Why?

What Do You Know?

Complete the What Do You Know? page. First, fill in the Venn diagram. Then describe the most important person in the Statue of Liberty's and Uncle Sam's histories.

Consider the main ideas of each of these articles and write them down. Then think about the ideas that both articles share. What do Lady Liberty and Uncle Sam have in common?

Discuss these questions to help you find the ideas these articles have in common:

- What are these two articles about? What do the subjects have in common?
- What is the story behind the Statue of Liberty and Uncle Sam? Why were they created? How are their histories alike?
- In your opinion, what is each a *symbol* for? Why might those values be important to Americans?
- Why do you think you were asked to read both articles together? What are the articles saying about American symbols?

When you finish your discussion, write ideas shared by these two articles on the What Do You Know? page.

When you are finished, you may bind your book of What Do You Know? pages and make a cover for it.

Name _____   **Date** _____

What Do You Know?

Complete the Venn diagram. Write five or more words in each circle, and two or more words where the circles overlap. Then answer the questions.

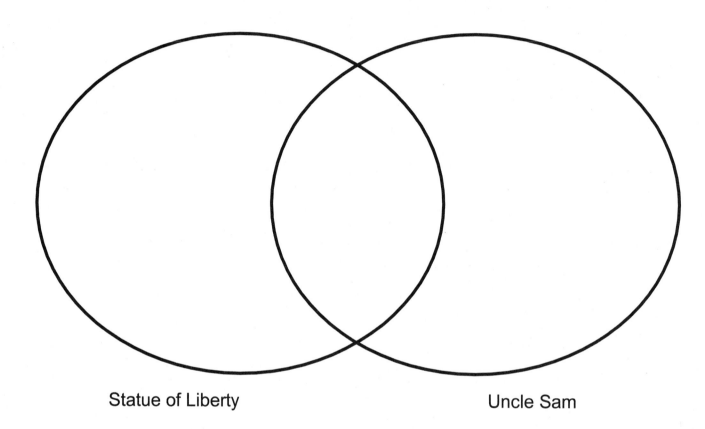

Statue of Liberty   Uncle Sam

Describe the most important person in the Statue of Liberty's history.

_____

_____

Describe the most important person in Uncle Sam's history.

_____

_____

_____

What Do You Know?

Write the main idea of "The Lady with the Green Skin."

_____

_____

Write the main idea of "Do You Know Your Uncle Sam?"

_____

_____

What ideas do these two articles have in common?

_____

_____

_____

Name _____   Date _____

Bard of Avon: Session 1

Chances are you've heard the name William Shakespeare. You may also know that he was a famous writer. But what did he write? Why is a man who lived more than 400 years ago still important today? Start reading *Bard of Avon* and begin to see why Shakespeare has fascinated people from all over the world for more than four centuries.

Vocabulary

You will find these words in today's reading.

bard: (n.) a poet
My friend's plays were so much like poetry, we started calling her the *Bard* of Boston.

guildhall: (n.) a public hall or building often used for meetings of local government officials
Members of the city council should never miss the weekly meetings in the town's *guildhall*.

trestles: (n.) pieces of wood that are arranged to act as a supportive framework for a stage or other structures
Because the play required a horse to walk on stage, the *trestles* supporting the stage had to be made of the strongest oak.

farces: (n.) works of literature, drama, or film characterized by broad humor and an improbable plot
Though *farces* are often unbelievable and silly, they can be enjoyable for audiences willing to trade reason and logic for humor and fun.

melodramas: (n.) works of literature, drama, or film characterized by extreme (sometimes unbelievable) situations and emotions

After being stabbed, the lead character in the *melodrama* staggered dramatically across the stage for a full minute, told his attacker that they were long-lost brothers, and died in his brother's arms just as the doctor arrived.

Think Ahead

1. Why do you think scholars and historians are interested in learning about William Shakespeare?
2. What do you think life was like during Shakespeare's time? How was it different from life today?
3. On a map, locate England, London, and Stratford-upon-Avon.

Read

Read the first 22 pages of *Bard of Avon*.

Questions

Answer the following questions in complete sentences in your Reading Notebook.

1. What was Shakespeare's family background?
2. When did young William Shakespeare likely first experience the theater?
3. Why did Shakespeare leave Stratford-upon-Avon for London?
4. How did Queen Elizabeth I feel about the theater?

Discuss

1. What did people think about the theater and actors in London during Shakespeare's time? Why?
2. How was Shakespeare able to make a living in the theater and support his family back in Stratford-upon-Avon?
3. How did the actors create special effects in their productions?
4. One of the University Wits described William Shakespeare as "an upstart crow; beautified with our feathers." What does this mean and why did the Wit say this about Shakespeare?

Fast Facts About Shakespeare

You have learned a lot about William Shakespeare already. Use the *Bard of Avon* to answer the questions on the Fast Facts About Shakespeare page. Save this page for future reference.

Name _____   Date _____

Fast Facts About Shakespeare

Using *Bard of Avon*, fill in the chart below to help you keep track of important facts about William Shakespeare and his times.

Shakespeare's hometown	
Shakespeare's father's job	
Shakespeare's school	
Subjects Shakespeare studied	
Shakespeare's wife's name	
Shakespeare's children's names	
City Shakespeare moved to	
James Burbage's first theater	
Courtyard audience members	
Queen of England in the late 1500s	
Powerful religious group	
One of the University Wits	
Name of Shakespeare's first patron	
Name of James Burbage's acting company	

Guidelines for Peer Discussion

Share your thoughts, ideas, questions, and feelings about a text with a peer or others. Listen carefully to what everyone has to say about the text. During your discussion, follow these guidelines.

1. Be prepared to discuss what you think about the text. You should have already read the assignment. Come prepared to discuss your ideas and use examples from the text to support your thoughts and answers.

2. You will be asked questions about the text. Be ready to answer them, and bring some questions of your own to ask others, such as:

   "Who was your favorite character? Why?"

   "What was your favorite part of the text? Why?"

   "What fact did you enjoy learning? Why do you find this fact interesting?"

   "What question would you ask if you had the chance to meet the author?"

3. Listen if it's not your turn to speak. Pay attention to what others say so that you can add your ideas. Speak clearly and in complete sentences.

4. If you don't understand what someone says, ask a question.

   "What do you mean when you say . . . ?"

   "Can you give an example of . . . ?"

5. If you don't agree with what someone says, explain why.

   "I don't agree with that because . . . "

6. Keep discussions positive! You can disagree, but don't argue. Be respectful.

Name _____   Date _____

Bard of Avon: Session 2

In the first part of *Bard of Avon*, you learned that William Shakespeare made quite an impression on the London theater scene when he arrived as a young man. In the second half of *Bard of Avon*, you will follow Shakespeare as he goes from talented young writer to a man of many masterpieces.

Vocabulary

You will find these words in today's reading.

bumpkin: (n.) an unsophisticated individual
The young man felt like a real *bumpkin* when he forgot to wear a suit to the opera.

slapstick: (adj.) physical humor using exaggerated horseplay
I don't like *slapstick* humor because I don't think it's funny to see people fall down and hit each other, even if they are only pretending.

Hercules: (n.) a hero from Greek mythology known for his incredible strength
When she lifted the heavy box all by herself, Sara felt like *Hercules*.

profound: (adj.) intense, extremely important
The graphic footage of the war had a *profound* effect on the members of the audience.

tranquil: (adj.) peaceful, serene
The sea was calm and *tranquil;* there was not a wave in sight.

Think Ahead

1. Summarize what you have learned about Shakespeare so far.
2. Have you ever seen or been in a play? What was the experience like?

Read

Bard of Avon pages 23-42

Questions

Answer the following questions in complete sentences in your Reading Notebook.

1. What are the three main types of plays that Shakespeare wrote?
2. What are the characteristics of each type of play?
3. Who was probably the first person to play the character of Falstaff?
4. Which Shakespeare play deals with Scottish history? What kind of play is it?
5. In what year did the Globe burn to the ground?

Discuss

1. Why did Shakespeare and other playwrights write certain parts for specific actors?
2. What kinds of dangers did Shakespeare face as a playwright in his time? Do you think he took a lot of risks? If so, why did he take those risks?
3. Who were some of the more famous actors during Shakespeare's time?
4. Who were the groundlings? How did they behave?
5. What are the titles of some of Shakespeare's most famous plays? What kind of plays are they?

The Globe: Then

The Globe was an extremely important place in the 1600s. Using *Bard of Avon* as a research tool, write one paragraph about the original Globe theater. Be sure to include any important details about the Globe that are discussed in *Bard of Avon*.

Name _____   Date _____

"A Midsummer Night's Dream": Session 1

Will Hermia be permitted to marry Lysander? How will going into the forest change the lives of the characters? Read the first two sections of this story based on William Shakespeare's play.

Vocabulary

You will find these words in today's reading.

filched: (v.) stole, took secretly and without permission
The burglar quietly entered the room and *filched* an expensive necklace.

wont: (adj.) accustomed, inclined
As he was *wont* to do, the lazy college student slept until noon.

dells: (n.) small and secluded valleys
While walking in the woods, the young lovers found quiet and privacy in the forest's lovely *dells*.

glades: (n.) clearings in wooded areas
The campers set up their tents in one of the forest's many *glades*.

gossamer: (n.) cobwebs floating in the air; something extremely light and delicate
During the hottest days of August, the girl wished her clothes were made of *gossamer*.

changeling: (n.) a mythological term for a human baby who was switched with a fairy child during infancy
Whenever the young boy acted mischievously, his mother would joke that she hoped the fairies were enjoying their *changeling*.

shrewd: (adj.) smart and clever

When the boy used his uncle's gift of three hens to start an egg business, everyone said he was *shrewd.*

knavish: (adj.) inclined toward mischief or trickery and deceit

The *knavish* student couldn't understand why his pranks were not appreciated.

bower: (n.) a natural garden or shelter

The *bower* was home to hundreds of varieties of wild flowers and trees.

Think Ahead

1. The title of this story is "A Midsummer Night's Dream." What are dreams like? Are dreams always logical or realistic? How might a play be like a dream?

2. In *Bard of Avon*, you read about three different types of stories that William Shakespeare wrote: tragedies, histories, and comedies. "A Midsummer Night's Dream" is a comedy. Based on your previous reading, what might you expect in a comedy?

Read

Read Sections 1 and 2 of "A Midsummer Night's Dream" in *Classics for Young Readers,* Vol. 5B, pages 6-12.

Questions

Answer the following questions in complete sentences in your Reading Notebook.

1. Where does the first section of the story take place?
2. Where does the second section of the story take place?
3. What does Hermia want at the beginning of the story?
4. Why does Hermia go to the forest?
5. Who are Oberon, Titania, and Puck?
6. What do Titania and Oberon argue about?

Discuss

1. Why is Helena unhappy?
2. What does Helena do? Is this a wise decision? What might Helena have done differently in the story?
3. How does Hermia feel about the Duke's decision? Do you agree or disagree with Hermia?
4. What does Oberon instruct Puck to do? Is this a good idea? Why or why not?

Confusing Couples

Keeping track of the couples in "A Midsummer Night's Dream" is confusing, but it's important to know who is with whom at different points in the story. The confusion helps make it a comedy, but to understand the joke, you need to know where the characters started out and with whom they wanted to be before the fairies got involved. Use the chart on the Confusing Couples page to keep track of the changing relationships in the story. Keep this page, because you will need it for the next lesson.

Character Cards

Can you imagine Helena chasing Demetrius? What is Puck doing? Use the character cards to help you see what the characters are doing. You may choose to act out part of the story using the characters as props. Write down important information about the characters on the back of each card. Color the characters if you wish.

Name _____   Date _____

Character Cards

Cut out each character card. On the back of the card, write important information that you have learned about the character. You may wish to pair the characters and move the cards around as the pairings change throughout the story.

Helena

Hermia

Lysander

Demetrius

Character Cards

Cut out each character card. On the back of the card, write important information that you have learned about the character. You may wish to pair the characters and move the cards around as the pairings change throughout the story.

Titania

Oberon

Puck

Bottom

Name _____   Date _____

Confusing Couples

Fill in the names of the characters that are paired at the end of each section of "A Midsummer Night's Dream." Use "=" to join two characters whose love is mutual. Use "—" to join two characters whose love is one-sided.

Section 1	Section 2	Section 3	Section 4	Section 5

Name _____   Date _____

"A Midsummer Night's Dream": Session 2

When you left them, Hermia, Helena, Lysander, and Demetrius were lost in the forest with a mischievous fairy named Puck. Will the young lovers find happiness or will confusion keep them apart? Will Oberon and Titania make up? Read the final three sections of this story based on William Shakespeare's play.

Vocabulary
You will find these words in today's reading.

espy: (v.) to see, to catch sight of
The secret agent hoped to *espy* the government official taking a bribe.

pretense: (n.) a false claim or show; a fiction
The frightened performer made a *pretense* of being quite confident in front of the audience.

dote: (v.) to be excessive in one's displays of fondness for someone or something
Though she knew she was spoiling Sara, Grandma could not help but *dote* on her only granddaughter.

Think Ahead
1. Summarize the events of the story's first two sections. Be sure to include
   - the conflicts in the story
   - the reason that the young lovers enter the forest
   - the situation among the fairies who live in the woods

2. Much of the humor in this story stems from confusion. Think of other funny stories, television shows, movies, or plays that you know. Is the humor in any of these a result of confusion? Why is confusion funny to readers and audience members?

3. Predict what will happen to the characters. As you read, you may wish to add to your Character Cards and move them into couples.

Read
Read Sections 3-5 of "A Midsummer Night's Dream" in *Classics for Young Readers,* Vol. 5B, pages 12-22.

Questions
Answer the following questions in complete sentences in your Reading Notebook.

1. Which characters are affected by Puck's mischief? How?
2. Why are the actors in the woods?
3. What does Puck do to Nick Bottom?
4. Who gets married at the end of the story?

Discuss
1. Why does Puck create all of the confusion in the woods? Does he do so intentionally?
2. Why might both audiences and performers particularly like the character of Puck?
3. Is the ending of this story happy? Why or why not?

Confusing Couples
Sort out the confusion. Write in the names of the couples and keep track of the changes in the pairs in Section 3, Section 4, and Section 5 of the story. Use the Confusing Couples page from an earlier lesson.

Now Playing

On poster board, create an advertisement for "A Midsummer Night's Dream." Be sure to indicate that the tale is a comedy by William Shakespeare and to include a drawing that depicts some of the characters or a scene from the story. Remember that audience members need to have their interest sparked, so include an attention-grabbing sentence or two in your advertisement.

Name _____   Date _____

"The Tempest": Session 1

You've left the woods of Athens and now find yourself on a deserted island, the home of a powerful magician and his daughter. What is life like for Prospero and Miranda and what will be the result of the violent tempest? Find out in this story based on William Shakespeare's play.

Vocabulary

You will find these words in today's reading.

corrupt: (adj.) immoral, lacking integrity
The *corrupt* judge was known to accept bribes.

mire: (n.) bog, swamp, marshy area
The hiker emerged from the *mire* a bit muddy, but almost home.

tempest: (n.) a violent storm
We thought it was going to be a summer shower, but when the winds got up to 50 miles an hour, we knew we were in a real *tempest.*

brine: (n.) salty water
Spending hours in the *brine,* the surfer insisted, was what made his skin so healthy.

Think Ahead

1. Much of "A Midsummer Night's Dream" is set in the woods. How does this setting affect the events of that story?

2. "The Tempest" is set on a deserted island. Consider how this setting might affect the story. Answer the following questions:
   - What would a person see or not see on a deserted island?
   - How would a person's life on a deserted island be different from the life of a person surrounded by people and civilization?

Read

Read Section 1 of "The Tempest" in *Classics for Young Readers,*
Vol. 5B, pages 23-29.

Questions

Answer the following questions in complete sentences in your
Reading Notebook.

1. Who lives on the island?
2. How old was Miranda when they arrived on the island?
3. Describe Prospero and Miranda's life before they arrived on the island.
4. Why did Prospero and Miranda leave Milan?
5. How did Prospero and Miranda arrive on the island?
6. Who is Ariel?
7. Why does Prospero bring Ferdinand to the island?

Discuss

1. How has living alone on an island affected Miranda's
   personality? Do you think she has been lonely?

2. Do you think Prospero uses his power responsibly? Support your
   answer with examples from the story. Consider the following:
   • Prospero causes the storm and the shipwreck but makes
     sure that all the passengers are safe.
   • Prospero freed Ariel but now insists that Ariel serve him.
   • Prospero does not allow Miranda to see or hear Ariel.

Two Views of Prospero

What do you think of Prospero? His behavior and actions seem to change depending on the characters he is with at the particular time. Explain these changes in two paragraphs in your Reading Notebook.

In the first paragraph, imagine that you are Miranda. Describe your father, Prospero. Remember that Miranda has had little contact with other creatures and that Prospero has been an extremely kind and loving father.

In the second paragraph, describe Prospero again, but this time imagine that you are Ariel. Remember that Prospero freed you from the wood, but he now forces you to serve him.

When you have finished writing, discuss the similarities and differences between these two views of the same person.

Name _____   Date _____

"The Tempest": Session 2

The second half of "The Tempest" brings major changes to the island shared by Prospero and Miranda. How will Miranda react to so many new faces? What will Prospero do to the men who betrayed him and stole his crown? Find out in the conclusion of this story based on the play by William Shakespeare.

Vocabulary

You will find these words in today's reading.

chide: (v.) to mildly scold or rebuke
When the young child spoke with his mouth full, his mother felt it necessary to *chide* him.

censure: (v.) to criticize
The angry director spent most of rehearsal *censuring* his poorly prepared actors.

vexations: (n.) acts of harassment
Tom mistook his teacher's honest attempts to help him learn for pointless *vexations*.

supplant: (v.) to steal the place of, especially by force
Nancy was very proud to be the first violin in the orchestra, but she was afraid that the second violinist was trying to *supplant* her.

Think Ahead

1. Summarize Section 1 of "The Tempest." In your summary, be sure to include:
   - A description of the characters
   - An explanation of their relationship to one another
   - The major events of the story
2. How do you think Miranda will react to Ferdinand? Why?
3. Predict what you think will happen next in the story. Give reasons for your prediction.

Read

Read Section 2 of "The Tempest" in *Classics for Young Readers,* Vol. 5B, pages 29-36.

Questions

Answer the following questions in complete sentences in your Reading Notebook.

1. Why is Ferdinand unhappy at the beginning of the section?
2. Why does Miranda mistake Ferdinand for a spirit?
3. What task does Prospero order Ferdinand to do and why?
4. How do Miranda and Ferdinand feel about each other? How do you know?
5. Who is Antonio?
6. How does Ariel treat Antonio and the king? Why?
7. What do Prospero and the king do for each other?
8. What happens to Ariel just before Prospero leaves the island?

Discuss

1. How does Miranda feel about all the new people she has met? Why do you think she feels this way?
2. Do you think Prospero's treatment of Ferdinand is fair? Why or why not?
3. Why do you think Prospero forgives Antonio and the king? Does this change the way you feel about Prospero?

"Brave New World"

At one point in "The Tempest," Miranda exclaims, "How many goodly creatures are there here! O brave new world that has such people in it!" She says this because of all the changes that have suddenly occurred on the island she previously shared with only her father. Ferdinand might have similar feelings of surprise after his experiences on the island. Pretend you are either Miranda or Ferdinand and write a diary entry about the events of the story and how you feel about those events. Explain how your life has changed because of what has happened.

The Last Laugh

Both of the stories that you read—"A Midsummer Night's Dream" and "The Tempest"—are based on Shakespearean comedies. Compare and contrast these two stories using The Last Laugh page. Remember what you learned about the comedies when you read *Bard of Avon.* Think about these characteristics as you compare and contrast the stories.

Name _____   Date _____

The Last Laugh

What makes these two plays comedies? Write a few words to describe them. Then compare and contrast their plots, settings, and some of their characters.

	A Midsummer Night's Dream	The Tempest
Setting	_____ _____	_____ _____
Confusion	_____ _____	_____ _____
Marriages	_____ _____	_____ _____
Feud and Resolution	_____ _____	_____ _____
Characters	Oberon_____ _____	Prospero_____ _____
Fairies or Spirits	Puck_____ _____	Ariel_____ _____

Name _____   Date _____

Dramatic Reading

You've learned about the life of William Shakespeare in *Bard of Avon*, and you've read stories based on two of his most famous plays. Now it's time to jump into Shakespeare's own words. Today, you'll have the chance to read some of the dialogue from Shakespeare's plays. With a little practice, you'll be able to hear what Shakespeare's original audiences heard about 400 years ago!

Think Ahead

1. Review the main ideas, events, and characters of *Bard of Avon*, "A Midsummer Night's Dream," and "The Tempest."

2. Shakespeare's language is very poetic. What are some of the other differences between Shakespeare's language and today's English? Why do actors perform these plays using Shakespeare's original words?

3. Just as books are sometimes divided into chapters, plays are sometimes divided into *scenes.* You will be reading scenes that are taken from the complete plays.

4. Today you will be reading a *script* of a play. The script shows the written words that the actors say on stage. The script also gives *stage directions,* which give the actors information about where to go on stage or how to say a particular line. Stage directions are usually written in parentheses. They are not read aloud. Find the stage directions in the following lines. Who will enter the scene?

> **PROSPERO:** Come away, servant; come; I am ready now. Approach, my Ariel. Come. *(Enter ARIEL)*
>
> **ARIEL:** All hail, great master! Grave sir, hail! I come…

Read

On the page entitled Center Stage, you will find scenes taken from William Shakespeare's *A Midsummer Night's Dream* and *The Tempest.* Read these scenes to yourself. Use the modern translations to help you understand the meaning of Shakespeare's language. (The word "exeunt" means exit. When you see it in the text, it means a character is leaving the stage.)

You can also listen to a sample from *A Midsummer Night's Dream.* Bring your Center Stage with you to the computer and follow the dialogue while you listen to actors from the Royal Shakespeare Company perform.

The Play's the Thing

Choose the scene from *A Midsummer Night's Dream* or *The Tempest* that you like the most. Which characters do you like best? Decide which scene you would like to act out. Read the modern translation of the scene.

Reread your scene aloud using Shakespeare's language. Get familiar with the way it sounds. Try to read Shakespeare's language in complete sentences. Don't stop reading at the end of each line. Try to pause or stop in the places where thoughts or ideas end, just like in a regular conversation. Think about the meaning of the words so you can read with good expression. Use the modern translation to help you understand Shakespeare's language.

When you feel comfortable with the dialogue and its meaning, choose a character to portray and read that character's dialogue aloud. Have a partner read the lines of the other character(s). After completing the entire dialogue, you may wish to attempt to commit a few lines to memory and perform the piece without using a script.

Name   Date

Center Stage

A Midsummer Night's Dream
ACT 2. SCENE 1.

(Enter a FAIRY at one door, and PUCK at another.)

Shakespeare's Original Text	Modern Translation

PUCK: The King doth keep his revels here tonight;
  Take heed the Queen come not within his sight;
  For Oberon is passing fell and wrath,
  Because that she as her attendant hath
  A lovely boy, stolen from an Indian king.
  She never had so sweet a changeling;
  And jealous Oberon would have the child
  Knight of his train, to trace the forests wild;
  But she perforce withholds the loved boy,
  Crowns him with flowers, and makes him all her joy.
  And now they never meet in grove or green,
  By fountain clear, or spangled starlight sheen,
  But they do square, that all their elves for fear
  Creep into acorn cups and hide them there.
	PUCK: The king will have his celebrations here tonight, so make sure he doesn't see the queen. Oberon is very angry with her because she is keeping a lovely changeling boy for herself and jealous Oberon wants him to be part of his group of attendants. Still, she is forcibly keeping Oberon from the boy, crowning the boy with flowers and lavishing attention on him. And for that reason Oberon and Titania never enjoy each other's company and act friendly, but always fight in such a nasty way that all of their elves get scared and hide.

FAIRY: Either I mistake your shape and making quite,
  Or else you are that shrewd and knavish sprite
  Call'd Robin Goodfellow. Are not you he
  That frights the maidens of the villagery,
  Skim milk, and sometimes labour in the quern,
  And bootless make the breathless housewife churn,
  And sometime make the drink to bear no barm,
	FAIRY: Maybe I'm wrong, but aren't you that clever and mischievous fairy called Robin Goodfellow? Aren't you the one who scares the women of the village by haunting the butter churn and spoiling the drinks that people usually enjoy? Don't you usually then

---

perforce: (adv.) by force of circumstances
sheen: (n.) shine
quern: (n.) a butter churn
barm: (n.) a type of yeast that forms during fermentation

Mislead night-wanderers, laughing at their harm?
Those that Hobgoblin call you, and sweet Puck,
You do their work, and they shall have good luck.
Are not you he?

PUCK: Thou speakest aright:
I am that merry wanderer of the night.
I jest to Oberon, and make him smile
When I a fat and bean-fed horse beguile,
Neighing in likeness of a filly foal;
And sometime lurk I in a gossip's bowl
In very likeness of a roasted crab,
And, when she drinks, against her lips I bob,
And on her withered dewlap pour the ale.
The wisest aunt, telling the saddest tale,
Sometime for three-foot stool mistaketh me;
Then slip I from her bum, down topples she,
And 'tailor' cries, and falls into a cough;
And then the whole quire hold their hips and laugh,
And waxen in their mirth, and neeze, and swear
A merrier hour was never wasted there.
But room, fairy, here comes Oberon.

laugh at their fright? Some people call you Hobgoblin and some call you Puck. You do certain things for them that they ask you to do. Aren't you that person?

PUCK: You're correct. I am that creature who plays tricks on others for Oberon's amusement. For example, I may trick a fat horse by neighing like a foal. And sometimes I make people hear invented gossip just to watch it spread and result in confusion. And sometimes, I turn myself into a stool that gives out when a woman tries to sit, causing her to fall down and making everyone around her laugh. It is so funny when I do these things. But wait, here comes Oberon.

beguile: (v.) to charm in a deceptive way
dewlap: (n.) loose skin under the neck of an animal or person
quire: (n.) a variant of the word "choir": an organized group of people or things
neeze: (v.) to sneeze

A Midsummer Night's Dream
ACT 4. SCENE 1.

Shakespeare's Original Text

TITANIA: Come, sit thee down upon this flow'ry bed,
  While I thy amiable cheeks do coy,
  And stick musk-roses in thy sleek smooth head,
  And kiss thy fair large ears, my gentle joy.

BOTTOM: Where's Peaseblossom?

PEASEBLOSSOM: Ready.

BOTTOM: Scratch my head, Peaseblossom.
  Where's Mounsieur Cobweb?

COBWEB: Ready.

BOTTOM. Mounsieur Cobweb; good mounsieur, get
  you your weapons in your hand and kill me a red-
  hipp'd humble-bee on the top of a thistle; and, good
  mounsieur, bring me the honey-bag. Do not fret
  yourself too much in the action, mounsieur; and, good
  mounsieur, have a care the honey-bag break not; I
  would be loath to have you overflown with a honey-
  bag, signior. Where's Mounsieur Mustardseed?

MUSTARDSEED: Ready.

BOTTOM: Give me your neaf, Mounsieur Mustardseed.
  Pray you, leave your curtsy, good mounsieur.

MUSTARDSEED: What's your will?

Modern Translation

TITANIA: Come, sit down in this flowerbed while I caress your beautiful cheeks and place flowers in your hair and kiss your large ears, my love.

BOTTOM: Where's Peaseblossom?

PEASEBLOSSOM: I'm here.

BOTTOM: Scratch my head, Peaseblossom. Where's Mister Cobweb?

COBWEB: I'm here.

BOTTOM: Mister Cobweb, good sir, get your weapons and kill a bee sitting on top of a flower for me. Then bring me the bee's honey. Be careful, however, when you kill the bee. Don't be too violent and make sure the bee's honey bag does not break. I'd hate to see you covered in honey if the bag were to break. Where is Mister Mustardseed?

MUSTARDSEED: I'm here.

BOTTOM: Give me your fist, Mister Mustardseed. Will you do me a favor?

MUSTARDSEED: What do you need?

---

coy: (v.) to caress or touch gently
mounsieur: (n.) a variant of the French word "monsieur": mister
signior: (n.) a variant of the Italian word "signor": mister
neaf: (n.) hand, fist

BOTTOM: Nothing, good mounsieur, but to help Cavalery Cobweb to scratch. I must to the barber's, mounsieur; for methinks I am marvellous hairy about the face; and I am such a tender ass, if my hair do but tickle me I must scratch.

TITANIA: What, wilt thou hear some music, my sweet love?

BOTTOM: I have a reasonable good ear in music. Let's have the tongs and the bones.

TITANIA: Or say, sweet love, what thou desirest to eat.

BOTTOM: Truly, a peck of provender; I could munch your good dry oats. Methinks I have a great desire to a bottle of hay. Good hay, sweet hay, hath no fellow.

TITANIA: I have a venturous fairy that shall seek The squirrel's hoard, and fetch thee new nuts.

BOTTOM: I had rather have a handful or two of dried peas. But, I pray you, let none of your people stir me; I have an exposition of sleep come upon me.

TITANIA: Sleep thou, and I will wind thee in my arms. Fairies, be gone, and be all ways away.
(Exeunt FAIRIES)
So doth the woodbine the sweet honeysuckle
Gently entwist; the female ivy so
Enrings the barky fingers of the elm.
O, how I love thee! How I dote on thee!

BOTTOM: Could you just help Sir Cobweb to scratch me? I need to go to the barber because I really need to shave. And I'm so sensitive that if my hair even tickles me, I must scratch it.

TITANIA: Would you like to hear some music, my love?

BOTTOM: I like music. Let's hear some music.

TITANIA: And what would you like to eat?

BOTTOM: To be honest, I'd love some animal feed or some dry oats. I'd also like some hay. Good hay is really remarkable food.

TITANIA: One of my fairy servants will find a squirrel's nest and get you some nuts.

BOTTOM: I'd rather just have some dried peas. But please don't let anyone wake me up. I'm feeling very sleepy.

TITANIA: You should sleep, and I'll hold you in my arms. Fairies, leave us alone. Just as the woodbine vines surround the honeysuckle, so will my arms surround you. Oh, how I love you and love caring for you!

---

provender: (n.) animal feed
woodbine: (n.) a type of vine that surrounds honeysuckles

The Tempest
ACT 1. SCENE 2.

Shakespeare's Original Text

PROSPERO: Come away, servant; come; I am
 ready now.
 Approach, my Ariel. Come. *(Enter ARIEL)*

ARIEL: All hail, great master! Grave sir, hail! I come
 To answer thy best pleasure; be't to fly,
 To swim, to dive into the fire, to ride
 On the curl'd clouds. To thy strong bidding task
 Ariel and all his quality.

PROSPERO: Hast thou, spirit,
 Perform'd to point the tempest that I bade thee?

ARIEL: To every article.
 I boarded the King's ship; now on the beak,
 Now in the waist, the deck, in every cabin,
 I flam'd amazement. Sometime I'd divide,
 And burn in many places; on the topmast,
 The yards, and bowsprit, would I flame distinctly,
 Then meet and join Jove's lightning, the precursors
 O' th' dreadful thunder-claps, more momentary
 And sight-outrunning were not; the fire and cracks
 Of sulphurous roaring the most mighty Neptune
 Seem to besiege, and make his bold waves tremble,
 Yea, his dread trident shake.

PROSPERO: Why, that's my spirit!
 But was not this nigh shore?

ARIEL: Close by, my master.

Modern Translation

PROSPERO: Come, servant. I'm ready
 now. Come on, Ariel.

ARIEL: Hail to you, my master. I come
 to serve you; to fly, swim, dive into
 fire, or ride on the clouds. I will do my
 best to do whatever you ask of me.

PROSPERO: Spirit, have you caused
 the storm like I asked you to?

ARIEL: Exactly as you asked. I boarded
 the King's ship as fire, and burned in
 several different places. I burned on
 the topmast, the yards, and the
 bowsprit. At the same time, I caused
 the heavens to erupt with thunder
 and lightning and the waves of the
 sea to swell. It seemed as if Neptune
 the god of the sea, was angry at the
 boat and was attempting to sink it.

PROSPERO: Great job, Ariel! But was
 this close to the shore?

ARIEL: Very close to the shore, master.

---

topmast: (n.) the highest pole rising from the deck of a ship
bowsprit: (n.) a large pole extending forward from the stem of a ship
trident: (n.) a three-pointed spear

PROSPERO. But are they, Ariel, safe?

ARIEL: Not a hair perish'd;
  On their sustaining garments not a blemish,
  But fresher than before; and, as thou bad'st me,
  In troops I have dispers'd them 'bout the isle.
  The King's son have I landed by himself,
  Whom I left cooling of the air with sighs
  In an odd angle of the isle, and sitting,
  His arms in this sad knot.
…
PROSPERO: Ariel, thy charge
  Exactly is perform'd.

PROSPERO: And are they safe, Ariel?

ARIEL: Not a hair on their head was harmed. Their clothes were not soiled at all, but actually nicer than before. They have washed ashore at different places on the island. I brought the king's son ashore alone. He is sitting by himself, wondering what to do, with his arms folded.

PROSPERO: Great job, Ariel. You did exactly what I wanted you to do.

The Tempest
ACT 3 SCENE 1

Shakespeare's Original Text

FERDINAND: I must remove
  Some thousands of these logs, and pile them up,
  Upon a sore injunction; my sweet mistress
  Weeps when she sees me work, and says such baseness
  Had never like executor. I forget;
  But these sweet thoughts do even refresh my labours,
  Most busy, least when I do it. *(Enter MIRANDA)*

MIRANDA: Alas, now; pray you,
  Work not so hard; I would the lightning had
  Burnt up those logs that you are enjoin'd to pile.
  Pray, set it down and rest you; when this burns,
  'Twill weep for having wearied you. My father
  Is hard at study; pray, now, rest yourself;
  He's safe for these three hours.

FERDINAND: O most dear mistress,
  The sun will set before I shall discharge
  What I must strive to do.

MIRANDA: If you'll sit down,
  I'll bear your logs the while; pray give me
  I'll carry it to the pile.

FERDINAND: No, precious creature;
  I had rather crack my sinews, break my back,
  Than you should such dishonour undergo,
  While I sit lazy by.

Modern Translation

FERDINAND: I have been ordered to move thousands of these logs and pile them up. The sweet woman cries when she sees me work and says that I am too noble for such lowly work. And her kindness makes this work seem easy.

MIRANDA: Please don't work so hard. I wish the lightning had burnt up these logs that you have been ordered to pile. Please, stop working and rest a while. My father is busy studying right now, so you can rest for at least three hours.

FERDINAND: Oh dear mistress, it will be night before I finish this task.

MIRANDA: If you sit, I'll do the work for a while. Please, give me that log, and I'll carry it.

FERDINAND: No, precious creature. I would rather tear all of my muscles and break my back than have you do my work for me.

---

baseness: (adj.) characterized by inferiority or low value
executor: (n.) one who completes a task or job
sinews: (n.) the tendons in human muscles

MIRANDA: It would become me
  As well as it does you; and I should do it
  With much more ease; for my good will is to it,
  And yours it is against.
  … You look wearily.

FERDINAND: No, noble mistress; 'tis fresh morning
  with me
  When you are by at night. I do beseech you,
  Chiefly that I might set it in my prayers,
  What is your name?

MIRANDA: Miranda—O my father,
  I have broke your hest to say so!

FERDINAND: Admir'd Miranda!
  What's dearest to the world! Full many a lady
  I have ey'd with best regard; and many a time
  Th' harmony of their tongues hath into bondage
  Brought my too diligent ear; for several virtues
  Have I lik'd several women, never any
  With so full soul, but some defect in her
  Did quarrel with the noblest grace she ow'd,
  And put it to the foil; but you, O you,
  So perfect and so peerless, are created
  Of every creature's best!

MIRANDA: I do not know
  One of my sex; no woman's face remember,
  Save, from my glass, mine own; nor have I seen
  More that I may call men than you, good friend,
  And my dear father. How features are abroad,
  I am skilless of; but, by my modesty,
  The jewel in my dower, I would not wish
  Any companion in the world but you;
  Nor can imagination form a shape,
  Besides yourself, to like of. But I prattle
  Something too wildly, and my father's precepts
  I therein do forget.

MIRANDA: It would be better for me to do it than you because I actually want to do it. You, however, don't want to do it. You seem very tired.

FERDINAND: No, noble woman. The darkest night feels like fresh morning when you are nearby. I do ask, mainly so I can include it in my prayers, what is your name?

MIRANDA: Miranda. Oh dear, I've disobeyed my father by telling you.

FERDINAND: Beautiful Miranda! What a lovely name. I've seen many women, but all of them had some kind of fault or personality flaw. But you are completely perfect. No one is your equal. Your personality incorporates the best qualities of others with none of their faults.

MIRANDA: I don't know any other women. I've never seen a woman's face except my own in the mirror. I've also never seen any men except you and my father. I have no idea what people look like elsewhere. To be honest, I must say that I want no one else in the world but you. I cannot even imagine another man who could hold a candle to you. But I'm talking too much and am forgetting that my father told me not to say too much to you.

---

dower: (n.) a variant of the word "dowry": a natural talent
prattle: (v.) to make empty or meaningless chatter

Name _____ Date _____

George Westinghouse and the Air Brake

In the late 1800s, George Westinghouse was one of America's finest inventors and one its greatest businessmen. Read and hear more about the life and achievements of Westinghouse, and then see one of his most important inventions in action.

Vocabulary

You will find these words in today's reading.

enrolled: (v.) became a student
After my dad finished college, he *enrolled* in medical school.

patented: (v.) established official ownership of an idea or invention
Thomas Edison patented the electric light bulb in 1880.

efficient: (adj.) productive; not wasteful
When I finished reading the book, Mrs. Wilkins congratulated me for my *efficient* use of my free time.

justly: (adv.) with justice; fairly
The honorable guard dealt *justly* with the prisoners.

engaged: (v.) activated; involved
Before the pilot took her hands off of the controls, she made sure that the autopilot was *engaged*.

Think Ahead

1. What qualities do you think make someone a good inventor? What qualities make someone a good businessperson?
2. Think about a time when you've seen a freight train—a train that is used to carry cargo or freight from one place to another. Why are freight trains good for moving products? What problems might arise from using freight trains to transport goods?
3. How do you think the brakes on a train work?
4. George Westinghouse grew up in New York, but he established his businesses in Pittsburgh, Pennsylvania. Locate New York and Pittsburgh on a map.

Read, Listen, and Watch

Read "George Westinghouse" and listen to "The Railway Air Brake." Then watch "The Westinghouse Air Brake in Action" on your computer."

Questions

Answer the following questions in complete sentences in your Reading Notebook.

1. What did George Westinghouse like to do at his father's machine shop when he was a boy?
2. The first passage says that Pittsburgh was "a bustling city in the 1860s." What does the word *bustling* mean?
3. What company did George Westinghouse found when he was just 22 years old?
4. In what ways were the brakes that Westinghouse invented different from the brakes used on trains before that?
5. Name three consequences of the invention of Westinghouse's brakes?

Discuss

1. Think about how important trains were to businesses in the late 1800s, a time before the car or the airplane had been invented. Consider also the problems that existed with train travel and with shipping goods by train at that time. Then explain what problems George Westinghouse tried to solve with his invention of the air brake and why the air brake Westinghouse invented was so useful and successful.
2. In your own words, restate how the brakes that Westinghouse invented used pressurized air to stop trains.
3. Why does the author of "The Railway Air Brake" begin the passage by describing the railroads before George Westinghouse's invention of his air brakes?

Animation

This lesson includes an animation that you watched online. Describe what the animation shows. Then tell how the animation helps you understand more about Westinghouse's invention.

George Westinghouse

George Westinghouse was a man who helped to change America. He was born in New York in 1846. His father owned a machine shop, and young George enjoyed spending time there. He soon learned how to take apart and rebuild many machines. He even tried to improve them with inventions of his own.

When George was 15, the Civil War began. Despite his age, Westinghouse bravely joined the fight. He served in the Union Army and the Navy. When the war ended, Westinghouse returned to New York.

Westinghouse enrolled in Union College, but he did not graduate. He left school to focus on work. He married Marguerite Erskine Walker in 1867. They eventually had one child. Soon after their wedding, they moved to Pittsburgh.

Pittsburgh was a growing city in the 1860s. It was home to many factories. The factories relied on railroads. Railroads brought raw materials to the city's factories. Railroads carried finished products to the rest of the country. Yet trains were not always safe. This gave Westinghouse an idea.

Westinghouse invented a new system of brakes for trains. His brakes used air pressure to work. In 1869, he patented his invention. He also founded the Westinghouse Air Brake Company. He was just 22 years old.

In the coming years, Westinghouse continued to improve on his air brakes. His company continued to make them. Railroad companies continued to buy them. By 1905, more than two million train cars and nearly 100 thousand locomotives used Westinghouse's brakes.

Yet George Westinghouse did not only invent brakes. He worked on problems related to signals between trains and stations. He developed ways to distribute natural gas, too. He also founded an electric company. Westinghouse Electric was formed in 1886.

Westinghouse Electric built the first hydroelectric power plant, which was at Niagara Falls. It provided power to the World's Fair in 1893. The company even challenged General Electric, which was led by Thomas Edison.

In his lifetime, George Westinghouse patented over 300 inventions. His companies helped make train travel safer and more efficient. They also helped to increase the use of electricity. Perhaps most important, they were known for treating their workers justly and paying them a fair wage. The brilliant George Westinghouse died in 1914.

Name _____   Date _____

A Second Look

Review the passages you read and heard and the animation you watched about George Westinghouse and the air brake. Then explore their similarities and differences to better understand them.

Think Ahead

1. Based on the reading you did in Lesson 1, what do you recall about the life of George Westinghouse?
2. What do you remember about his achievements? How did Westinghouse's air-brake work?
3. Think of a food that you like, but that someone you know does not. If you were both to write about that food, how might your passages be similar? How might they be different? What are some reasons for these similarities and differences?

Read, Listen, and Watch Again

Reread "George Westinghouse." Then listen to "The Railway Air Brake" and watch "The Westinghouse Air Brake in Action" on your computer once more.

Questions

Answer the following questions in complete sentences in your Reading Notebook.

1. Read this sentence: "Westinghouse Electric's largest factories were built in East Pittsburgh, Pennsylvania." In which passage would this sentence best fit?
2. Read this sentence: "When the brakes engaged, they pressed on the wheels of the train, which caused them to stop moving." In which passage would this sentence best fit?
3. Why might an animation of how manual brakes worked on trains be helpful to viewers of "The Westinghouse Air Brake in Action"?

4. Think about what you heard in "The Railway Air Brake" and what you saw in "The Westinghouse Air Brake in Action." Then explain why teams of brakemen were no longer needed on trains that used Westinghouse's invention.

5. How is the description of the air brake in "George Westinghouse" different from the description of the air brake in "The Railway Air Brake"?

Compare and Contrast

Follow the directions on the Compare and Contrast page to examine the ways that the passages you read and the animation you watched are alike and how they are different.

Name _____   Date _____

Compare and Contrast

Read each statement in the column on the left. Think about what you read, heard, or saw in the selections. Place an X under the selections the statements describe.

	"George Westinghouse"	"The Railway Air Brake"	"The Westinghouse Air Brake in Action"
The selection contains language that reveals the author's feelings about the subject.			
The language of the selection does not reveal the author's feelings about the subject of the passage or animation.			
The selection tells events in chronological, or time, order.			
The selection describes a problem before explaining its solution.			
The selection focuses on several events that happen over a long period of time.			
The selection focuses on a few events that happen over a relatively short period of time.			
The selection uses images or other visual aids to help convey its points.			
The main purpose of the selection is to inform people or help them understand its subject.			

Name _____   Date _____

Conduct Research

Do some research to learn about another important inventor and something he or she invented. Then begin to work on a project that you will present about your research.

Think Ahead

1. You have learned about George Westinghouse and one of his most famous inventions: the railway air brake. Do you know any other famous inventors? If so, which ones and what did they invent? If not, which inventions interest you? Why?

2. You have researched a topic before. What do you know about presenting information that you find? Is it okay to copy information from a source and present it as your own?

Your Assignment

Over the next several days, you will complete a research project and give an oral presentation. Your assignment has three parts:

1. Write a brief report on an inventor's life and his or her invention. The report should tell about the person's life, but also describe the person's invention and explain the invention's importance. It should answer this question: How did the invention change people's lives? The report should be 2–3 paragraphs and must contain information from at least two reliable sources.

2. Use the report to help craft a short speech about the inventor and his or her invention. The speech should mention the most important points from the report. The speech should be 3–4 minutes long.

3. Create a visual aid—a drawing, a movie, or a slide show—that will help people better understand the speech. The visual aid might show the inventor or the invention the speech focuses on.

Choose an Inventor and an Invention

Read the list of inventors and inventions. Think about which one interests you the most. Consider which inventor and invention you want to learn more about. Then select the person and the invention that will be the focus of your research project and presentation. Circle your choice now.

Elias Howe: the sewing machine

Robert Fulton: the steamboat

Samuel Morse: the telegraph

Josephine Garis Cochran: the dishwasher

Mary Anderson: windshield wipers

Garrett A. Morgan: the gas mask

Grace Murray Hopper: the compiler (computer device)

George Washington Carver: numerous peanut products

Use Reliable Sources

When doing research, it is important to always use reliable sources. Reliable sources are those that can be trusted to contain factual information.

Printed encyclopedias and books are considered to be reliable sources. Printed magazine and newspaper articles are also reliable.

Online, web sites with URLs ending in .gov, .edu, and .org are usually reliable.

Some web sites with URLs ending in .com are reliable. Others are not.

Web sites with URLs ending in .info or .biz are not reliable. Sites created by people who are not experts in a field and sites that allow anyone to contribute to them are not reliable, either.

Wikipedia is not a reliable source of information.

Complete the Reliable Sources sheet to review what are and are not appropriate sources for a research project.

Take Notes

As you find reliable sources and read about the inventor you've chosen and his or her invention, you should take notes. Notes are a record of the important details and information that you learn. Your notes should cover these kinds of facts:

- where and when the inventor was born
- why he or she came up with the invention
- how the invention works
- how the invention changed people's lives

You will use the notes you take to help you write your research report.

Print the Take Notes page now. Follow the directions on it to begin your research.

Name _____   Date _____

Reliable Sources

Below is a list of possible sources that the author of the Westinghouse selections discovered while researching.

Read the title, description, and URL (if it is an online source) of each source below. Think about whether each source can be trusted to contain true and accurate information. Then, on the line provided, write "R" under to those that are reliable sources and "NR" under those that are not reliable sources.

1. "George Westinghouse: A Hundred Thousand Horsepower Man": an article that appeared in *The New York Times* on March 6, 1904

   _____

2. *George Westinghouse: His Life and Achievements*: a book by Francis E. Leupp that was published in 1919

   _____

3. "The Westinghouse Air Brake Company": a website created and maintained by the Library of Congress (http://memory.loc.gov/papr/west/westair.html)

   _____

4. "What Did George Westinghouse Invent?": a website on which users can ask questions to be answered by other users (http://www.ask.com/question/what-did-george-westinghouse-invent)

   _____

5. "George Westinghouse": a website about Westinghouse that allows users to change and modify content (http://en.wikipedia.org/wiki/George_Westinghouse)

   _____

6. "Inventor of the Week: George Westinghouse, Jr.": a website created and maintained by the Massachusetts Institute of Technology (http://web.mit.edu/invent/iow/westinghouse.html)

   _____

Name _____   Date _____

Take Notes

Use this page to take notes as you research the inventor and invention(s) you've chosen. You may print additional copies of this page to take more notes, if needed.

Remember that when taking notes it is important to put what you learn in your own words and to record the sources you used to find information. If you use another person's words, put them in quotation marks and give the writer credit.

Inventor's Name: _____

Invention: _____

Notes on the inventor's life, the invention, and the impact of the invention:

_____

_____

_____

_____

_____

_____

_____

_____

346

_____

_____

_____

_____

_____

_____

_____

_____

_____

_____

_____

Sources:

_____

_____

_____

_____

Name _____   Date _____

Write a Research Report

Finish your research and then write a brief report on a famous inventor and his or her invention.

Finish Taking Notes

Use the Take Notes sheet to finish recording important details and facts about the life and accomplishments of the inventor you chose and his or her invention. Remember to use reliable sources and keep track of where you found the information you've written down.

Write Now

Now begin to write the report on an inventor's life and invention. Be sure to include key details about when and where the inventor lived, as well as how he or she came up with the invention and how the invention worked. Also describe how the invention changed people's lives.

Remember that the report should be at least two paragraphs and must contain information from at least two reliable sources. Use the Write Now pages.

Name _____ Date _____

Write Now

Use these pages to write your paragraphs on the inventor and the invention(s) you've researched. Write the title of your report on the line below. You may print additional copies of these pages if you need more space.

- In your first paragraph, introduce your inventor and give a brief overview of his or her life.
- In your second paragraph, describe the invention he or she created. Tell how it works and why it was needed.
- In your third paragraph, explain how the invention changed people's lives.

_____

_____

_____

_____

_____

_____

_____

_____

_____

_____

_____

_____

_____

_____

_____

_____

_____

_____

Sources:

_____

_____

_____

_____

Name _____ Date _____

Practice a Presentation

Finish writing your report and then craft a short speech about your inventor and his or her invention. Create a visual aid to accompany your speech.

Finish Writing

Use the Write Now sheet to finish the report about the life and accomplishments of the inventor you chose and his or her invention. Remember to describe how the invention changed people's lives. Your finished report should be at least two paragraphs long and must contain information from at least two reliable sources.

Speech

Once you have finished writing, use your report to create a short speech about your inventor and his or her invention. The speech should not be just you reading your report aloud. Instead, it should contain the report's most important and interesting information, and should present that information in the same order. The speech should take 2–3 minutes to deliver.

Follow the directions on the Craft a Speech page to organize the information that will be included in your speech. You may add extra information that you find interesting, if you wish. Then use the Give a Speech sheet to help you as you practice delivering your speech.

Visual Aid

When delivering a speech, it is often helpful to show the audience pictures, drawings, slide shows, or other visual aids. These can help those hearing your speech to better understand and picture what you are saying.

Consider the content of your speech. Think about the inventor and the invention that you will describe. Then choose a visual aid that you think will make a good companion to your speech. You may choose to include

- a drawing of the invention
- a diagram that shows how the invention works
- a slide show that incorporates pictures of life before and after the invention

It is up to you which visual aid to use. It is also up to you to find or create the visual aid you select. You may decide to draw a picture, map, or diagram of your own. Or you may decide to show a picture, map, drawing, or diagram that you find from a reliable source. If so, be sure to give that source credit.

Name _____   Date _____

Craft a Speech

Use this page to craft your speech on the inventor and the invention(s) you've researched and written about. Fill in the blanks about your speech's title and subject below. Then fill in the sections that follow using information from your report. Your speech should present the most important and interesting information from your report and present that information in the same logical order.

The title of my speech is: _____

My inventor's name is: _____

He/she was born in the year: _____

His/her birthplace was: _____

My inventor invented: _____

This invention solved the following problem(s):

_____

_____

The invention worked like this:

_____

_____

_____

_____

Here is how the invention changed people's lives:

_____

_____

_____

_____

Name _____   Date _____

Give a Speech

Follow the steps as you practice giving your speech on the inventor and the invention(s) you've researched and written a report about.

1. Review your completed Craft a Speech pages. They should contain all of the information about your inventor and his or her invention that you will include in your speech. Review the information several times.

2. Practice delivering your speech. Talk about the details you've written down about your inventor's life, the invention itself, and the invention's impact. You do not need to read or state what is on your Craft a Speech pages exactly.

3. Speak in complete sentences.
   Be natural and friendly, but use formal, standard English.
   Do not make grammatical errors.

4. Focus on speaking slowly and with a clear voice. Do not speak too loudly. Do not mumble. Remember that your audience needs to hear and understand everything you say.

5. Speak with confidence and enthusiasm.

6. Deliver your speech in front of a mirror. Stand up straight and make eye contact with your own reflection as much as possible. Do not fidget.

7. Think about what the best time or times are to show your visual aid. Remember that the visual aid should be related to a key point that you make during your speech. Practice delivering the speech and explaining what your visual aid shows (or will show).

8. If possible, make a video or audio recording of your speech. Seeing yourself deliver the speech can help you notice areas that need improvement. Consider sharing the recording with a peer or friend who can give helpful feedback.

Name _____   Date _____

Deliver a Presentation

Deliver the speech about your inventor and his or her invention. Present a visual aid to accompany your speech.

Make a Presentation

Review your Give a Speech sheet once more. Then deliver the speech you crafted and present a visual aid to go with it. Your presentation should last 2-3 minutes.

As you give your presentation, remember:

- Talk about the most important and interesting points in your report.

- Include key details about the inventor, what the invention does and how it works, and how the invention changed people's lives.

- Touch on points in a logical order.

- Refer to your visual aid when appropriate.

- Speak clearly, at the appropriate speed and volume, and with enthusiasm.

- Speak in complete sentences.

- Use formal, standard English.

- Do not make grammatical errors in your speech.

- Stand up straight and maintain eye contact as much as possible.

Name _____   Date _____

Don Quixote: Chapters 1-3

Stories of brave knights slaying dragons and rescuing damsels in distress have been around for centuries. Perhaps you have even read a few. Why is a 1605 story by Miguel de Cervantes about an old knight named Don Quixote special? You are about to find out. Read the funny and charming adventures of Don Quixote as he sets out to fight for people who need help. Armed with only his good will and his imagination, Quixote is a most unusual knight.

Pronunciation

Cervantes (suhr-VAHN-tayz)

Quixana (kee-HAHN-ah)

Quixote (kee-HOH-tay)

Rocinante (roh-see-NAHN-tay)

Aldonza Lorenzo (ahl-DOHN-zah loh-REHN-zoh)

Dulcinea del Toboso (duhl-see-NAY-ah del toh-BOH-soh)

Señor Castellano (seh-NYOR cahs-tay-YAHN-oh)

Vocabulary

You will find these words in today's reading.

breeches: (n.) short pants reaching to just below the knee
Before an important riding competition, Jane made sure to feed her horse his favorite meal and to wear her lucky *breeches*.

chivalry: (n.) the system of customs and qualities that characterized the ideal knight in the Middle Ages
For his test on medieval history, Edward had to read several articles on the importance of the code of *chivalry* that knights were supposed to follow.

steed: (n.) horse
The brave, young prince mounted his *steed* and galloped off to lead his troops into battle.

garret: (n.) a sparsely decorated room, usually just under the roof of a home
The poor young artist lived simply in a *garret* she rented for little money in a Paris home.

homage: (n.) an expression of respect; a tribute
The retiring athlete paid *homage* to her parents and to the coaches who taught her the game.

swineherd: (n.) one who tends to pigs or boars
While walking along the lonely country road, Stephen came across a *swineherd* bringing his flock of pigs to market.

alighting: (v.) stepping down off of something; dismounting
Alighting from a city bus before it reaches a complete stop can be dangerous.

boon: (n.) a fortunate occurrence; a blessing
The rainy week was a *boon* to farmers whose crops were in danger of drying out.

valorous: (adj.) brave; valiant
The wounded soldier received a medal for his *valorous* conduct during the war.

doleful: (adj.) sad
The loss of a loved one is always a *doleful* experience.

base: (adj.) inferior; low
The rude comedian's act was filled with *base* jokes and insulting humor.

churl: (n.) a low-class individual; a rude person
By acting like a *churl*, the wedding guest ensured that he would not be invited to any future family functions.

Think Ahead

1. Miguel de Cervantes was born in 1547 near Madrid, Spain. Cervantes joined the army and fought in several important battles in the 1570s. From 1575 to 1580, Cervantes was held prisoner by pirates who sought a ransom from his family. After his release, Cervantes returned to Madrid where he married and began to write. The first part of *Don Quixote* appeared in 1605. The novel was wildly popular and made Cervantes famous. He published the second part of *Don Quixote* 10 years later.

2. Chivalry is the code of conduct that knights lived by. Knights were honorable and brave men who did noble deeds in the name of a lady. What do you know about knights?

3. Do you remember reading "St. George and the Dragon"? What did you learn about knights and their behavior from that story?

4. When is it good to use one's imagination? Is it ever not good?

Read

Chapters 1-3 of *Don Quixote,* pages 4-27

Questions

Answer the following questions in complete sentences in your Reading Notebook.

1. At the beginning of the story, how does Mr. Quixana spend his days?
2. Who is Dulcinea del Toboso?
3. Where is the first place Don Quixote stops after he leaves home?
4. What does the innkeeper do for Don Quixote?
5. In Chapter 3, why is the farmer whipping his servant?
6. Describe how Don Quixote handles the situation with the farmer.

Discuss

1. Why do you think the tales of knights appeal to Mr. Quixana? Why does he admire the knights?
2. Does Don Quixote act like a knight? Why or why not?
3. How would you describe Don Quixote? Use details from the story to support your answer.

Interview: Part 1

There is more than one way to look at any situation. It all depends on your *perspective*—on how you see and think about the situation. Mr. Quixana sees himself as a knight on a noble quest for his lady, Dulcinea. But the other characters in this story have a different perspective on Don Quixote. How does Don Quixote appear to them? Remember that even when Don Quixote does something that appears foolish, he has noble reasons for his action. And, he continues to do nice things for the other characters in the story. Answer the questions on the Interview: Part 1 page.

Visualize It

The author of *Don Quixote* includes a lot of description in the story. Review the descriptions of Don Quixote and Rocinante on pages 7 and 8. Draw a picture of Don Quixote and his horse that includes the details that you have read. Then consider how Don Quixote's imagination differs from his reality. If you like, you may draw another picture of Don Quixote the way he sees himself. Save your picture for the next lesson.

Name _____   Date _____

Interview: Part 1

Imagine that you are a character in Don Quixote's story.
In complete sentences, answer the questions
below from that character's perspective.

Your character: _____

1. How do you know Don Quixote?

_____

_____

_____

2. How would you describe Don Quixote?

_____

_____

_____

3. Briefly tell about a recent encounter you had with Don Quixote.

_____

_____

_____

Interview: Part 1

4. Describe at least one positive thing you have seen Don Quixote do. Explain why you believe he did this. (You may say more than one positive thing if you like.)

_____

_____

_____

_____

_____

_____

_____

Guidelines for Peer Discussion

Share your thoughts, ideas, questions, and feelings about a text with a peer or others. Listen carefully to what everyone has to say about the text. During your discussion, follow these guidelines.

1. Be prepared to discuss what you think about the text. You should have already read the assignment. Come prepared to discuss your ideas and use examples from the text to support your thoughts and answers.

2. You will be asked questions about the text. Be ready to answer them, and bring some questions of your own to ask others, such as:

   "Who was your favorite character? Why?"

   "What was your favorite part of the text? Why?"

   "What fact did you enjoy learning? Why do you find this fact interesting?"

   "What question would you ask if you had the chance to meet the author?"

3. Listen if it's not your turn to speak. Pay attention to what others say so that you can add your ideas. Speak clearly and in complete sentences.

4. If you don't understand what someone says, ask a question.

   "What do you mean when you say . . . ?"

   "Can you give an example of . . . ?"

5. If you don't agree with what someone says, explain why.

   "I don't agree with that because . . . "

6. Keep discussions positive! You can disagree, but don't argue. Be respectful.

Name _____   Date _____

Don Quixote: Chapters 4-6

Don Quixote has been dubbed a knight and has started his quest to fight injustice. How will the people react to Don Quixote as he searches for adventure?

Vocabulary

You will find these words in today's reading.

plight: (n.) an unfortunate situation
The concerned celebrity helped to draw attention to the *plight* of people living in regions with poor medical care.

pluck: (n.) willingness to struggle against the odds; admirable determination
In the championship game, the underdog team won over the crowd with their tremendous *pluck.*

halter: (n.) a rope used to tie or lead an animal
Donna led the stubborn horse out of the barn by the *halter.*

curate: (n.) a member of the clergy
When he had a problem, Stephen felt comfortable turning to the town *curate* for advice.

fortitude: (n.) strength
Completing a marathon requires equal parts mental *fortitude* and physical strength.

notorious: (adj.) generally known and talked about in an unfavorable way
After the highly publicized trial, the defendant was *notorious,* even though he was found not guilty of the crime.

squire: (n.) a knight's servant

Lancelot, Gawaine, and other knights of King Arthur's Round Table traveled with *squires* who were their servants.

Think Ahead

1. Summarize the main points from the first three chapters of *Don Quixote.* Include the following in your summary:
   - How Don Quixote acts before he decides to become a knight
   - How his friends and family react to his decision
   - What Don Quixote looks like
   - The encounters he has with other people in Chapters 1-3

2. Would it be a good idea to keep Don Quixote from his books? Why or why not?

3. What is a sidekick? Would a sidekick be useful to Don Quixote?

4. What does a squire do for a knight?

Read

Chapters 4-6 of *Don Quixote*, pages 27-40

Questions

Answer the following questions in complete sentences in your Reading Notebook.

1. What does Don Quixote do when he sees the merchants?
2. How do the merchants treat Don Quixote?
3. Describe the encounter between the plowman and Don Quixote.
4. Why do Don Quixote's friends board up his library?
5. Who is Freston?
6. What does Don Quixote promise to Sancho Panza in return for Sancho's services?

Discuss

1. After Don Quixote falls off of his horse, Cervantes writes that the merchants were amused: "His sorry plight amused them no less than his wonderful pluck." Why is Don Quixote's pluck an important part of his personality? How does his pluck affect the way other characters see him?

2. Why do Don Quixote's niece and housekeeper tell him that an enchanter has made his books and library disappear? Are they being cruel or kind to him? Use examples from the text to support your answer.

3. Describe Sancho Panza using examples from the text.

Interview: Part 2

Choose another character from today's chapters and complete an interview from his perspective. You may select one of the merchants or the plowman whom Don Quixote meets in Chapter 4. Save this page for a later lesson.

Focus on Language: Quixotic

Sometimes, a character or a work of literature has such a strong effect on society that the ideas it stands for become part of our language. This is the case with Don Quixote. His character inspired the word *quixotic.* What ideas do you think Don Quixote represents? Think about this before looking up the word *quixotic* in your dictionary. Were you right?

Name _____ Date _____

Interview: Part 2

Imagine that you are one of the merchants or the plowman whom Don Quixote meets in Chapter 4. In complete sentences, answer the questions below from that character's perspective.

Your character: _____

1. How do you know Don Quixote?

_____

_____

_____

2. How would you describe Don Quixote?

_____

_____

_____

3. Briefly tell about a recent encounter you had with Don Quixote.

_____

_____

_____

_____

Interview: Part 2

4. Describe at least one positive thing you have seen Don Quixote do. Explain why you believe he did this. (You may say more than one positive thing if you like.)

_____

_____

_____

_____

_____

_____

_____

Name _____ Date _____

Don Quixote: Chapters 7-9

Don Quixote has fallen on some hard times, but he manages to rebound quickly. With his new squire, Sancho Panza, he bravely rides out again in search of adventure and to stand up for the oppressed. Will they free the unfairly imprisoned? Or will the dangers of the real world again land Don Quixote in trouble?

Pronunciation
Montiel (mahn-TYEL)
Sierra Morena (SYER-rah moh-RAY-nah)
Gines de Passamonte (hee-NAYS day pah-sah-MOHN-tay)

Vocabulary
You will find these words in today's reading.

gaunt: (adj.) excessively skinny to the point of being unhealthy
After being lost in the woods for six days, John returned to his family looking *gaunt* and feeling exhausted.

beseech: (v.) to beg or ask for earnestly
"I *beseech* you," cried the woman to the judge. "Please don't send my son to jail."

galleys: (n.) oar-propelled war ships that prisoners were often sentenced to work on
During the Middle Ages, prisoners sentenced to the *galleys* worked terribly hard on these ships.

rogues: (n.) scoundrels, criminals
The band of *rogues* traveled the countryside, bringing trouble and destruction with them wherever they went.

toiling: (v.) working extremely hard
After he retired, the old man would often think about the years he spent *toiling* in the coal mines.

routed: (v.) decisively defeated
The Eagles kicked off the season with a bang when they *routed* the Cowboys.

hastened: (v.) moved quickly
During the scavenger hunt, Melissa's team *hastened* to complete the easy tasks first.

skulk: (v.) to lurk or sneak around as if trying to hide something
The untrustworthy businessman was known to *skulk* around the office, attempting to eavesdrop on the conversations of his coworkers.

tarry: (v.) to delay doing something; to wait or linger
Aunt Polly ordered Tom not to *tarry* because the painting of the fence needed to be finished that day.

pommel: (n.) a knob at the front of a saddle
Kelly lifted the saddle off of her favorite horse by the *pommel*.

stealthily: (adv.) slowly and secretively
The international spy *stealthily* made her way past the security guards and into the office of a high-ranking government official.

ingenuity: (n.) skill or cleverness in inventing something
I didn't have a pattern for the dress I was sewing, but I was able to sketch one out on a paper bag and was very proud of my own *ingenuity*.

Think Ahead

1. Summarize the story so far. Be sure to include:
   - What happens to Don Quixote when he encounters the merchants
   - The role that his imagination plays in the story
   - The local villager whom Quixote chooses as his squire

2. What type of relationship do you expect Don Quixote and Sancho Panza to have?

3. *Idealists* are people who are guided by ideals, or the way they think things should be, rather than the way things are. Idealists tend to place their ideals above practical considerations. How is Don Quixote an idealist? Is Sancho Panza likely to be an idealist?

Read

Chapters 7-9 of *Don Quixote,* pages 40-54

Questions

Answer the following questions in complete sentences in your Reading Notebook.

1. What does Don Quixote see when he looks at the windmills? How does he respond?
2. Why does Don Quixote free the prisoners he meets in Chapter 8?
3. Who is Gines de Passamonte?
4. What does Gines de Passamonte do to Sancho Panza?

Discuss

1. The phrase "tilting at windmills" refers to a trip or a plan that is out of the ordinary and is viewed by most people as foolish or pointless. For instance, if someone is fighting for a cause that seems hopeless, we might say that he is just tilting at windmills. This expression refers to Don Quixote's battle with the windmills. Can you think of a reason when it might be good to go tilting at windmills?

2. Although he goes about it in a funny way, Don Quixote's desire to help the poor and fight injustice is very serious. Don Quixote's idealism is one of the *themes* or big ideas of this story. What other idealistic characters do you know who fight injustice?

3. If Don Quixote is an idealist, how would you describe Sancho Panza? Use examples from the story to support your answer.

4. After the experience with the prisoners, Don Quixote says to Sancho, "There is a proverb I desire you to remember. It is this: One might as well throw water into the sea as to do a kindness to rogues." What does this mean?

Interview: Part 3

Describe another episode in Don Quixote's adventures from the perspective of Gines de Passamonte. Save this page for a later lesson.

Tilting at Windmills

On a separate sheet of paper, draw a windmill. If you are unfamiliar with what windmills look like, find a picture of one in an encyclopedia or on the Internet. When you have finished drawing the windmill, make adjustments to your picture so that the windmill begins to resemble a giant. Feel free to add features to the windmill to make the resemblance stronger. When you are finished, discuss your picture and Don Quixote's quests "tilting at windmills." Do any of his quests seem worthwhile? Why or why not?

Name _____   Date _____

Interview: Part 3

Imagine that you are Gines de Passamonte. In complete sentences, answer the questions below from his perspective.

Your character: Gines de Passamonte

1. How do you know Don Quixote?

_____

_____

_____

2. How would you describe Don Quixote?

_____

_____

_____

3. Briefly tell about a recent encounter you had with Don Quixote.

_____

_____

_____

_____

Interview: Part 3

4. Describe at least one positive thing you have seen Don Quixote do. Explain why you believe he did this. (You may say more than one positive thing if you like.)

_____

_____

_____

_____

_____

_____

_____

_____

Name _____ Date _____

Don Quixote: Chapters 10-12

How will Don Quixote react to his latest setback? Learn how Don Quixote tries to demonstrate his devotion to Dulcinea and how his friends from home find their way back into the story.

Vocabulary

You will find these words in today's reading.

dales: (n.) valleys
Sarah always felt a sense of calm looking out over the hills and *dales* that surrounded her home.

proverbs: (n.) short words of advice or maxims
Proverbs are often used to teach simple, but important lessons.

strew: (v.) to disperse, spread, or scatter
The lazy farmer *strew* seeds across his fields without any real plan or pattern.

malady: (n.) a sickness or a disease
Smallpox was an unfortunate and deadly *malady* that has thankfully now been eliminated from society.

rebuke: (v.) to reprimand or criticize
Eliot's nastiness to his little brother made his mother *rebuke* him often.

victuals : (n.) food
We packed canned goods, dried fruit, and other long lasting *victuals* to bring on our camping trip.

sallying: (v.) setting out; departing
In the famous painting, the brave knight is shown *sallying* forth to defeat the wicked dragon.

idle: (adj.) inactive
At age 80, Charlie insisted that the reason he remained sharp and healthy was that he never sat *idle* for very long.

Think Ahead

1. Summarize the main points of the story so far. Be sure to include:
   - Don Quixote's devotion to Dulcinea
   - The incident with the windmills
   - What happens when Don Quixote helps free several convicted criminals

2. Knights usually dedicate their service to one lady. In Don Quixote's case, that lady is Dulcinea. Aside from performing heroic tasks in her name, what else might Don Quixote do to impress Dulcinea?

Read
Chapters 10-12 of *Don Quixote,* pages 54-67

Questions
Answer the following questions in complete sentences in your Reading Notebook.

1. What does Don Quixote plan to do in the forest to impress Dulcinea?
2. How do the curate and the barber convince Don Quixote to ride with them out of the forest?
3. How does Sancho Panza recover his beloved donkey?
4. Why does Sancho Panza come to see Don Quixote in Chapter 12? How does his niece react?
5. What does Don Quixote tell Sancho Panza in response to the squire's demands?
6. Who encourages Don Quixote to ride out again in Chapter 12?

Discuss

1. Why do you think the curate and the barber wear disguises when they go to find Don Quixote?
2. Are Don Quixote's friends helpful to him or do they make life more difficult for him?
3. Why does Samson Carrasco urge Don Quixote to continue on his quests?

Interview: Part 4

Complete the Interview: Part 4 page. Answer the questions from the perspective of Sancho Panza. Save this page for a later lesson.

Visualize It

How do you think Sancho Panza and Don Quixote look riding together? Draw a picture of them, or add Sancho Panza and his donkey to your drawing of Don Quixote and Rocinante that you completed in the first lesson. Try to capture the personalities and characteristics of both men in your drawing. For example, how would Rocinante look compared to Sancho's donkey? What would each man be wearing as they leave the town? Who would be leading the way?

Name _____ Date _____

Interview: Part 4

Imagine that you are Sancho Panza. In complete sentences, answer the questions below from his perspective.

Your character: Sancho Panza

1. How do you know Don Quixote?

_____

_____

_____

2. How would you describe Don Quixote?

_____

_____

_____

3. Briefly tell about a recent encounter you had with Don Quixote.

_____

_____

_____

_____

Interview: Part 4

4. Describe at least one positive thing you have seen Don Quixote do. Explain why you believe he did this. (You may say more than one positive thing if you like.)

_____

_____

_____

_____

_____

_____

Name _____   Date _____

Don Quixote: Chapters 13-15

What will happen to Don Quixote in the last three chapters of his story? Will he finally meet his beloved Dulcinea? Will his friends and family convince him to stay at home and live quietly? Read on and find out.

Vocabulary
You will find these words in today's reading.

forebodings: (n.) feelings or predictions of negative events to come
Before attempting the dangerous trick, the magician was filled with dark *forebodings*.

palfrey: (n.) a small, saddled horse
The princess looked elegant as she rode into the courtyard atop her prized *palfrey*.

haughtiness: (n.) excessive pride; snobbishness
The arrogant teenager carried himself with such *haughtiness* that his teachers enjoyed teaching him to be humble and modest.

abhor: (v.) to detest or hate
Claire's parents taught her to *abhor* all forms of bigotry and prejudice.

vanquish: (v.) to overcome in battle
The two soldiers faced each other bravely, each with the desire to *vanquish* his opponent.

forfeit: (adj.) lost by an error or taken away
The rules of the game state that your turn is *forfeit* if you roll the dice off the game board.

Think Ahead

1. Summarize of the story of *Don Quixote.* Be sure to include the following main events from the last lesson:
   - Don Quixote's devotion to Dulcinea
   - His attempts to impress her by physically punishing himself
   - The efforts of Quixote's friends and family to get him to give up being a knight

2. What do you think would happen if Don Quixote ever met Dulcinea?

3. Predict how Don Quixote's story will end.

Read

Chapters 13-15 of *Don Quixote,* pages 68-80

Questions

Answer the following questions in complete sentences in your Reading Notebook.

1. Does Sancho Panza bring Dulcinea to Don Quixote? Why or why not?
2. What does the Knight of the White Moon make Don Quixote promise to do?
3. Who is the Knight of the White Moon?
4. What happens to Don Quixote at the end of this story?

Discuss

1. Why does Samson Carrasco confront Don Quixote in Chapter 14?
2. Why do you think Don Quixote's mind clears at the end of the story?
3. How does the last chapter of the story affect the way you view Don Quixote?

Interview: Part 5

For your final interview, pretend that you are Samson Carrasco. Answer the questions from his perspective. Then gather all of your interview pages for the next activity.

Eulogize Don Quixote

A eulogy is a speech that is usually given at a funeral. Eulogies praise a person's life, recount the person's accomplishments, and discuss the positive effect he or she had on other people. Use the interviews you have completed over the course of this unit to help you compose a eulogy for Don Quixote. Be sure to include specific examples from the story that help illustrate Don Quixote's life, his personality, and how other people viewed him. Complete this activity in your Reading Notebook. Then deliver your eulogy aloud.

Name _____   Date _____

Interview: Part 5

Imagine that you are Samson Carrasco. In complete sentences, answer the questions below from
his perspective.

Your character: Samson Carrasco

1. How do you know Don Quixote?

_____

_____

_____

2. How would you describe Don Quixote?

_____

_____

_____

3. Briefly tell about a recent encounter you had with Don Quixote.

_____

_____

_____

Interview: Part 5

4. Describe at least one positive thing you have seen Don Quixote do. Explain why you believe he did this. (You may say more than one positive thing if you like.)

_____

_____

_____

_____

_____

_____

_____

Name _____   Date _____

"The Red-Headed League": Session 1

Having red hair has never caused so much confusion, until
Sherlock Holmes steps in and unravels the mystery.

Vocabulary

You will find these words in today's reading.

intrusion: (n.) an act of coming or going without an invitation
When Mrs. Whaler unexpectedly burst into our living room, she
shouted, "Excuse my *intrusion,* but there's been an accident outside!"

bob: (n.) a nod
My grandpa gave a *bob* of his head to tell me that I had spelled the
word correctly.

deduce: (v.) to use clues to make a specific conclusion
From the mess in the kitchen, Sally *deduced* that her brother
had been cooking, not her mother.

vacancy: (n.) an empty space or position
When my mother got her new job, she filled a *vacancy* in the
accounting office.

dejected: (adj.) sad in spirits
Jerome really wanted to play Romeo in our production of
Romeo and Juliet, so he felt *dejected* when he learned he was
cast as a townsperson.

bashful: (adj.) shy
The little girl felt *bashful* in front of her parents' guests and did
not want to sing the alphabet song for the company.

dissolved: (v.) ended
When we turned 11, we *dissolved* the club we'd had in our
backyard for 5 years because we thought it was for babies.

Think Ahead

1. What do detectives do? What is the root word of *detective?*

2. Sherlock Holmes is a famous detective in literature. He is known for his logic, his deductive reasoning, his pipe, and his deerstalker cap. Do you know anything about Sherlock Holmes? Look at the illustration on page 44.

3. Sherlock Holmes lives at 221B Baker Street in London. There is a Sherlock Holmes museum at the address today! London has been an important city for many centuries. Do you know anything about it? Name three things you know about London, then find the city on a map.

Read

Part 1 of "The Red-Headed League" in *Classics for Young Readers,* Vol. 5B, pages 38-43

Questions

Answer the following questions in complete sentences in your Reading Notebook.

1. Who is Dr. Watson?

2. How does Sherlock Holmes know Jabez Wilson has done manual labor?

3. Why is Mr. Wilson's assistant willing to work for half wages?

4. What is Mr. Wilson's one complaint about his assistant, Vincent Spaulding?

Discuss

1. Does Dr. Watson admire Sherlock Holmes? Use examples from the story to support your answer.

2. Mr. Wilson goes to see Sherlock Holmes to investigate the closing of the Red-Headed League. When Mr. Wilson explains his situation to Sherlock Holmes, the detective says, "I think graver problems hang from it than might at first appear." What does Holmes means?

Facts, Inferences, and Deductions

You know what a *fact* is. It is a piece of information that can be proven. For example, Jabez Wilson has rough hands. Do you remember what an *inference* is? An inference is a general conclusion you draw based on facts and observation. For example, Sherlock Holmes infers that Wilson has been a manual laborer because of his rough hands.

But inferences can be taken one more step—to a deduction. A *deduction* is a specific conclusion based on additional facts and observation. A deduction is the result of a series of logical steps. For example, because Holmes has inferred that Wilson is a manual laborer, Holmes may look for additional clues to deduce the specific work Wilson has done.

Deductive reasoning relies on careful attention to facts and observations. Deductive reasoning is an important tool whether you are reading literature, doing mathematics, or making a decision about which sneakers provide the best quality for the money.

Now you be the detective. Turn to the Facts, Inferences, and Deductions page to work through the logical steps needed to solve a case. Will you arrive at the same conclusion as Sherlock Holmes?

Name _____

Date _____

Facts, Inferences, and Deductions

Think about Part 1 of this story and follow three steps. First, notice important facts in the case. Then make a general inference about the information you have. Finally, make a specific deduction about the information. To illustrate the process, all three steps have been completed for you in the first example. The first two steps are completed in the second example. Complete the rest of the chart. In the last row, write a fact, inference, and deduction of your own.

FACT	INFERENCE	DEDUCTION
Vincent Spaulding frequently goes to the cellar to develop photographs.	He loves photography. He wants to be alone.	He might not be developing photography in the cellar.
Mr. Ross stares at Wilson's hair and then gives him the job at the Red-Headed League.	Mr. Ross recognizes Mr. Wilson.	
Mr. Wilson's job requires that he leave his office for 4 hours a day.		
The Red-Headed League is dissolved.		
Sherlock Holmes asks if Spaulding has pierced ears.		

Guidelines for Peer Discussion

Share your thoughts, ideas, questions, and feelings about a text with a peer or others. Listen carefully to what everyone has to say about the text. During your discussion, follow these guidelines.

1. Be prepared to discuss what you think about the text. You should have already read the assignment. Come prepared to discuss your ideas and use examples from the text to support your thoughts and answers.

2. You will be asked questions about the text. Be ready to answer them, and bring some questions of your own to ask others, such as:

   "Who was your favorite character? Why?"

   "What was your favorite part of the text? Why?"

   "What fact did you enjoy learning? Why do you find this fact interesting?"

   "What question would you ask if you had the chance to meet the author?"

3. Listen if it's not your turn to speak. Pay attention to what others say so that you can add your ideas. Speak clearly and in complete sentences.

4. If you don't understand what someone says, ask a question.

   "What do you mean when you say . . . ?"

   "Can you give an example of . . . ?"

5. If you don't agree with what someone says, explain why.

   "I don't agree with that because . . . "

6. Keep discussions positive! You can disagree, but don't argue. Be respectful.

Name _____ Date _____

"The Red-Headed League": Session 2

Does Sherlock Holmes know what he is doing? Will he explain why Wilson lost his position with the Red-Headed League?

Vocabulary
You will find these words in today's reading.

dingy: (adj.) dirty and run-down
The white sweater Janine got for Christmas last year is already getting *dingy;* it looks almost gray.

vault: (n.) a large space used for keeping something secure
Because they are so rare and valuable, some of the ancient Egyptian texts had to be kept in a *vault* rather than displayed.

vulnerable: (adj.) open to attack or damage
We didn't want to build our house too close to the river because we were afraid that we would be *vulnerable* to flood damage.

expedition: (n.) an outing or trip with a purpose
Mountain climbers go on *expeditions* to climb to new heights.

perched: (v.) sat on gently
My aunt had so many flowers in her hospital room that I *perched* on the end of her bed to keep from knocking anything over.

Think Ahead
1. Summarize the story so far.
2. Whom do you trust in the story at this point? Explain your answer.

Read
Parts 2 and 3 of "The Red-Headed League" in *Classics for Young Readers,* Vol. 5B, pages 43–50

Questions

Answer the following questions in complete sentences in your Reading Notebook.

1. Why does Sherlock Holmes want to see the knees of the pants that Wilson's assistant wears?
2. Why does Sherlock Holmes tap on the pavement and floor?
3. Why do John Clay and his partner create the Red-Headed League?
4. Why is Saturday the best day for breaking into the bank?

Discuss

1. Sherlock Holmes asks Watson to bring his revolver to their 10 o'clock meeting. Why do you think he does this? Use your deductive reasoning skills to determine what Holmes thinks will happen.

2. *Point of view* is the perspective from which a story is told. This story is told from Watson's point of view because he is the narrator. Why is Watson a good narrator for the story?

3. How does Sherlock Holmes treat the criminal? How does he treat the policeman? What does this tell you about Holmes?

Character Studies

We learn about characters by paying attention to what they say and do, and what others say about them. And sometimes, to understand a character, we go beyond the words in the story. We *make inferences.* To make an inference, or *infer,* means to think about the evidence in the story, and then draw conclusions based on that evidence.

Create character studies for Dr. Watson and Sherlock Holmes on the Character Study pages. Think about the characteristics that you have observed and make inferences about the two characters. Then, find examples in the story that support the characteristics that you have chosen. Save these character study pages. You will need them in a later lesson.

Saxe-Coburg Square

Detectives often take careful notes, including diagrams and maps. When Holmes and Watson go to Saxe-Coburg Square, Holmes pays careful attention to the shops.

Now you are going to collect information and complete a map of Saxe-Coburg Square. Turn to the Saxe-Coburg Square page and follow these steps:

1. Turn to page 43 in the story. Reread the paragraph that begins "Holmes and I traveled by Underground…." On page 44, reread the paragraph that begins "'Let me see,' said Holmes, standing at the corner…."

2. On the map, label Saxe-Coburg Square, City and Suburban Bank, and McFarlane's carriage-building shop.

3. With a marker or crayon, draw an X over the most important locations in the story. Discuss why they are important.

Name _____   Date _____

Doctor Watson Character Study

In the left column, record four characteristics or traits you see in Doctor Watson. In the right column, record quotations or details from the text that support the characteristic. Two examples are given. Record four more. You will complete this study in Lesson 4. You will also use this study in a writing assignment in Lesson 6.

Characteristic	Evidence from the Text
polite	"I apologized for my intrusion and was about to leave"
not as observant as Holmes	"I did not gain much from my inspection"

Name

Date

Saxe-Coburg Square

Use the details from your book and the directions on your Student Guide to complete this map of Saxe-Coburg Square.

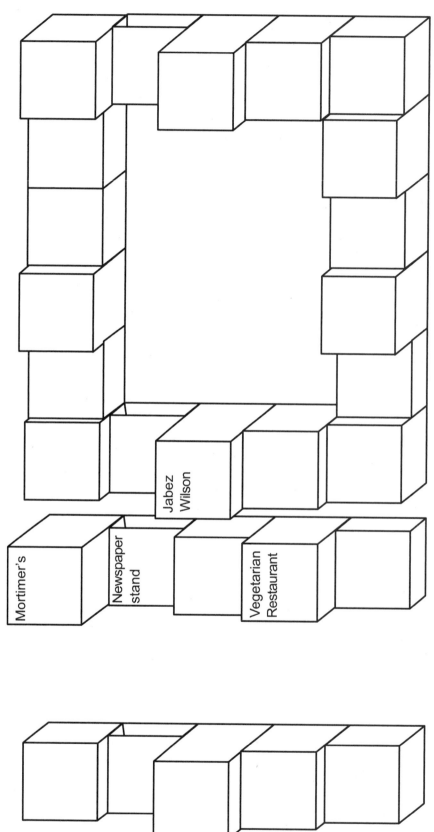

Mortimer's

Newspaper stand

Jabez Wilson

Vegetarian Restaurant

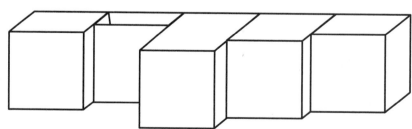

Name _____   Date _____

Sherlock Holmes Character Study

In the left column, record four characteristics or traits you see in Sherlock Holmes. In the right column, record quotations or details from the text that support the characteristic. Two examples are given. Record four more. You will complete this study in Lesson 4. You will also use this study in a writing assignment in Lesson 6.

Characteristic	Evidence from the Text
fond of Doctor Watson	"my dear Watson" "my partner in many of my most successful cases"
very observant	he concludes that Wilson has done manual labor, been to China, and has been writing a lot recently

Name _____   Date _____

"The Adventure of the Blue Carbuncle": Session 1

An unclaimed hat and goose turn out to be worth a lot more than their original owner expected. See how Sherlock Holmes uses these physical clues to solve a new case.

Vocabulary

You will find these words in today's reading.

billycock: (n.) a man's felt hat
The hero in the old movie always wore his *billycock* upon his head when he was tracking the criminals.

grizzled: (adj.) gray
The old *grizzled* horse lived years longer than we expected.

lime-cream: (n.) a hair styling cream with a distinct smell
Mr. Howard walked into the house after his haircut, and his wife laughed and said, "They put *lime-cream* in your hair this time!"

crop: (n.) a part of a bird's neck that stores food
The butcher showed us the *crop* of the turkey he had butchered for us.

carbuncle: (n.) a large jewel
The biggest *carbuncle* I'll ever own is a fake one from the gumball machine.

souvenirs: (n.) reminders or keepsakes
When the Taylors visited the Grand Canyon, the kids bought postcards as *souvenirs*.

Think Ahead
1. Review "The Red-Headed League." What tools does Sherlock Holmes use to solve his crimes?
2. What is a detective story? List three words to describe what you expect from a detective story.

Read
Parts 1 and 2 of "The Adventure of the Blue Carbuncle" in *Classics for Young Readers,* Vol. 5B, pages 51-61.

Questions
Answer the following questions in complete sentences in your Reading Notebook.

1. How does Sherlock Holmes intend to figure out who the owner of the goose is?
2. What shocking thing does Peterson discover in the goose?
3. Why is John Horner being held for the crime?
4. Why is Sherlock Holmes sure that the owner of the hat and goose will respond to the ad in the paper?
5. Why doesn't Henry Baker place an advertisement about his lost things?
6. What does Baker do that proves he was not involved in the crime?
7. Why does Sherlock Holmes want to solve the case about the goose?

Discuss
1. When Watson examines the hat, he says, "I can't see anything." But Holmes says, "…you can see everything…." The men are talking about the same hat. Why do they have different responses?

2. Do you think it is important for Holmes to find the owner of the hat and goose? Explain your answer.

Sensory Writing

Authors often appeal to a reader's five senses. The five senses are sight, sound, smell, touch, and taste. Details that appeal to the senses are called *sensory details.* For example, in "The Adventure of the Blue Carbuncle," Doyle writes about Holmes's "purple dressing gown." This detail appeals to the sense of sight. He also writes "among a pile of crumpled morning newspapers." This detail appeals to the senses of sight *and* sound—can you hear the sound of the newspaper crumpling?

Authors use sensory details to give a reader a more complete picture of the setting and events in a story. Look for sensory details in Parts 1 and 2 of this story and record them on the Sensory Writing page.

Sensing the Solution

Why do you think that sensory details are important in a detective story? How does Sherlock Holmes depend on his senses, particularly sight, to investigate the mystery cases? Look back to the chart you completed on the Sensory Writing page and consider how these details might help Sherlock Holmes make deductions. Discuss your ideas.

Name

Date

Sensory Writing

In the following table record all the sensory details you find in today's reading in the correct column. Several examples are given to spark your thinking and help you find others.

Sight	Sound	Smell	Touch	Taste
purple dressing gown	crumpled morning newspaper		warmed my hands before his crackling fire	
crumpled morning newspaper	warmed my hands before his crackling fire		sharp frost	
old, shabby, black hat			windows thick with ice crystals	
windows thick with ice crystals				

"The Adventure of the Blue Carbuncle": Session 2

Have you ever heard of a *wild goose chase?* Holmes and Watson are certainly on one in this adventure. Will they solve the mystery of the goose?

Vocabulary

You will find these words in today's reading.

nipper: (n.) a young boy
Grandpa O'Leary liked to tell stories about his childhood when he was a mischievous *nipper* in Ireland.

sovereign: (n.) an old gold coin used in Great Britain
In Charles Dickens's novels, the characters pay for things with *sovereigns.*

obstinate: (adj.) stubborn
I tried to retrieve my slipper from the puppy, but it was *obstinate* and would not let go.

hubbub: (n.) noise and confusion
After the accident, there was such a *hubbub* in the street that I couldn't tell what was going on.

quavering: (adj.) trembling
Annabelle's *quavering* voice and knocking knees told me that she was nervous.

bulged: (adj.) jutted out; swelled
The little girl was so astonished by the magician's show that her eyes grew wide and *bulged* out.

parched: (adj.) dry

After gardening in the very hot weather, my throat was terribly *parched* and I needed a glass of water.

Think Ahead

1. Summarize the story so far.
2. What facts about the goose does Sherlock Holmes know so far?
3. Predict a solution to the case.

Read

Parts 3 and 4 of "The Adventure of the Blue Carbuncle" in *Classics for Young Readers,* Vol. 5B, pages 61-68

Questions

Answer the following questions in complete sentences in your Reading Notebook.

1. Why is Breckinridge furious when Holmes asks him where the geese are from?
2. Why does Holmes make a bet that the goose is country-bred?
3. Why does Holmes believe Breckinridge will respond to the bet?
4. What does Holmes mean when he says, "You know, it laid an egg after it was dead—the prettiest, brightest little blue egg ever seen"?
5. How does the goose end up with Henry Baker?

Discuss

1. Explain how Sherlock Holmes gets the Breckinridge salesman to tell him where the geese are from.
2. Discuss the path of the goose that swallowed the carbuncle. You might want to draw a diagram or flowchart.
3. If Holmes values justice, why does he let James Ryder go free at the end of the story?
4. After he finishes telling his story, James Ryder tells Holmes, "I never even touched the wealth for which I sold my character." What does he mean by this? How does he sell his character?

Character Studies

Now you are going to complete the Sherlock Holmes and Doctor Watson Character Studies you began in Lesson 2. Using new information from "The Adventure of the Blue Carbuncle," add to your list of characteristics. If Holmes or Watson shows a characteristic already on the chart, be sure to add evidence from this story.

When finished, circle the three most important characteristics of each character. You will use these studies for a writing assignment in Lesson 6.

Criminal Treatment

How does Sherlock Holmes treat the criminal in "The Red-Headed League"? How does it differ from the way he treats the criminal in "The Adventure of the Blue Carbuncle"? In your Reading Notebook, write two sentences comparing Holmes's attitude toward these characters.

Name _____ Date _____

"The Real Sherlock Holmes"

Could any real person be as smart as Sherlock Holmes? Read about Sir Arthur Conan Doyle's inspiration for his character.

Vocabulary
You will find these words in today's reading.

deerstalker: (adj.) a hunting cap with a flap on the front and back
The hunters gathered their rifles and their *deerstalker* hats before leaving on the Thanksgiving hunt.

Freemason: (n.) a secret club for grown men
The *Freemasons* meet in the town hall, but nobody knows what they do when they meet.

asthmatic: (adj.) having asthma, which is a disorder that makes breathing difficult and causes coughing and wheezing
Mrs. Pizzler was so *asthmatic* that she could not go to the movies because her coughing distracted the other moviegoers.

romantic: (adj.) marked by imagination and an emotional appeal to what is adventurous, heroic, or idealistic
Billy doesn't really have a good reason for believing that his father is a secret agent; that's just his *romantic* ideas.

Think Ahead
1. Write three sentences describing the fictional Sherlock Holmes.
2. The "real" Sherlock Holmes, Dr. Joseph Bell, was from Edinburgh, Scotland. Find Edinburgh on a map.

Read
"The Real Sherlock Holmes" in *Classics for Young Readers,* Vol. 5B, pages 69-74

Questions
Answer the following questions in complete sentences in your Reading Notebook.

1. What was the relationship between Dr. Joseph Bell and Arthur Conan Doyle?
2. Why did Doyle first write a detective story?
3. List three examples of Dr. Bell's deductive reasoning.

Discuss
1. The author of the article writes "So Conan Doyle invented his scientific detective, Sherlock Holmes." How is Holmes a *scientific detective?* Give examples from any of the readings in this unit.

2. Dr. Bell told his students that if they wanted to be good doctors, they must "learn to use their eyes properly." He told them, "Most people see, but they do not observe." What is the difference between seeing and observing? How did Dr. Bell use his eyes?

Venn Diagram
You have read about Sherlock Holmes and Dr. Joseph Bell. They have some similarities, don't they? But they are not the same person. To think about the ways they are similar as well as different, complete the Venn Diagram page.

Failure of Deductive Reasoning
At the end of "The Real Sherlock Holmes" the author tells us about an incident in which Dr. Bell's deductive reasoning skills fail. Reread that section; it begins "One day he and his pupils…" (page 74). Discuss why his deduction is not accurate. What conclusion can you draw about deductive reasoning? Does it always work? Why or why not?

Name _____

Date _____

Venn Diagram

Under Dr. Bell's name, record characteristics that are his alone. Do the same under Sherlock Holmes. In the section where the two circles overlap, record the characteristics that both men have.

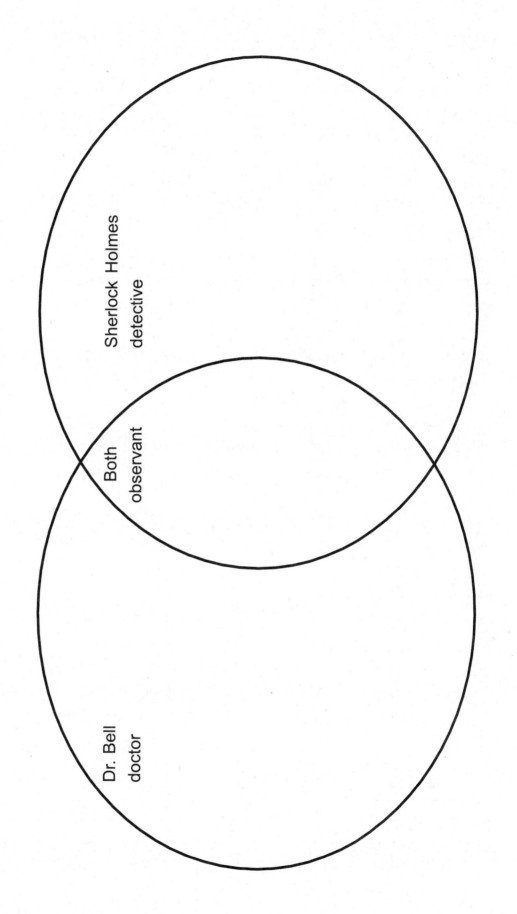

Sherlock Holmes
detective

Both
observant

Dr. Bell
doctor

Name _____   Date _____

Sherlock Holmes and Doctor Watson

In this lesson, you will do several activities to review the plots, deductive reasoning, and characters in "The Red-Headed League" and "The Adventure of the Blue Carbuncle."

Story Timelines

Create a timeline for "The Red-Headed League" and "The Adventure of the Blue Carbuncle," putting key events in order. To start, create a list of the main events in each story.

For example, in "The Red-Headed League" you might start by listing the following:

- Watson goes to Holmes's house.
- Watson meets Mr. Jabez Wilson.
- Wilson tells his story about the Red-Headed League.
- Holmes asks Wilson some questions.

Put the events on a vertical line in the order in which they occur. Do this for both stories.

Marking Deductions

Do you remember the meaning of *deduction?* A deduction is a specific conclusion based on facts and observations. Look back at the timelines you just created for the two stories. Use a marker or crayon to place an X wherever Sherlock Holmes made a deduction. Explain what happened and how he made the deduction.

Complementary Characters

Holmes and Watson make a pretty good team, don't they? They *complement* each other. To complement means to make complete or to be a very good counterpart. Characters who complement each other can share some characteristics, or they may have very different strengths. Look back at the Character Studies you created in Lessons 2 and 4. Review the information you gathered. Notice how the traits of each character are shown through the specific details of the stories.

Now in your Reading Notebook, write a paragraph explaining *how* the two characters complement each other. Be sure to use evidence from the text for support. You probably have most of this material in your Character Studies. Decide how these characters help each other or why they make a good team.

Name _____   Date _____

Native Songs

Today's poems are translations of chants and songs from different Native American peoples. Through chant and song, the people gave thanks, celebrated, laughed, mourned, and passed wisdom from one generation to the next.

First Reading: "Little Puppy"

Vocabulary

You will find these words in today's first reading.

fluted: (adj.) marked by long grooves
The walls of the canyon had become *fluted* by the streams of water wearing away the rock for thousands of years.

hogan: (n.) the traditional house built by the Navajo, usually with six or eight sides, with a frame made of logs and sticks, and covered with mud
The door of a Navajo *hogan* faces east toward the rising sun.

Think Ahead

Today's first poem comes from the Dinè people, also known as the Navajo, of the American Southwest. Look at the map that goes with today's lesson and locate this region.

Read

Read "Little Puppy" (page 146) once silently and a second time aloud.

Discuss

1. Describe the speaker in the poem. What job does he do?
2. Identify words or phrases in the poem that describe the setting.
3. Why do you think the speaker is asking the little puppy to come with him?

Second Reading: "The Grass on the Mountain"

Vocabulary
You will find these words in today's second reading.

mesquite: (n.) a thorny shrub or tree that grows mainly in Mexico and the Southwestern United States
The rattlesnake slept coiled under the *mesquite*.

chia: (n.) a plant whose seeds were part of the diet of some Southwestern Native Americans
You can find seed cakes made of *chia* in some natural food stores today.

Think Ahead
The next poem is told in the voice of one of the Paiute people. On the map, find the region of the Paiute.

Read
Read "The Grass on the Mountain" (page 147) once silently and a second time aloud.

Discuss
1. Describe the setting in the poem. Where does the speaker live? What time of year is it? Identify words in the poem that support your answer.
2. Where have the deer and bighorn sheep gone, and why?
3. Why are the speaker and his people tired of chia seeds, dried deer meat, and the "smoking smell of garments"?
4. What do the speaker and his people long for?
5. What words would you use to describe the tone of this poem?

Third Reading: "A Song of Greatness"

Vocabulary

You will find this word in today's third reading.

esteem: (v.) to think highly of, to respect
The good king was *esteemed* by all the people in his kingdom.

Think Ahead

The next poem is from the Chippewa people. On the map, find the region of the Chippewa.

Many Native Americans honor their ancestors and respect the older members of society. They believe that being old means being wise and being connected to times when great deeds and great heroes were common. Stories of these great deeds and heroes were told and repeated from generation to generation. The next poem from the Chippewa people shows this connection between the old and the young, the past and the future.

Read

Read "A Song of Greatness" (page 148) once silently and a second time aloud.

Discuss

1. Who do you think the "old men" in the poem are? What do they tell stories of?
2. What do the stories told by the old men make the speaker think about himself?
3. The title is "A Song of Greatness." Who or what in the poem is great? Explain your answer.

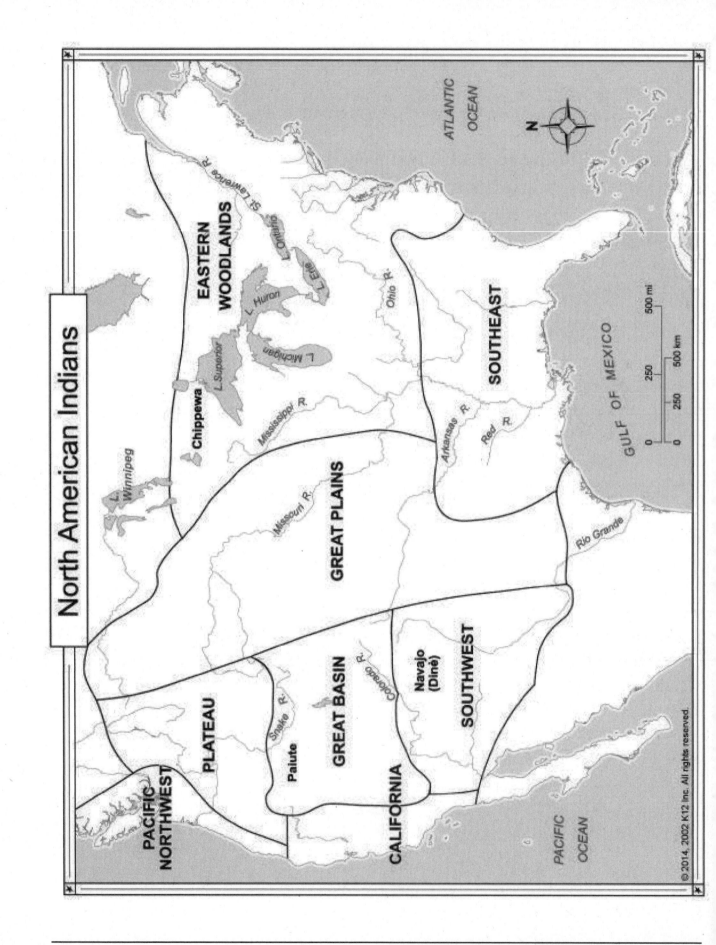

North American Indians

Guidelines for Peer Discussion

Share your thoughts, ideas, questions, and feelings about a text with a peer or others. Listen carefully to what everyone has to say about the text. During your discussion, follow these guidelines.

1. Be prepared to discuss what you think about the text. You should have already read the assignment. Come prepared to discuss your ideas and use examples from the text to support your thoughts and answers.

2. You will be asked questions about the text. Be ready to answer them, and bring some questions of your own to ask others, such as:

   "Who was your favorite character? Why?"

   "What was your favorite part of the text? Why?"

   "What fact did you enjoy learning? Why do you find this fact interesting?"

   "What question would you ask if you had the chance to meet the author?"

3. Listen if it's not your turn to speak. Pay attention to what others say so that you can add your ideas. Speak clearly and in complete sentences.

4. If you don't understand what someone says, ask a question.

   "What do you mean when you say . . . ?"

   "Can you give an example of . . . ?"

5. If you don't agree with what someone says, explain why.

   "I don't agree with that because . . . "

6. Keep discussions positive! You can disagree, but don't argue. Be respectful.

Name _____   Date _____

Patriotic Songs as Poetry

The three selections you'll read today are the first stanzas of songs you have probably sung many times. In History, you might have learned how some of these songs came to be written. Today, you'll examine these songs as poems.

First Reading: "America the Beautiful"

Vocabulary

You will find these words in today's first reading.

spacious: (adj.) vast, extending for a great distance
When we moved from an apartment in the city to a house in the country, our yard seemed *spacious*.

amber: (adj.) a yellow-brownish color
The cat's *amber* eyes shone in the dark.

majesty: (n.) greatness, grandness, splendor
Although the king disguised himself in ragged robes, he could not hide the *majesty* of his character.

Think Ahead

Katherine Lee Bates was born in 1859 in the whaling village of Falmouth, Massachusetts. She grew up to become a professor of literature at a college in Massachusetts.

In 1893, she was invited to teach a summer class in Colorado Springs, at the foothills of the Rocky Mountains. While she was there, she and a group of fellow teachers climbed Pike's Peak. As she stood on Pike's Peak, she looked out at mountains and prairies stretching as far as the eye could see. And it was at this moment, she later wrote, that "the opening lines of the hymn floated into my mind."

The "hymn" is "America the Beautiful." Katherine Lee Bates wrote it as a poem, and a few years later it was set to music.

Read
Read the first stanza of "America the Beautiful" (page 150) once silently and a second time aloud.

Discuss
1. Imagery is language that appeals to the senses, that makes readers see, hear, smell, taste, or feel things in their imagination. The first stanza of "America the Beautiful" appeals most to your sense of sight. On the lines below, write three visual images from the poem.

   _____

   _____

   _____

2. Imagine that you are explaining the song to a younger child. In your own words, tell the child what you think these phrases mean:
   • "purple mountain majesties"
   • "the fruited plain"
   • "crown thy good with brotherhood"

3. What do you think is the main impression about America that the poet is expressing?

Second Reading: "The Star-Spangled Banner"

Vocabulary
You will find these words in today's second reading.

spangle: (v.) to sprinkle with shiny, glittering materials
The modern sculpture was *spangled* with bits of bright metal and colored glass.

hail: (v.) to salute, to greet or welcome enthusiastically
As the popular president entered the room, the crowd *hailed* him with cheers and applause.

perilous: (adj.) dangerous, risky
Although it was a *perilous* task from which he might not return alive, the brave knight did not hesitate to undertake it.

rampart: (n.) a wall-like barrier, usually of raised earth or rock, built to protect a town or fort
The invaders could not get past the *ramparts* that surrounded the castle.

gallantly: (adv.) in a splendid, spirited, noble manner
With their heads held high, the show horses trotted *gallantly* into the ring.

Think Ahead
In your History studies, you might have learned the story behind the national anthem of the United States.

It was September of 1814. From a ship anchored in the Baltimore harbor, a young American lawyer, Francis Scott Key, watched anxiously as British ships opened fire on Fort McHenry, which guarded the city of Baltimore. The British bombarded the fort, and the cannons of the fort fired back. The night sky glowed with the red glare of the bursting bombs.

When dawn broke, Key and his companions strained to see through the smoke and morning fog. Then they saw it—the American flag, still waving over the walls of Fort McHenry. The British attack had failed.

As the British fleet sailed away, Key rushed to write down the words of a poem that filled his heart. Within weeks, this poem, called "Bombardment of Fort McHenry," appeared in many American newspapers.

Before long, Americans were proudly singing the poem to the tune of a popular melody. In 1931, the United States officially adopted the poem, now called "The Star-Spangled Banner," as our national anthem.

Read

Read the first stanza of "The Star-Spangled Banner" (page 150) once silently and a second time aloud.

Discuss

1. Look again at the first two lines of the poem. In those lines, to whom is the speaker speaking? In your own words, what is he asking?

2. The first two lines ask a question. Imagine they were written instead as a statement; for example:

   O look, where I see, by the dawn's early light,
   That which proudly we hailed at the twilight's last gleaming.

   Compare that with the real opening lines:

   O say, can you see, by the dawn's early light,
   What so proudly we hailed at the twilight's last gleaming?

   What difference does it make that the real opening lines are written as a *question* directed to *you?*

3. The poem uses imagery to help us imagine the scene. Identify two examples of imagery that appeal to sight, and one that appeals to hearing:

sight: _____

sight: _____

hearing: _____

4. Recall the historical facts behind the poem. The flag the speaker is so anxious to see flies over Fort McHenry in Baltimore, Maryland. But in the last two lines of the stanza, the speaker does not mention any specific fort, city, or state. Instead, he asks:

O say, does that Star-Spangled Banner yet wave
O'er the land of the free and the home of the brave?

What difference does it make that the speaker does not refer to a specific location but instead to "the land of the free and the home of the brave"? How does that change the significance of the flag?

5. In the blank below, write the rhyme scheme of the stanza:

_____

Third Reading: "This Land Is Your Land"

Think Ahead
"This Land Is Your Land" is probably the best known of the more than 1,000 songs written by the American folk singer and composer, Woody Guthrie (1912-1967).

Before you read, gather a map of the United States.

Read
Read "This Land Is Your Land" (page 149) once silently and a second time aloud.

Discuss
1. Identify the metaphor in the first line:

   _____ = _____

2. Read through the verse, beginning with "This land is your land…." As you read, pause to locate each of the following on your map of the United States:
   - California
   - the "New York island" (that is, Manhattan Island)
   - where the "redwood forest" grows (in northern California and into Oregon)
   - the "Gulf Stream waters" (the warm ocean current that flows from the Gulf of Mexico, around the southern tip of Florida, and up the southeastern coast of the United States)

   Read the lines again, and this time point to each of the four locations as you name each one. Describe the movement your finger is making on the map. Why do you think the song names these places?

3. If you say, "This is my book," then you express ownership—the book belongs to you. The song says, "This land is your land, this land is my land." But neither you nor I *own* this land. In what sense is this land "yours" and "mine"?

4. In a work of literature, a *theme* is the big, important idea, the message the writer is trying to communicate. In your own words, what is the theme of "This Land Is Your Land"?

Activity

Sing Out
If you haven't already sung today's readings, go ahead and sing them now!

Name _____   Date _____

Three Portraits

Today's poems present figures from American history who have become almost legendary: Christopher Columbus, George Washington, and Abraham Lincoln.

First Reading: "Columbus"

Vocabulary

You will find these words in today's first reading.

mutinous: (adj., from the noun *mutiny*) being a part of a rebellion, trying to overthrow those who are in charge
The *mutinous* sailors captured the captain and tied him to the mast.

wan: (adj.) feeble, sickly, weak, pale from sickness
When she spent weeks in bed with the flu, Sally became *wan* and thin.

swarthy: (adj.) having a dark facial appearance
After spending hours working at the smoky forge, the blacksmith looked sweaty and *swarthy.*

naught: (n., pron.) an old-fashioned word meaning "nothing at all"
We have tried and tried, but all our efforts have come to *naught.*

blanch: (v.) to remove the color from; to grow pale or white
Even a fly scares Mindy, so when she saw the big spider climbing the wall, her face *blanched.*

unfurl: (v.) to open; to unroll
The messenger stood before the crowd, *unfurled* the rolled parchment, and read an announcement from the king.

Think Ahead

When you were little, perhaps you learned this rhyme: "In fourteen-hundred ninety-two, Columbus sailed the ocean blue." Unlike that simple rhyme, the real story of Columbus is more complex. Part of his story is heroic and inspiring, but another part is dark and sad, especially from the perspective of the native peoples in the lands Columbus found.

While the historical facts about Columbus are complicated, there is no doubt he has become an almost legendary figure. He boldly sailed across unknown seas, encountered a new world, and changed the course of history. This heroic figure is the Columbus celebrated in today's first poem.

Before you read, find the following on a world map or globe:
- The Azores: a chain of islands off the coast of Portugal
- The Gates of Hercules: rocks that frame the east entrance of the Straits of Gibraltar

Read

Read "Columbus" (page 151) once silently and a second time aloud.

Discuss

1. Two characters speak in this poem. In the blanks below, identify each speaker:

   _____

   _____

2. *Characterization* is the way in which a writer reveals what a character is like, for example, through the character's appearance, or through what he or she says and does. In this poem, each speaker is characterized mainly by what he says.

How is the mate characterized by what he says? Go back and read the words he speaks and then describe him on the lines below:

_____

_____

3. The "brave Admiral," Columbus, repeatedly says "Sail on!" How do these words characterize him?

_____

_____

4. At one point, the mate uses figurative language to describe the sea:
    "This mad sea shows his teeth tonight.
   He curls his lip, he lies in wait,
      With lifted teeth, as if to bite!"

   What kind of figurative language is the mate using? Explain your answer.

5. What kind of figurative language does the poet use when he says that Columbus's "words leapt like a leaping sword"? Explain your answer.

6. The poet says that Columbus gave the new world "its grandest lesson: 'On! sail on!'" In your own words, explain that "lesson."

Second Reading: "George Washington"

Vocabulary
You will find these words in today's second reading.

tar: (n.) a slang word for "sailor"
"Aye, mateys," said the old sailor, "the life of a jolly *tar* is full of adventure."

aghast: (adj.) horrified, shocked
My mother was *aghast* when she saw the huge blueberry stain on the new white carpet.

shin: (v.) to climb up something by hugging it with arms and legs
As part of their training, the soldiers had to *shin* up a tall pole.

staid: (adj.) serious
In London, the *staid* guards in front of Buckingham Palace never smile at tourists.

renown: (n.) the state of being widely known and honored
The poet won many prizes and gained great *renown.*

specimen: (n.) an individual or part that is typical of a whole group
The scientist showed us the finest *specimen* in his collection of fossils.

Think Ahead

Can you recall two facts about George Washington?

George Washington was perhaps the most respected and beloved of all the "founding fathers." When the American Revolution ended and the United States gained its independence, there were some people in the new nation who wanted to make Washington our first *king!* Think how very different many things might now be if Washington had decided to rule as a king.

In the next poem, you will hear two different voices. One voice is indicated by *italics.* The other voice responds to what the first voice says.

Read

Read "George Washington" (page 153) once silently and a second time aloud.

424

Discuss

1. In each of the first three stanzas, the first voice (in *italics*) describes what George Washington *might* have become, while the second voice describes what happened instead. In the chart below, briefly summarize the contrasts in the second and third stanzas. (The contrast in the first stanza has been filled in for you.)

Stanza Number	What he *might* have become	What happened instead
1	a famous British admiral, sailing the seas for King George	George's mother was very upset and did not want him to go to sea, so he remained at home.
2		
3		

2. What picture of the "real" George Washington emerges from this poem? What adjectives would you use to describe him?

3. The final stanza of the poem expresses an important theme in these lines:

> But, when you think about him now,
> From here to Valley Forge,
> Remember this—he might have been
> A highly different specimen,
> And, where on earth would we be, then?
> I'm glad that George was George.

In your own words, explain the theme expressed in those lines.

Third Reading: "Abraham Lincoln"

Vocabulary

You will find these words in today's third reading.

gait: (n.) a way of walking
He walked with a steady, even *gait.*

toil: (n.) hard work; (v.) to work hard and long
At harvest time, a farmer's days are filled with *toil* as he works
to bring in the crops before the first frost.

Think Ahead

There are certain historical facts that you probably remember
about Abraham Lincoln. Can you recall two facts about him?
Beyond these facts, you probably have a mental *image* of Lincoln.
When you think of him, what picture comes to mind?

As you read the next poem, think about how the poet
characterizes Abraham Lincoln. Notice the ways she reveals what
Lincoln was like, for example, through his appearance, through
what he does, and through what others say about him.

Read

Read "Abraham Lincoln" (page 155) once silently and a second
time aloud.

Discuss

1. Identify words and phrases in the poem that describe Lincoln's
   appearance.

2. How does the poet describe Lincoln's background? Identify
   words and phrases in the poem that tell where he came from
   and what he did before he became president.

3. Every stanza begins with the same word: "Remember." In your own words, briefly summarize what you think the poet *most* wants us to remember about Abraham Lincoln.

_____

_____

_____

Optional Activities

Say It with Feeling!

Do a dramatic reading of either "Columbus" or "George Washington."

To prepare for "Columbus," think about how Columbus and the mate are characterized. How will you sound when you read the words spoken by the mate? What kind of voice will you use for Columbus's repeated words ("Sail on!")?

For "George Washington," think about how you should say lines in *italics* and how you should change your tone and voice for the other lines. You might want to have a partner join you for performing this poem: One of you can read the lines in italics, and the other can read the remaining lines.

For an extra challenge, memorize and recite one or more stanzas of either poem.

Portrait of a Hero

Write your own poem about a hero you admire. Follow the steps on the Portrait of a Hero page.

Name _____   Date _____

Portrait of a Hero

Write your own poem about a present-day hero.

A. First, choose your hero. Your hero can be a famous person or someone you look upon as a personal hero.

_____

B. What has this person accomplished that makes him or her a hero in your eyes?

_____

_____

_____

C. Make a list of words or phrases that describe your hero. Include one simile and one metaphor.

_____

_____

_____

Simile: _____

Metaphor: _____

D. What is the main impression that you want the reader of your poem to remember about your hero?

_____

Portrait of a Hero

E. Reread your responses to the previous questions. Keeping the main impression in mind, select words and phrases and arrange them into lines and stanzas to create your poem. Your poem does not have to rhyme.

_____

_____

_____

_____

_____

_____

_____

_____

_____

Name _____   Date _____

The Varied Carols I Hear

On many United States coins, you will find this motto: *e pluribus unum.* Those Latin words mean "one out of many." They express the idea that America is one nation of many diverse people, an idea at the heart of today's poems.

First Reading: "I Hear America Singing"

Vocabulary

You will find these words in today's first reading.

blithe: (adj.) carefree, happy
Singing a *blithe* song, the children merrily skipped along.

robust: (adj.) full of strength, health, energy
Ever since he started exercising regularly, Dan has been feeling *robust.*

Think Ahead

In 1855, Walt Whitman, a poet whom no one had ever heard of before, published a slender volume of poems called *Leaves of Grass.* Few people read the poems. Of those who did, many were puzzled or even offended. "These poems do not rhyme," they said. "They are not about polite subjects."

But one of the greatest and most respected writers of the time, Ralph Waldo Emerson, recognized the genius of Walt Whitman's work. In a letter to Whitman, he said, "I greet you at the beginning of a great career."

Walt Whitman is now recognized as an original and important voice in American poetry. He wrote most of his poetry as *free verse*—the lines vary in length, and they do not rhyme. Some say that the freedom of Whitman's verse reflects the freedom of the American spirit.

Read

Read "I Hear America Singing" (page 156) once silently and a second time aloud.

Discuss

1. Who are the people that the speaker hears singing? What do these people have in common?

2. What do you think the speaker means when he says that he hears "each singing what belongs to him or her and to none else"?

3. What words would you use to describe the tone of the poem?

4. Identify three adjectives that describe the singing or songs that the speaker hears.

   _____   _____   _____

5. What picture of America is painted by the poem?

Second Reading: "I, Too"

Think Ahead

Langston Hughes was an African American poet who lived from 1902 to 1967. In the next poem you will read, Langston Hughes echoes Walt Whitman's idea of "America singing," but adds something new to it.

Read
Read "I, Too" (page 157) once silently and a second time aloud.

Discuss
1. Who is the speaker in this poem?

2. How does the speaker respond when "they send [him] to eat in the kitchen"? What does he say will happen "tomorrow"?

3. The speaker says, "I, too, sing America," and "I, too, am America." These statements suggest that the speaker is not just one particular person, but that he is a *symbol* of many people— he stands for them and represents them. How is the speaker's situation symbolic of the situation of other people in America?

Third Reading: "The New Colossus"

Vocabulary
You will find these words in today's third reading.

brazen: (adj.) (1) made of brass; *or*, (2) boldly scornful
(1) The sculptor made a *brazen* statue of a cat. (2) The *brazen* child tipped his plate of spinach onto the floor right in front of his mother's eyes.

astride: (adv.) with legs spread on either side of something
The lumberjack sat *astride* the log as it drifted down the river.

exiles: (n.) people who are forced to leave their home country
During World War II, many *exiles* from Europe came to America.

pomp: (n.) a fancy show of wealth or power
The king was crowned in a ceremony of great *pomp*.

huddle: (v.) to crowd together
The puppies in the basket *huddled* against their mother.

wretched: (adj.) miserable
The boy felt *wretched* when he realized he had lost his grandfather's valuable pocketwatch.

refuse (REH-fyoos): (n.) useless items thrown away
Each week the garbage men collect the *refuse* from the dumpsters in the city.

teeming: (adj.) filled with or bearing life
The boy pulled one fish after another out of the *teeming* stream.

tempest-tost: a poetic expression meaning "thrown about by a storm"

Think Ahead

In a recent lesson, you read about the Statue of Liberty. Since 1886, when construction was completed, the Statue has stood proudly in New York Harbor, greeting millions of immigrants to America.

The poem you are about to read was written by Emma Lazarus to help raise money to build a pedestal for the Statue of Liberty. The poem is now engraved on a plaque at the base of the statue.

Emma Lazarus's poem compares the Statue of Liberty to an ancient statue, the Colossus of Rhodes, built by the Greeks more than 2,000 years ago. The Greeks erected this gigantic bronze statue after they had won an important victory. The Colossus stood at the entrance to a harbor. Legend says that the statue stood astride the harbor, and that ships passed between its legs. In fact, the Colossus stood on a hill overlooking the harbor. Even so, it was an impressive figure, meant to make visitors see the Greeks as strong and powerful.

Read

Read "The New Colossus" (page 158) once silently and a second time aloud.

Discuss

1. The poem opens with a contrast: the "New Colossus," our Statue of Liberty, is "not like the brazen giant of Greek fame." This contrast begins with appearance. The ancient Greek Colossus was a "brazen giant" with "conquering limbs." Identify specific words and phrases in the poem that describe the appearance of the Statue of Liberty, and write them on the lines below:

   _____

   _____

2. The poet has the Statue of Liberty say these words: "I lift my lamp beside the golden door." The lamp is the torch held high in one of the Statue's hands. The poet turns the torch into a symbol: "From her beacon-hand glows world-wide welcome." What do you think the torch is a symbol of?

3. In ancient Greece, the Colossus of Rhodes was intended to convey a message of the Greeks' strength and power. In contrast, what message does the Statue of Liberty communicate? Pay special attention to the last five lines of the poem.

4. In the final line of the poem, what do you think the "golden door" might be?

Name _____   Date _____

A Ride in the Night

Meet a very brave young boy named Will Clark. As you read about the courage he displayed to help the American cause during the Revolutionary War, think about the problems he faced and how he managed to stay calm in the face of danger.

Vocabulary

You will find these words in today's reading.

ford: (n.) a shallow section of a river that is suitable for crossing
Tom waded across the river at Zuckerman's *ford* and continued on his journey.

yonder: (adv.) indicating the direction of a place that is relatively far away but still within sight
"Once we climb *yonder* hill," Sam said, "we'll have a view of the whole town."

hominy grits: (n.) a hot breakfast side dish of coarse grains that is especially popular in the South
On cold winter mornings, the smell of *hominy grits* and frying bacon made waking up a pleasure for Elizabeth.

mare: (n.) a female horse
The old *mare* spent most of the day eating hay in the field, but she could still gallop quite fast when she wanted to.

stammer: (v.) to struggle and make involuntary stops while speaking
During her job interview, Janice was nervous and *stammered* while giving some of her answers.

shan't: (v.) shall not
"I *shan't* forget this," cried the old man after he was rescued by the brave young knight.

keen: (adj.) eager, sharp, intense
Sylvia listened to the directions that the skydiving instructor gave her with a *keen* ear.

astride: (adv.) a way of sitting with one leg on either side of something
Jason sat *astride* his father's horse and imagined riding off into the sunset.

muzzle: (n.) a covering placed on an animal's mouth to prevent eating or biting
Cara could not walk her pit bull without its *muzzle* for fear that it would bite someone.

briars: (n.) prickly masses of plants and twigs
Doug spent about an hour removing thorns from his legs after getting lost in the woods and wandering through the *briars* to get home.

Think Ahead

1. The Revolutionary War was fought between the 13 American colonies and Great Britain from 1775 to 1781. The first shots were fired at Lexington and Concord, Massachusetts, in 1775. The colonists were fighting for the right to govern themselves and be free from British rule. George Washington was the leading general of the Continental Army. This story takes place in those times.

2. The stories in this unit are about real people who showed great courage when they were still very young. The stories are based on fact; however, they contain parts that are fiction. When real

events from history are mixed with fictional events, we call this type of story *historical fiction*. As you read, see if you can find the facts.

Read

"A Ride in the Night" in *Classics for Young Readers,* Vol. 5B, pages 108-116

Questions

Answer the following questions in complete sentences in your Reading Notebook.

1. Why was John Clark unable to deliver the horses to Coleman?
2. Why did Will and York not immediately rush down to the tavern when they saw it?
3. Who was in the tavern when Will first entered?
4. What lie did Will tell the British soldiers?
5. Who was the innkeeper?

Discuss

1. Have you ever heard the expression, "Think fast on your feet"? What do you think this means? What can someone who can think fast on his or her feet do? How does Will think fast on his feet in this story?

2. What qualities did Will Clark show during his mission that helped him deliver the horses successfully?

3. Why were the British troops quick to dismiss the idea that Will Clark could have been working for the Continental Army?

Conflict and Resolution: Part 1

A *conflict* is a clash or struggle between people, ideas, or feelings. As you read the stories in this unit, you will find that people have different kinds of conflicts.

A person can have a conflict with:

- Another person or group of people. For example, in the story "Don Quixote," Don Quixote has a real conflict with his friends who do not want him to read his books about chivalry and knights. He has imaginary conflicts with Freston and other enemies.

- His or her own thoughts and feelings. For example, in the story "Beauty and the Beast," when the Beast allows Beauty to return to visit her family, Beauty experiences a conflict in her own feelings. Her loyalty to the Beast makes her want to return to him, but her love for her family makes her want to stay with them.

- His or her society or the natural world. For example, in the story "The Tempest" the king and the prince are washed upon on Prospero's island because of a violent storm. They have a conflict with the natural world.

In a story, as in real life, characters usually need to *resolve*, or work out, their conflicts. Resolving conflicts requires courage—the courage to face problems rather than run away from them. Having conflicts with other people is hard, but having conflicts within yourself can be even harder.

In "A Ride in the Night," there are several conflicts that we see. Follow the directions to fill in the Conflict and Resolution: Part 1 page with details from "A Ride in the Night."

Letter of Praise

"I thought it was all over when you walked in on the King's men," said Mr. Coleman. "It wasn't safe for me to give you a signal of any kind. But you played your part well. You're a bright lad—a lad to help build America."

Imagine that you are George Coleman, the innkeeper to whom young Will Clark delivered the horses in 1779. You are impressed by the way the young person handled himself under pressure. Why? What qualities did Will Clark display that impressed you? Write a letter to John and Ann Clark, Will's parents, explaining what you saw Will do and why they should know about it. Be sure to include information about the situation Will was in, what he did, and what might have happened if Will had not acted appropriately. Support your ideas with examples from the text.

Name _____   Date _____

Conflict and Resolution: Part 1

A person can have a conflict with:
- Another person or group of people
- His or her own thoughts and feelings
- His or her society or the natural world

In a story, as in real life, people usually need to *resolve*, or work out, their conflicts.

Answer the questions below on "A Ride in the Night" in complete sentences.

1. Describe the conflict between Will Clark and the British soldier in the tavern.

_____

_____

_____

2. How does Will Clark feel during the conflict with the British soldier in the tavern?

_____

_____

_____

3. What does Will Clark do to resolve the conflict with the British soldier in the tavern?

_____

_____

_____

Conflict and Resolution: Part 1

4. Do you think that Will resolved the conflict in an appropriate way? Why or why not?

_____

_____

_____

5. What could he have done differently? What do you admire about Will's behavior and the way he resolved the conflict?

_____

_____

_____

Guidelines for Peer Discussion

Share your thoughts, ideas, questions, and feelings about a text with a peer or others. Listen carefully to what everyone has to say about the text. During your discussion, follow these guidelines.

1. Be prepared to discuss what you think about the text. You should have already read the assignment. Come prepared to discuss your ideas and use examples from the text to support your thoughts and answers.

2. You will be asked questions about the text. Be ready to answer them, and bring some questions of your own to ask others, such as:

   "Who was your favorite character? Why?"

   "What was your favorite part of the text? Why?"

   "What fact did you enjoy learning? Why do you find this fact interesting?"

   "What question would you ask if you had the chance to meet the author?"

3. Listen if it's not your turn to speak. Pay attention to what others say so that you can add your ideas. Speak clearly and in complete sentences.

4. If you don't understand what someone says, ask a question.

   "What do you mean when you say . . . ?"

   "Can you give an example of . . . ?"

5. If you don't agree with what someone says, explain why.

   "I don't agree with that because . . . "

6. Keep discussions positive! You can disagree, but don't argue. Be respectful.

Name _____ Date _____

"Young Frederick Douglass: The Slave Who Learned to Read"

What is the power of reading? How can an education change a life? What will a person risk to get an education? Witness the answer to these questions as you read about Frederick Douglass, a person whose uncommon bravery changed the direction of his life.

Vocabulary

You will find these words in today's reading.

orator: (n.) an accomplished public speaker
The presidential candidate knew that his skills as an *orator* would be tested each time he stepped up to the microphone to answer a question.

eloquent: (adj.) fluent or smooth while speaking
Though he was not used to making speeches, the young man felt comfortable in front of a crowd and was quite *eloquent*.

dialogue: (n.) a piece of writing in which two or more characters talk to each other
The story about Socrates was written as a *dialogue* between Socrates and his student, Plato.

starboard: (n.) facing forward, the right side of a boat
The ship's captain turned his boat hard to the *starboard* side.

larboard: (n.) facing forward, the left side of a boat; also called the port side
The *larboard* side of the boat needed repairs after it crashed into the dock.

poised: (adj.) balanced and exhibiting self-control
As her country's national anthem was played, the gold medallist remained *poised* and proud.

tarpaulin: (n.) a material such as plastic or rubber that protects exposed areas

As he set out to sea, the sailor put on his *tarpaulin* hat and heavy overcoat.

neckerchief: (n.) a square piece of cloth worn around the neck

When the cold wind blew, Edward was glad to have his *neckerchief* to help keep him warm.

abolitionist: (n.) one who does not support slavery

The diary of the 19th century *abolitionist* offered a fascinating look at the private life of a woman who helped free hundreds of slaves.

integration: (n.) the act of including all different races and religions in every aspect of society on the basis of equality

In the 1950s, the *integration* of public schools was an important goal in the Civil Rights Movement.

Think Ahead

1. Before the Civil War (1861-1865), slavery was legal in several states in America. Millions of African Americans were denied their freedom and were forced to work for the white "masters" who owned them. The work done by slaves ranged from backbreaking farm labor to domestic work to manual labor in towns and large cities. Except in extremely rare cases, slaves were not paid for their work. Also, because slaves were considered property rather than people, they were frequently mistreated and abused.

2. In this story, you will read about one man who was born a slave, but grew up to be a famous orator and writer. Think about slavery and the courage this man must have had as you read about Frederick Douglass.

Read

"Young Frederick Douglass: The Slave Who Learned to Read" in *Classics for Young Readers,* Vol. 5B, pages 117-124

Questions

Answer the following questions in complete sentences in your Reading Notebook.

1. How did Mr. Auld react when his wife told him that Frederick was learning to read?
2. What did the writing contests teach young Frederick?
3. How did Frederick manage to escape slavery?
4. Why did Frederick Douglass go to see an abolitionist after arriving in New York?
5. By the time he died at age 78, what jobs had Frederick Douglass held?

Discuss

1. Why did white slave owners consider it dangerous to educate slaves?
2. Why did Frederick Douglass want to escape? What was he risking by attempting to escape?
3. Why do you think the freed sailor helped Frederick Douglass?

Conflict and Resolution: Part 2

Remember that a conflict is a clash or struggle between people, ideas, or feelings. There are different types of conflicts. A person can have a conflict with another person or group of people, with himself or herself, or with society or the natural world. A person can experience more than one type of conflict at the same time.

Resolving conflicts requires courage—the courage to face problems rather than run away from them. In "Young Frederick Douglass: The Slave Who Learned to Read," there are several conflicts. Fill in the Conflict and Resolution: Part 2 page with details from this story.

Learning to Read

Think about the following excerpt from the story:

> "Mr. Auld sent Frederick out of the room. Then he began
> to lecture his wife. Teaching a slave to read was against
> the law, he told her. A slave who could read would be
> 'spoiled.' He would get ideas. He'd want to write as well,
> and if he could write, there was no telling what mischief
> he'd dream up."

After hearing Mr. Auld say these things to his wife, young Frederick Douglass was determined to learn to read. What were the consequences of this decision? Was Mr. Auld right to be concerned about his wife teaching Frederick to read? In your Reading Notebook, write two paragraphs on what happened as a result of Frederick deciding to learn to read. Use the text to help you find specific examples of how an education changed the course of Frederick Douglass's life.

Name _____   Date _____

Conflict and Resolution: Part 2

A person can have a conflict with:
- Another person or group of people
- His or her own thoughts and feelings
- His or her society or the natural world

In a story, as in real life, people usually need to *resolve*, or work out, their conflicts.

Answer the questions below on "Young Frederick Douglass: The Slave Who Learned to Read" in complete sentences.

1. Describe the conflict between Frederick Douglass and society.

   _____

   _____

   _____

2. What does Frederick Douglass do to resolve the conflict between himself and society?

   _____

   _____

   _____

Conflict and Resolution: Part 2

3. Do you agree with Frederick Douglass's way of resolving the conflict between society and himself? Why or why not?

_____

_____

_____

4. What could he have done differently? What do you admire about his behavior and the way he resolved his conflict?

_____

_____

_____

Name _____   Date _____

"Run, Kate Shelley, Run"

It was a dark and stormy night in Iowa over a hundred years ago when a young girl named Kate Shelley showed the kind of bravery that legends are made of. Learn about Kate Shelley, her courageous deeds, and the consequences of her actions as you read this story. Enjoy!

Vocabulary

You will find these words in today's reading.

bluffs: (n.) steep banks along the side of a river
From high atop her perch on the *bluffs*, Becky liked to watch the river rushing past below.

trestle: (n.) a frame of wood or iron built to support a road or rail bridge
The old *trestle* bridge was rusted and unsafe, so the mayor decided it had to be demolished.

pilings: (n.) columns of wood or iron that are driven into the ground to support weight
The bridge's *pilings* were strong enough to support hundreds of cars at a time.

Think Ahead

1. In the late 1880s, there were no airports or airplanes, no cars or buses. People who wanted to travel long distances in relatively short amounts of time had two choices: they could take a boat or they could take a train. In places like Iowa, where young Kate Shelley lived, geography ruled out boat travel. So trains were extremely important. The railroads were not only used to help people travel, but also to ship goods and products from place to place. As a result, the railroads also provided jobs to many people.

2. The stories in this unit are about real people who displayed great courage when they were young. Remember, the stories are based on fact; however, they contain parts that are fiction. When real events from history are mixed with fictional events, we call this type of story *historical fiction*. As you read, see if you can find the facts.

Read

"Run, Kate Shelley, Run" in *Classics for Young Readers,* Vol. 5B, pages 125-130

Questions

Answer the following questions in complete sentences in your Reading Notebook.

1. Why was Kate Shelley able to recognize each train engine by the sound of its whistle?
2. Where did the train accident occur?
3. Why did Kate Shelley run over a mile to the Moingona railroad station?
4. About how many lives did Kate Shelley save that night in 1881?
5. In what ways did the railroad workers continue to honor Kate Shelley?

Discuss

1. What inspired Kate Shelley to continue in her rescue attempt, despite the danger? Provide examples from the text that support your answer.

2. What were the consequences of Kate Shelley's father's decision to teach his daughter about the railroads?

3. The author of this story uses figurative language in her descriptions. Figurative language uses figures of speech such as metaphor, simile, and personification, for poetic effect rather than for precise, factual meaning. Here is an example: "After nearly a week of rain, the creek was a wild bull, roaring and leaping, crashing against the high bluffs that caged it in on either side." What mood does this figurative language create? Why would the author use a metaphor that compares the creek to a wild bull? How does this description help readers understand Kate Shelley's situation?

Conflict and Resolution: Part 3

You have read about two other young people who use their courage to resolve a conflict. What conflict does Kate Shelley face? Fill in the Conflict and Resolution: Part 3 page with details from this story.

Memorial

When Kate Shelley died, the Order of Railway Conductors and Brakemen dedicated a plaque to her memory. Now imagine that you are in charge of creating a monument to honor Kate Shelley. Will it be a statue of her, a plaque, a sculpture of a train, or some other form of monument? On a separate sheet of paper, draw your idea for a Kate Shelley memorial. Remember that memorials should, in some way, reflect the life and accomplishments of the person being honored. When you have finished, discuss your ideas and why you chose to honor Kate Shelley as you did.

Name _____   Date _____

Conflict and Resolution: Part 3

A person can have a conflict with:
- Another person or group of people
- His or her own thoughts and feelings
- His or her society or the natural world

In a story, as in real life, people usually need to *resolve*, or work out, their conflicts.

Answer the questions below on "Run, Kate Shelley, Run" in complete sentences.

1. Describe Kate Shelley's conflict with the natural world.

   _____

   _____

   _____

2. Describe Kate Shelley's conflict with herself.

   _____

   _____

   _____

3. How does Kate Shelley resolve the conflicts she faces?

   _____

   _____

   _____

Conflict and Resolution: Part 3

4. Do you think Kate Shelley resolved her conflicts in an appropriate way? Why or why not?

_____

_____

_____

5. What could she have done differently? What do you admire about her behavior and the way she resolved her conflict?

_____

_____

_____

Name _____ Date _____

Young and Brave Review

Review the events of the stories in this unit and complete the two activities below.

Think Ahead

Review "A Ride in the Night," "Young Frederick Douglass: The Slave Who Learned to Read," and "Run, Kate Shelley, Run." Discuss the events of each story and the challenges faced by the people in this unit. Do you admire these individuals? Why? Which of their qualities or actions were admirable?

Compare and Contrast

After reviewing the events of the stories in this unit, fill in the Compare and Contrast page to show how Will Clark, Frederick Douglass, and Kate Shelley were alike and how they were different. Be prepared to discuss your responses when you finish.

Interview

Play the role of Will Clark, Frederick Douglass, or Kate Shelley and answer the questions on the Interview page as that person would have answered them. You may wish to review the events of your person's story and his or her personality before beginning.

Name _____ Date _____

Interview

Imagine that you are Will Clark, Frederick Douglass, or Kate Shelley. A newspaper reporter has heard of you and wants to write an article about your brave deeds. Answer the interview questions below as completely as you can.

Who are you:

1. Why did you decide to act so courageously?

_____

_____

_____

_____

2. Were you ever afraid? When?

_____

_____

_____

_____

Interview

3. How were you able to overcome your fears?

_____

_____

_____

_____

4. What advice would you give to other young people who face conflicts that they must try to resolve?

_____

_____

_____

_____

Name _____ Date _____

Compare and Contrast

Based on what you've learned from reading about Will Clark, Frederick Douglass, and Kate Shelley, complete the chart. When you have finished, discuss your answers. How were these people were similar to one another? How did their ability to overcome fear help them accomplish their goals?

	Will Clark	Frederick Douglass	Kate Shelley
Personality Traits			
Helped by These People			
Important Choices Made			
Fears Overcome			
Major Accomplishments as Young People			

Name _____   Date _____

"Sky-bright Axe"

In the northern parts of the United States, in states such as Maine, Michigan, Wisconsin, Minnesota, and the Dakotas, a story is told about a giant lumberjack and his enormous blue ox. That lumberjack's name is Paul Bunyan, and his ox is known as Babe. Meet both Paul Bunyan and Babe as you read about their legendary deeds. As you read, think about the exaggerations in the story and the traits that make Paul Bunyan a hero.

Vocabulary

You will find these words in today's reading.

gale: (n.) a strong wind, often at sea or along the coast
The sailboat moved along at great speed thanks to the powerful *gale* that blew in from the west.

griddles: (n.) flat, metal cooking surfaces or pans
The smell of pancakes on the *griddle* always helped Maria get out of bed in the morning.

hitched: (v.) attached or fastened to something for the purposes of pulling
The tow-truck driver *hitched* up the broken-down car to his truck and headed for the garage.

spraddled: (v.) spread out; a combination of straddled and sprawled
The gymnast lay *spraddled* on the mat, thinking only about performing a flawless routine.

maul: (n.) a heavy, wooden-headed hammer
Frederick used his father's heavy *maul* to split wood for the fire at his mountain cabin.

crooning: (v.) singing in a soothing way
The sound of Frank Sinatra *crooning* on the radio on Sunday afternoons always made Tim think of his grandmother.

Think Ahead

1. In this unit, you will read several tall tales. A tall tale is a story that tells the wildly exaggerated adventures of North American folk heroes. The hero is always a person who seems larger-than-life and is known for his or her exceptional strength, skill, intelligence, dedication, and courage. Some of the heroes in tall tales, such as Johnny Appleseed, were real people. Others, such as Paul Bunyan, were probably invented with their stories.

2. Many American tall tales began to take shape during the 1800s as the country was expanding westward. People in different parts of the country would tell stories about heroes who lived and worked in their region. Why do you think these pioneers would want to tell tales of heroes who accomplished great things in the new land? (Hint: Think about how hard the lives of the pioneers were.)

3. The story of Paul Bunyan is one of America's most famous and best-loved tall tales. The legendary Paul Bunyan and his blue ox, Babe, inspired the lumberjacks who cleared the forests of North America in the 1800s. As the country grew and people moved to the wooded regions of Michigan, Wisconsin, Minnesota, and the Dakotas, the logging industry boomed. Lumberjacks cleared the land for homes and supplied the timber used as building material in the rest of the country. The lumberjacks often lived together in logging camps, where tall tales about the incredible accomplishments of the mythical Paul Bunyan grew as different storytellers added their own unique details to the story.

Read

"Sky-bright Axe" in *American Tall Tales,* pages 11-23

Questions

Answer the following questions in complete sentences in your Reading Notebook.

1. What advice does Paul Bunyan's mother give to him?
2. Who is Babe?
3. How do Paul Bunyan and Babe change the logging road in Wisconsin?
4. Why does the King of Sweden write to Paul Bunyan?
5. How does Paul Bunyan decide to feed Ole while he figures out how to cut down the giant cornstalk?

Discuss

1. Have you ever heard the term "gentle giant"? What is a gentle giant? Would you consider Paul Bunyan a gentle giant? Why or why not?

2. How does Paul Bunyan help shape the American landscape? What does he do?

3. Hyperbole is a figure of speech that uses exaggeration for emphasis or often for comic effect. Tall tales are full of hyperbole that makes the stories fun and the characters memorable. For example, when discussing the very cold winter, the story says, "That very same winter, men's words froze in front of their mouths and hung stiff in the air." (p. 18). Find other sentences or passages in the story that use hyperbole to create a fun or memorable image. Explain how these examples help you see Paul Bunyan and why you like them.

Telling Tall Tales!

You've seen how hyperbole makes Paul Bunyan a larger-than-life hero in "Sky-bright Axe." Now exaggerate your own details to create your own tall tale. Fill in the blanks of the story provided on the Telling Tall Tales page. Use your imagination to make the tale as tall as possible.

Hero Cards

The hero in a tall tale is a larger-than-life person whose great accomplishments are the result of his or her exceptional size, strength, skill, intelligence, and/or bravery. On one side of three separate index cards, write three different deeds that Paul Bunyan does in "Sky-bright Axe." On the other side of each card, write the heroic characteristic or personality trait that the deed is an example of. When you have finished, discuss your responses and why you chose them. Save these cards for a later lesson.

Name _____   Date _____

Telling Tall Tales

Many years ago, there lived a _____ named_____.
                              name of a job   female name of the hero

She was famous in_____because of her incredible _____
                  name of a state   physical characteristic

and her wonderful_____. In addition to these things,_____was
                 positive personality trait   hero's name

extremely_____. In fact, she was so_____that
         2nd physical characteristic   2nd physical characteristic

she could easily_____.
                impressive physical feat related to 2nd physical characteristic

Naturally, the people around_____often turned to her for help.
                             hero's name

Over the course of several years,_____helped the local people to ____
                                 hero's name

_____ ,_____, and, on one occasion, to ____
  1st helpful deed   2nd helpful deed

_____ . But the most famous thing
        3rd and most impressive helpful deed

that_____ever did was when she single-handedly _____
    hero's name   impossible feat

_____
                    impossible feat continued

_____.
                    impossible feat continued

This amazing accomplishment made her the subject of songs and stories all over

_____. In fact, if you go there today, people will tell you that the
  name of a state

next time they have a problem that is just too big for them to handle, they know

_____ will return to give them a helping hand.
  hero's name

Name _____   Date _____

"Coyote Cowboy"

What do you think of when you hear the word *cowboy?* In this story, you will meet the legendary Pecos Bill—one of the most famous cowboy heroes of all time.

Vocabulary

You will find these words in today's reading.

sagebrush: (n.) a small shrub common in the western and southwestern United States
The cowboy loved the smell of *sagebrush* that grew on the plains.

bear grass: (n.) a plant whose leaves look like thick and rough blades of grass
Denise watched the wind blow the *bear grass* out in the field near her Texas home.

yucca plants: (n.) white-blossomed plants that live mainly in warm, dry climates such as the southwestern United States
Carl sold several of his paintings at the art show, including the one he painted of the *yucca plants* that grow near his home in New Mexico.

greasewood: (n.) a thorny shrub, white or dull gray in color, that grows in the western United States
The rancher looked out of his windows, but there was nothing to see except *greasewood* plants and wide open space.

Gila monsters: (n.) large black and orange reptiles that live in the southwestern United States
The *Gila monsters* at the zoo reminded Amanda of the picture of the dragon in her favorite book.

cyclone: (n.) a tornado
The family left their home when they saw the twisting funnel of the
cyclone headed their way.

varmints: (n.) animals that are considered pests or nuisances and
are not protected by hunting laws
By never cleaning and always leaving half-eaten food lying around
his home, Jack practically invited all kinds of *varmints* to move in and
share his house.

Think Ahead

1. What is a tall tale? What are some characteristics of tall tales? Why
    did tall tales come about, how were they passed along to different
    audiences, and why do they remain popular?

2. The story of Pecos Bill has its roots in Texas and the southwestern
    United States, which is also where the tale takes place. In the 1800s,
    cattle ranching was an important business in this part of the country.
    Cowboys cared for the cattle, transported them, and defended the
    herd from outlaws. Being a cowboy could be dangerous, and
    although this danger attracted some, it kept many others away. The
    life of the cowboy was often lonely as long nights needed to be
    passed during cattle drives from ranch to ranch. It was probably
    during these long nights around the campfire that the legend of Pecos
    Bill began.

3. What do you picture when you think of a cowboy? Chances are, the
    picture that you have in your mind of a cowboy—the strong, silent
    type who will bravely face down any villain—was influenced by the
    legend of Pecos Bill. As his story was passed from person to person,
    the character of Pecos Bill became more and more heroic. Pecos Bill
    became the ultimate cowboy. Think about other cowboy stories you
    know as you read this tale.

Read

"Coyote Cowboy" in *American Tall Tales,* pages 24-36

Questions

Answer the following questions in complete sentences in your Reading Notebook.

1. What animals raised young Pecos Bill?
2. How does Pecos Bill invent the lasso?
3. Why is Pecos Bill's horse named the Widow-Maker?
4. How does Pecos Bill end the drought in Texas and other parts of the Southwest?
5. Who is Pecos Bill's wife?

Discuss

1. How does Pecos Bill influence cowboys and how they behave? Provide examples from the story to support your answer.

2. What does it mean to be larger-than-life? How is Pecos Bill larger-than-life? Provide examples from the story to support your answer.

3. Just as "Sky-bright Axe" is filled with hyperbole that describes the life and deeds of Paul Bunyan, the language in this story helps to create our image of Pecos Bill. How does the language help you create a mental picture of Pecos Bill? How would you describe him?

Exaggerations

As you know, exaggerations are an important part of tall tales. While reading the story of Pecos Bill, you probably noticed many examples of hyperbole. Follow the directions on the Exaggerations page to go back through "Coyote Cowboy" and find several examples of hyperbole. When you have finished, discuss how these examples made Pecos Bill a unique and larger-than-life character.

Hero Cards

Continue the activity you began in the first lesson of this unit and explore the heroic deeds of Pecos Bill. On one side of three separate index cards, write three different deeds that Pecos Bill does in "Coyote Cowboy." On the other side of each card, write the heroic characteristic or personality trait that the deed is an example of. When you have finished, discuss your responses and why you chose them. Save these cards for a later lesson.

Name _____   **Date** _____

Exaggerations

The story of Pecos Bill is filled with exaggerations. These incredible details help to make Pecos Bill a larger-than-life character. Fill in the blanks below with sentences or passages from the text of "Coyote Cowboy" that display the trait named. When you are finished, discuss the passages you chose.

Example:
Strength: "Bill wrestled the bear and tossed it around until the bear put its paws over its head and begged for mercy."

1. Speed: _____

_____

2. Cowboy skill: _____

_____

3. Inventiveness: _____

_____

4. Bravery: _____

_____

Name _____   Date _____

"Hammerman"

During the 1800s, railroads sprang up all over America. Naturally, tall tales began to appear about some of the people who built the railroads. The most famous of those tales is that of John Henry, the steel-driving man.

Vocabulary

You will find these words in today's reading.

gnawing: (v.) biting or chewing; bothering
After lying to his boss about being sick, Marshall felt a *gnawing* sense of guilt the entire day.

singed: (v.) mildly burned, often in a way that removes hair
While wrestling with her sister near the fireplace, Jackie accidentally *singed* the ends of her hair.

Think Ahead

1. Review the characteristics of tall tales. How did they originate? Who were their original audiences?

2. The railroad industry plays a big part in John Henry's story. As the United States expanded during the 1800s, sending people and materials great distances became necessary. There were no highways or airplanes at the time, so trains were very important. Building the railroads was extremely difficult and demanding work. Gradually, as technology advanced, machines were invented that made the job easier. However, the arrival of machines often meant that not as many workers were needed. It was not uncommon for people to lose their jobs because a machine replaced them.

Read

"Hammerman" in *American Tall Tales*, pages 88-100.

Questions
Answer the following questions in complete sentences in your Reading Notebook.

1. At first, the foreman does not want to give John Henry a job. Why?
2. Who is John Henry's assistant?
3. For what railroad does John Henry eventually work?
4. Who is Polly Ann?
5. Why does Cap'n Tommy agree to the contest between John Henry and the machine?
6. What happens to John Henry at the end of the story?

Discuss
1. The *theme* is the big idea or lesson of the story. What is the lesson of John Henry's story? What do John Henry's efforts prove?
2. What other examples can you think of where man has challenged machine?
3. Find sentences or passages in the story that use hyperbole to create a strong image of John Henry. Explain how these passages help you see John Henry and why the language appeals to you.

Audiences
As you know, different tall tales originated in different parts of the country. How did each region influence the tall tales that began there? Answer the questions on Paul Bunyan, Pecos Bill, and John Henry on the Audiences page. When you have finished, be prepared to discuss your answers.

Hero Cards
Continue the activity you began in the first two lessons of this unit and explore the heroic deeds of John Henry. On one side of three separate index cards, write three different deeds that John Henry does in "Hammerman." On the other side of each card, write the heroic characteristic or personality trait that the deed is an example of. When you have finished, discuss your responses and why you chose them. Save these cards for a later lesson.

Name _____   Date _____

Audiences

Answer the questions below on Paul Bunyan, Pecos Bill, and John Henry. Feel free to use *American Tall Tales* if you need to look up an answer.

1. Where do the stories of Paul Bunyan, Pecos Bill, and John Henry take place?

   _____

   _____

   _____

2. What job does each of the heroes of these stories hold?

   _____

   _____

   _____

3. Were these jobs unusual, or were they done by many ordinary people as well?

   _____

   _____

   _____

Audiences

4. Why would characters performing these jobs be popular in these parts of the country?

_____

_____

_____

5. What effect would stories about these heroes have on the people who originally listened to them?

_____

_____

_____

Name _____   Date _____

A Visual Story

Learn how a picture or a series of pictures can tell a story. Then examine how one student created a visual story based on events in "Sky-Bright Axe." Finally, prepare to create a visual story of your own based on the events of one of the tall tales you read.

Pictures Say a Thousand Words
Explore how a picture or a series of pictures can be used to tell an effective visual story.

Paul Bunyan in Pictures
Learn how one student used several events in "Sky-Bright Axe" to craft a visual story about Paul Bunyan and Babe, the blue ox.

Your Assignment
Now it's time to choose which tall tale you will use for the visual story that you will create. Think about each story you read. Then reread your favorite tall tale. As you read, consider which events in that tall tale you might like to illustrate and make part of the visual story you will create.

You may choose to use events from "Sky-Bright Axe" as the basis for your visual story, but you may not use the same events that Jesse used in her visual story.

Name _____   Date _____

Create Your Own Visual Story

Create an outline that contains notes and ideas for your visual story. Then use the outline to help you create your visual story, which should include at least three pictures with captions. Finally, explain and share your visual story.

Outline Your Visual Story

Print the Model Outline page and read the outline Jesse completed for her visual story. Next, print the Visual Story Outline page and follow the directions to take notes and plan the images and captions that will be a part of your visual story.

Produce Your Visual Story

Gather several sheets of paper, as well as colored pencils, markers, or crayons.

Then, using your completed Visual Story Outline sheet as a guide, create your visual story by drawing the pictures and writing out the captions you have planned. Use a stapler or a paper clip to attach the pages of your completed visual story together.

Finally, review your completed story and practice presenting it to an audience. Use this checklist as you practice presenting your visual story.

Presentation Checklist

- Present your story in the proper order, showing pictures in the order that events occur in the story.

- Use your captions to help you remember what each picture shows, but do not read the captions directly.

- Speak clearly.

- Speak with enthusiasm and expression.

- Speak at an appropriate pace: not too fast or too slow.

- Show confidence and pride in your depiction of events from the story.

- Stand up straight.

- Look at your audience as much as possible.

- Direct your audience's attention to key details in the pictures you've created.

- Practice presenting your visual story several times so that you know what to say and are comfortable speaking about your work.

Also consider videotaping one of your practice presentations. Watching yourself is a great way to notice your own strengths and spot weaknesses in the presentation that you can then work to improve.

Explain and Share Your Visual Story

Now it's time to share your completed visual story with your Learning Coach. Present your story, giving your Learning Coach time to look at each picture and read each caption.

Remember: As you explain each picture in your story, state what the picture shows and why you decided to include the details you did. Point out those elements in your visual story that you included in order to show an important moment or express a key idea from the text.

Answer any questions that your Learning Coach may have about what you were trying to show in your visual story, the pictures you drew, and the captions you wrote.

Finally, consider sharing your visual story with peers, family members, or friends.

Once you have finished, complete the Self-Evaluation page and discuss it with your Learning Coach.

Model Outline

Review Jesse's completed outline. Use it as an example as you complete your own outline.

Notes

Visual Story Subject: ____ Paul Bunyan and Babe _____

_____

Background Information: __Paul Bunyan meets Babe during the Winter of the__

__Blue Snow. He is out for a walk, when he trips over Babe, who is as big as a__

__mountain.____

Key Events: __Paul and Babe see the twisted logging road in Wisconsin. Paul__

__hitches Babe's harness to one end of the twisted road. Babe pulls on the road and__

__straightens it out.__

Pictures & Captions

Picture 1: Paul Bunyan out for a walk during the Winter of the Blue Snow

Caption: It was the Winter of the Blue Snow, and Paul Bunyan was out for a walk.

Picture 2: Paul trips over Babe (their first meeting)

Caption: Suddenly, Paul tripped over something the size of a mountain. It was Babe, a giant blue ox who was soon to be Paul Bunyan's best friend.

Picture 3: Paul and Babe stand next to a very, very twisted logging road

Caption: In Wisconsin, Paul and Babe came upon a logging road that was so crooked the loggers would start home and meet themselves coming back.

Picture 4: Babe is being hitched to one end of the curvy logging road by Paul

Caption: If anyone could pull that crooked road straight, it was Babe, so Paul Bunyan hitched her harness to one end of the road.

Picture 5: Babe and Paul look proud as they stand next to the straight road

Caption: When Babe finished, the logging road was as straight as a railroad tie, and Paul Bunyan was bursting with pride.

Name _____   Date _____

Visual Story Outline

Now that you have reread your favorite tall tale, complete this outline.

Write which story events you will show. This is your subject.

Jot down any background information or details that you will need to show your audience through pictures.

Next, list the key events from the story that you will show.

Finally, give brief descriptions of each picture in your visual story. Write captions to go with each picture. Your captions should be short but tell what is happening or how the characters feel.

Your visual story must contain at least three pictures and captions. You may do more if you like.

Visual Story Outline

Notes

Visual Story Subject: _____

_____

Background Information: _____

_____

_____

Key Events: _____

_____

_____

_____

Pictures & Captions

Picture 1: _____

Caption: _____

_____

Picture 2: _____

Caption: _____

_____

Picture 3: _____

Caption: _____

_____

Picture 4: _____

Caption: _____

_____

Picture 5: _____

Caption: _____

_____

_____

Name _____ Date _____

Self-Evaluation

After you present your visual story, review your own efforts to create and share your work. Use these questions to guide your review.

Purpose and Content

1. Did my presentation tell about the events of an American tall tale? A. Yes   B. No

2. What important events did the visual story show? Were all the main events represented in the visual story? If not, what was missing?

_____

_____

_____

_____

3. Why did I choose the pictures I did? How did the pictures make one or more of the events or details easier to understand or clearer?

_____

_____

4. Did the captions of each picture in the visual story help audiences understand what was being depicted in the image and why the events were important?
A. Yes   B. No

5. Which parts of the visual story were strongest? Which parts could have been improved?

_____

_____

Structure and Organization

1. Did the visual story have a beginning, a middle, and an end? If not, how should I have changed or reorganized the story?

_____

_____

2. Were any key events left out of the visual story? If so, where should I have included them?

_____

_____

Grammar and Mechanics

1. Did I speak in complete sentences? If not, where should I have focused on improving my speech?

_____

_____

2.   Did I make eye contact with the audience as much as possible? If not, note when should I have tried to make eye contact?

_____

_____

3.   Did I speak clearly, at an appropriate pace, and at an appropriate volume? If not, when did I mumble, speak too quickly, or speak too softly or too loudly?

_____

_____

4.   Did I speak with enthusiasm, expression, and confidence? If not, when did my tone falter?

_____

_____

5.   Did I maintain good posture throughout the presentation? If not, where did I slouch or have poor posture?

_____

_____

6.   What could have been done to improve the presentation?

_____

_____

_____

Name _____   Date _____

Exploration Day

Choose another tall tale and read about the heroic deeds and amazing actions of its hero!

Think Ahead
1. How are the heroes in the tall tales you've read similar? How are they different?
2. Describe the language of tall tales. What are some of its characteristics? Is it usually boring and plain? Are the details strictly realistic and believable?

Read
one of the other stories in *American Tall Tales*

Questions
Answer the following questions in complete sentences in your Reading Notebook.

1. What region of the country is the hero of this tall tale from?
2. What special skills, talents, or strengths does the hero of this story show?
3. How do the hero's skills, talents, or strengths help the hero accomplish difficult tasks?
4. Provide two examples of exaggeration in the story.

Discuss
1. As you know, tall tales use creative language to entertain readers and make their stories and heroes more memorable. Scan through the tall tale you just read, and choose one sentence or passage that uses language that is particularly creative. Discuss the meaning of the sentence or passage and why it appeals to you. Explain how the language helps create an image of the hero of this tale.

Discuss

1. As you know, tall tales use creative language to entertain readers and make their stories and heroes more memorable. Scan through the tall tale you just read, and choose one sentence or passage that uses language that is particularly creative. Discuss the meaning of the sentence or passage and why it appeals to you. Explain how the language helps create an image of the hero of this tale.

2. How is the hero of this tall tale similar to Paul Bunyan, Pecos Bill, and John Henry? Use examples from the story to support your points.

Picture It!

On a separate sheet of paper, draw a picture of the hero from the tall tale you just read. Show the hero doing something from the story that you feel shows one or more of the hero's extraordinary qualities. For example, if you were drawing a picture of Pecos Bill, you might show him riding the cyclone. When you have finished your drawing, discuss the picture and why you chose to show the hero as you did.

Hero Cards

Continue this activity with the hero of the tall tale you just read. On one side of three separate index cards, write three different deeds done by the hero of this story. On the other side of each card, write the heroic characteristic or personality trait that the deed is an example of. When you have finished, discuss your responses and why you chose them. Save these cards for a later lesson.

Name _____   Date _____

Activity Day

Review the events of the stories in this unit and complete the two activities below.

Think Ahead

Why did tall tales develop? What are some characteristics of tall tales? Name several heroes from the tall tales you've read. How are these heroes similar?

Match Up

As you know, tall tales often use exaggeration. During this unit, you have completed several activities that focus on exaggeration and how it affects the story and the hero. Now complete the Match Up page, which asks you to match the passages provided with the character whose size, strength, or skill is being exaggerated. Each character will match up with two passages.

Hero Hall of Fame

Use the Hero Cards that you have created over the course of this unit to help you complete the Hero Hall of Fame pages. You should have four sets of cards. On each page, you will write a short paragraph about why each hero deserves to be in the Hall of Fame. Use the examples from the stories from your Hero Cards to help support your response. Then, in the box provided, draw something that represents the hero being described. Your drawing should be of an object that was important to each person.

Name _____   Date _____

Match Up

Throughout this unit, you have read stories that rely on exaggeration to make their heroes larger-than-life. Can you now recognize which exaggeration describes each character? Below you will find six passages that use exaggeration to describe one of the heroes from this unit. In the space next to each passage, write in the appropriate hero's name—Paul Bunyan, Pecos Bill, or John Henry.

1. Then he settled down to working the regular way, pounding in the drills with four or five strokes of a twenty-pound sledge. He worked so fast that his helpers had to keep buckets of water ready to pour on his hammers so they wouldn't catch fire.

   _____

2. Then he would stand straddle-legged and swing the axe in a wide circle, yelling "T-I-M-B-E-R-R-R! Look out!" With every swing and every yell, a hundred trees would come whooshing down.

   _____

3. [His] chest swelled up so with pride that it broke one of his suspenders. The broken suspender whizzed up into the sky like a long rubber band. Just then, thousands of wild ducks were flying overhead. The suspender wrapped itself around the ducks and strangled the whole flock.

   _____

4. He invented spurs for them to wear on their boots. He taught them how to round up the cattle and drive the herds to railroad stations where they could be shipped to market.

   _____

Match Up

5. He began swinging a hammer in each hand. Sparks flew so fast and hot they singed his face. The hammers heated up until they glowed like torches.

_____

6. When he was as high as the top of the cyclone, he jumped and landed astraddle its black, spinning shoulders.

_____

Name _____   Date _____

Hero Hall of Fame

Use the Hero Cards that you have created over the course of this unit to help you fill in the page below with details from the hero's tall tale. In the box at the bottom of the page, draw an object or symbol that you think represents this hero.

_____
Hero's Name

belongs in the Hero Hall of Fame because

_____

_____

_____

_____

_____

_____

_____

Name _____   Date _____

Hero Hall of Fame

Use the Hero Cards that you have created over the course of this unit to help you fill in the page below with details from the hero's tall tale. In the box at the bottom of the page, draw an object or symbol that you think represents this hero.

_____
Hero's Name

belongs in the Hero Hall of Fame because

_____

_____

_____

_____

_____

_____

_____

Name _____   Date _____

Hero Hall of Fame

Use the Hero Cards that you have created over the course of this unit to help you fill in the page below with details from the hero's tall tale. In the box at the bottom of the page, draw an object or symbol that you think represents this hero.

_____
Hero's Name

belongs in the Hero Hall of Fame because

_____

_____

_____

_____

_____

_____

_____

Name _____ **Date** _____

Hero Hall of Fame

Use the Hero Cards that you have created over the course of this unit to help you fill in the page below with details from the hero's tall tale. In the box at the bottom of the page, draw an object or symbol that you think represents this hero.

_____
Hero's Name

belongs in the Hero Hall of Fame because

_____

_____

_____

_____

_____

_____

_____

Name _____ Date _____

Semester Review

Review the skills you've learned and the stories and poems you've read this semester.

Young People in Action

In the Young and Brave unit, you read about real people who made a difference in American history. Review or reread one of the stories from the unit and do the following things:

- Summarize the plot of the story.
- Describe the person the story is about.
- Discuss the theme—the big idea—of the story.
- Describe some of the important choices the person made, why he/she made them, and the consequences of those choices.
- Identify the conflict in the story, how the person dealt with this conflict, and the resolution of the problems. Remember that a *conflict* is a clash or struggle between people, ideas, or feelings. A person can have a conflict with another person or group of people, his or her own thoughts or feelings, or society.

Read Aloud!

Choose two of the poems below to read aloud or act out. After you finish:

- Tell what the poems are about and who the speakers are.
- Point out rhyming couplets and use letters to write the rhyme schemes of the poems.
- Find similes, metaphors, personification, and examples of figurative language in the poems.

- Locate alliteration in the poems. If there is no alliteration, make up a line that alliterates that could fit in or after the poem.
- Discuss the possible symbolic meanings of the poems.

Poems:
"Travel" (page 132)
"Sea Fever" (page 137)
"The Road Not Taken" (page 144)
"Abraham Lincoln" (page 155)
"I, Too" (page 157)

Elementary!

This semester, you met one of the most famous characters of all time: Sherlock Holmes. Spend some time reviewing what you know about Holmes and the stories about him. Feel free to consult the stories to refresh your memory.

- Who is Sherlock Holmes?
- What does he do?
- Describe his character.
- Compare Holmes to his friend and partner, Dr. Watson. How are the two men similar? How are they different? How did you notice these differences?

Now listen to the first section of a brief story about Sherlock Holmes. As you listen, write down the important details from the story on the Taking Notes page. When the first section of the story is complete, discuss the problem that Holmes faces. Predict what he will do. Make an inference about what will happen using what you know about Sherlock Holmes.

- What skills will Holmes rely on to solve this case?
- Who will Holmes say is responsible for Vladimir's disappearance?
- Why will he identify this person?

After you have discussed the conflict and made your prediction, listen to the second section of the story. When you finish the story, discuss the solution and the accuracy of your prediction.

Matching

This semester has introduced you to many important authors, characters, terms, and ideas. Review some of the important things that you learned by completing the Matching page.

Identification, Please

Follow the directions on the Identification, Please page. Name the person or character described by each passage. When you have finished, discuss which characters or people you liked most from this semester's reading.

Name _____   Date _____

Taking Notes

During this semester, you practiced taking notes while listening to text being read aloud. Brush up on those skills with this activity. As you listen to the passage about Sherlock Holmes, take notes about the questions on this page.

1. Where is Sherlock Holmes when the woman comes to see him?

_____

2. How does the woman act as she tells her story?

_____

3. What happens to Vladimir?

_____

4. Why does Vladimir go for a walk?

_____

5. What does Vladimir do for a living?

_____

6. Where are the woman and Vladimir from?

_____

7. How does the woman act when the chief-of-police enters the room?

_____
_____

Name _____ Date _____

Matching

During this semester, you came across many important authors, characters, terms, and ideas. How much do you remember? Match the items in the left column with the correct description on the right.

1. The Globe ____
2. Sherlock Holmes ____
3. Don Quixote ____
4. William Shakespeare ____
5. Tall tale ____

a. A famous fictional detective created by Arthur Conan Doyle. His partner is Dr. Watson.

b. A story in which a larger-than-life hero performs amazing feats. These are often specific to certain regions of the country.

c. The London theater most associated with William Shakespeare.

d. The British playwright who wrote such masterpieces as *A Midsummer Night's Dream*, *The Tempest*, *Romeo and Juliet*, and *Hamlet*.

e. The name taken by an old man who imagines himself to be a knight whose job it is to stand up for the weak and oppressed.

Name _____   Date _____

Identification, Please

During this semester, you read about some memorable characters and incredible people. In this activity, demonstrate just how memorable they are. Fill in the space next to each description below with the name of the appropriate character or person. You may refer to the text if needed.

Characters:

Jo March	Paul Bunyan	Pecos Bill	Frederick Douglass
Don Quixote	Kate Shelley	Sherlock Holmes	Will Clark

1. _____

This fifteen-year-old ran over a mile through a driving rainstorm in Iowa in the late 1800s to report one train wreck and stop another from happening. In doing so, she showed great courage and helped to save the lives of about 200 people. For her heroic efforts, she was forever respected by the people who worked on the railroads.

2. _____

This giant woodsman had a blue ox named Babe for a best friend. He helped to clear the forests in many of the states in the northern part of America. In fact, he specifically cleared out North Dakota for the King of Sweden, so that the extra Swedes in that country could come to America. With Babe's help, he also created the lakes in Minnesota, the Mississippi River, and the Grand Canyon.

3. _____

On his horse, Rocinante, this would-be knight rides off in search of adventure. Along the way, he acquires a squire named Sancho Panza and performs deeds for his beloved Dulcinea. Of course, in reality, the knight is really just an old man who has read too many books about knights. Nevertheless, he does find a great deal of adventure during his travels.

Identification, Please

4. _____

While their father is away serving as a chaplain in the Union Army during the Civil War, this young girl and her three sisters spend their days trying to deal with the hardships they face. As the holidays approach, she befriends a boy named Laurie who is ill. She reads to him and keeps him company as he gets better. Then, when her father gets sick, she selflessly sells her long hair to provide much-needed money to her family.

5. _____

This person was born into slavery in the 1800s. As a young man, he quickly learned that an education could perhaps help him achieve freedom. He taught himself to read and write. He managed to escape slavery with the help of another freed man. He eventually made his way to New York, where he became a well- known and eloquent abolitionist.

6. _____

This famous cowboy was raised by coyotes for several years. When he returned to human society, he used a rattlesnake for a lasso and taught the other cowboys how to sing songs. His horse was named Widow-Maker. One day, he rode a cyclone all the way from Texas to California. He eventually married a woman named Slue-Foot Sue.

7. _____

This famous London detective lives at 221B Baker Street and solves cases with the help of his partner, Dr. Watson. He relies mainly on his superior powers of observation and logic. He is based on a real person who was a professor at Edinburgh University in the late 1800s.

8. _____

This young boy helped the American Army during the Revolutionary War. He delivered horses to a man named George Coleman when his father was unable to do so. While bringing the horses to Coleman, the boy came face to face with enemy British soldiers. By thinking quickly and remaining calm, he was able to avoid being caught and complete his mission successfully.